NATURE IN AMERICAN PHILOSOPHY

STUDIES IN PHILOSOPHY AND THE HISTORY OF PHILOSOPHY

General Editor: Jude P. Dougherty

Studies in Philosophy
and the History of Philosophy Volume 42

Nature in American Philosophy

Edited by Jean De Groot

THE CATHOLIC UNIVERSITY OF AMERICA PRESS
Washington, D.C.

The paper used in this publication meets the minimum requirements of the American National Standards for Information Science—Permanence of Paper for Printed Library materials, ANSI Z39.48-1984.
∞

LIBRARY OF CONGRESS CATALOGING-IN-PUBLICATION DATA
Nature in American philosophy / edited by Jean De Groot.— 1st ed.
p. cm. — (Studies in philosophy and the history of philosophy ; v. 42)
Includes bibliographical references and indices.
ISBN 978-0-8132-3206-5 (alk. paper)
1. Philosophy of nature. 2. Philosophy, American. I. De Groot, Jean. II. Title. III. Series.
B21.S78 vol. 42
[BD581]
100 s—dc22
[113/.09]
2003023169

Contents

Acknowledgments

The papers presented in this volume were lectures given in the series *Nature in American Philosophy* presented at The Catholic University of America in the Fall semester, 2000. Thanks are due to the Thomas and Dorothy Leavey Foundation and the George Dougherty Foundation, both of which contributed generously to make the series possible. Gratitude is also due to the School of Philosophy, for its financial support of the project.

As organizer of the series and editor of the volume, I wish to thank the present dean of the School of Philosophy, Fr. Kurt Pritzl, O.P., for his collaboration in planning and his enthusiasm in bringing the project to fruition. I wish also to thank Brian Fox and Bryan Atchison, whose research and editorial work contributed so much to the present form of the volume. Thanks are due also to Ms. Gabrielle Fenlon, who worked patiently and painstakingly on the bibliography, and to Ms. Jasie Hinson. Special thanks are due to Dr. David McGonagle, director of the Press, for supporting the idea of illustrations in the volume and for obtaining the permissions to use the paintings included in the last essay, by Nicholas Rescher. I thank Prof. Rescher himself for his help in making these available for use in this volume.

Introduction

JEAN DE GROOT

The papers in this volume all provide insight on the theme of nature as it was a theme in classical American philosophy in the nineteenth and early twentieth centuries. They were originally presented in a series of lectures, *Nature in American Philosophy*, held at The Catholic University of America in Fall, 2000. The series honored the dean emeritus of the School of Philosophy, Prof. Jude P. Dougherty, who has a long and continuing interest in American philosophy that began with his own doctoral dissertation on John Dewey.[1]

The themes of *nature* and *community* are striking in their prominence in American philosophy of this period and figure importantly in this book. Indeed, these two themes, taken separately or interwoven, yield up the distinctive characteristics of classical American philosophy.[2] One can speculate that these themes arose from the special nineteenth-century experience of settling the continent. Nature was ubiquitous, even oppressive. What seemed a vast natural landscape imposed itself upon American imagination alternatively as an obstacle to be overcome, a source of grandeur and beauty, and a resource to be used for the satisfaction of ambition.[3] The social nature of the human being was taken for granted in this context. Cooperation was essential to settling

1. Jude P. Dougherty, *Recent American Naturalism: An Exposition and Critique* (Washington, D.C.: Catholic University of America Press, 1960).

2. On themes in American philosophy, see Peter Caws, ed., *Two Centuries of Philosophy in America* (Oxford: Blackwell, 1980), and John E. Smith, *America's Philosophical Vision* (Chicago: University of Chicago Press, 1992). For responses to Smith's vision, see the papers in *Transactions of the Charles S. Peirce Society* 31, no. 1 (1995). For a short account of themes in classical American philosophy, see the introduction to *Pragmatism and Classical American Philosophy: Essential Readings and Interpretive Essays*, ed. John J. Stuhr (Oxford: Oxford University Press, 2000), 1–9.

3. The effect of nature on American character was noted by Alexis de Tocqueville, *Democracy in America*, trans. Harvey Mansfield and Delba Winthrop (Chicago: University of Chicago Press, 2000), 264–73, 290–91, and by Lord James Bryce, *The American Commonwealth*, vol. 3 (London: Macmillian, 1883), 50, 497, 620–21. The most famous development of the theme of wilderness as forming American national character is Frederick

the land and beginning civilized life, and society provided a necessary solace and release.[4] The religious communities of Protestant America provided the strength to endure hardship. The immediacy of American involvement with these themes of nature and community—life in an untamed natural environment, in which basic human resources provided the means of survival—imparted the stamp that American intellectual concerns in general would retain for a hundred years.

By the mid-twentieth century, however, both these themes of classical American philosophy were in eclipse. A wild American nature had been tamed remarkably quickly and came to be seen as a fragile remnant to be preserved. In community life, hardship and mutual need were replaced by affluence, Cold War, and an emerging new conflict between different concepts of a free society. John Dewey was the most important and prolific American philosopher of the twentieth century to treat nature and community in the terms of classical American philosophy.[5] At mid-century, political philosophy, presumably the natural home for a discussion of community, was declared moribund, though a philosophical concept of community still thrived in the ideal of a scientific community pursuing the truth.[6] In spite of the importance of sci-

---

Jackson Turner, "The Significance of the Frontier in American History," *Report of the American Historical Association* (1893): 199–227, which appears as chapter 1 of Turner's *The Frontier in American History* (New York: H. Holt, 1920). More recently, John McDermott developed the theme of the "press of environment" and its influence on American thought, drawing on early American sources and contemporary commentary in *The Culture of Experience: Philosophical Essays in the American Grain* (New York: New York University Press, 1976), 1–20. Like most contemporary students of classical American philosophy, McDermott is concerned with the concept of experience, not nature. His analysis illustrates the relation of the two themes, however, and suggests the origin of the American focus on experience in the encounter with nature.

4. See Lord Bryce, *Commonwealth:* "Colonists need one another's aid more constantly than the dwellers in an old country, are thrown more upon one another, even when they live scattered in woods or prairies, are more interested in one another's welfare" (615).

5. On nature, see in particular Dewey's *Experience and Nature* (Chicago: Open Court, 1925). His social and political philosophy appeared in *Individualism: Old and New* (New York: Minton, Balch, 1930), *Liberalism and Social Action* (New York: Putnam, 1935), and *Freedom and Culture* (New York: Putnam, 1939). John Stuhr says of Dewey, "[I]n the widest sense, all of Dewey's philosophy—a comprehensive account of experience, inquiry and logic, education, morality, religion, and art—simply *is* social and political philosophy. For Dewey, social and political philosophy—and not metaphysics or epistemology—is First Philosophy" ("Dewey's Social and Political Philosophy," in *Reading Dewey: Interpretations for a Postmodern Generation,* ed. Larry A. Hickman [Bloomington: Indiana University Press, 1998], 85). For other philosophers of the mid-twentieth century working in the American tradition, see Sidney Hook, *American Philosophers at Work* (New York: Criterion Books, 1956), and John E. Smith, *The Spirit of American Philosophy* (New York: Oxford University Press, 1963). See also the work of philosophers associated with the Society for the Advancement of American Philosophy and their initiation in 1965 of the journal *Transactions of the Charles S. Peirce Society.*

6. On the death of political philosophy at mid-century, see Peter Laslett, *Philosophy,*

ence to twentieth-century philosophy, American philosophers were largely silent on the theme of nature, except as it figured tangentially in discussions of the logic of science.

More generally, beginning around 1930, American philosophers submitted themselves to the bracing atmosphere of logical positivism, which made American romanticism and idealism seem outmoded. Subsequently, the new 'international style' of philosophy, analytic philosophy, was embraced enthusiastically in this country. Pragmatism was reconceived in relation to logical positivism and analytic philosophy.[7] From 1950 until 1985, it became harder to find philosophers at the leading universities in the United States willing to identify themselves as *American philosophers* engaged in a continuing tradition stretching back to the eighteenth and nineteenth centuries.

Fortunately, the decline of interest in American philosophy was never universal and has proven to be short-lived. There has been a redirection of mainstream philosophical concern to classical American philosophy. Prominent examples include the writings of Richard Rorty and Stanley Cavell.[8] This involvement of American philosophy in contemporary philosophizing has been reinforced by a renewal of scholarly interest in American pragmatism, a renewal given luster by the seriousness with which European philosophers began to take Peirce and James.[9] It is still the case, however, that the *philosophy of nature* is not a

Politics, and Society, series 1 (Oxford: Blackwell, 1956), vii–xv. American political philosophy regained center stage with John Rawls's *A Theory of Justice* (Cambridge, Mass.: Harvard University Press, 1971). Judged by some as too individualistic, Rawls's philosophy elicited communitarian reactions. Among these were Michael Sandel, *Liberalism and the Limits of Justice* (London: Cambridge University Press, 1982), and Michael Walzer, *Spheres of Justice* (New York: Basic Books, 1983). On community in science, see Daniel J. Wilson, *Science, Community, and the Transformation of American Philosophy, 1860–1930* (Chicago: University of Chicago Press, 1990), 9–10, 121–49.

7. See C. I. Lewis, "Pragmatism and Current Thought," *Journal of Philosophy* 27, no. 9 (1930): 238–46; also Rudolph Carnap's delineation of 'pragmatics' in "Meaning and Synonymy in Natural Languages," and "On Some Concepts of Pragmatics," in *Meaning and Necessity*, 2d ed. (Chicago: University of Chicago Press, 1956); also Wilfrid Sellars, "Pure Pragmatics and Epistemology," *Philosophy of Science* 14, no. 3 (1947): 181–202. W. V. O. Quine dissociates his own position on truth from pragmatism in *Word and Object* (Cambridge, Mass.: MIT Press, 1960), 23.

8. See Richard Rorty, *Philosophy and the Mirror of Nature* (Princeton: Princeton University Press, 1979) and *Consequences of Pragmatism* (Minneapolis: University of Minnesota Press, 1982); also, Stanley Cavell, *Senses of Walden* (New York: Viking, 1972), *In Quest of the Ordinary: Lines of Skepticism and Romanticism* (Chicago: University of Chicago Press, 1988), *Conditions Handsome and Unhandsome: The Constitution of Emersonian Perfectionism* (Chicago: University of Chicago Press, 1990).

9. On the European interest in American pragmatism, see the series of introductions by Apel and Bernstein in Karl-Otto Apel, *Charles S. Peirce: From Pragmatism to Pragmaticism*, trans. John M. Krois (Atlantic Highlands, N.J.: Humanities Press, 1995), vii–xxvii, and Apel's chapter 1, "Peirce and the Contemporary Function of Pragmatism," 1–13. For

topic in this revival, despite the importance of nature in American philosophy of the nineteenth century. It was with this state of affairs in mind that the present volume was conceived. In this series, nature is understood broadly, for the papers treat the Kantian background of American thought on nature, as well as metaphysical issues related to nature and reflections on human nature from the standpoints of history, law, and psychology. Similarly, classical American philosophy is construed broadly to include Emerson and Thoreau, as well as Tocqueville and the most recent interpretations of Dewey.

It is remarkable that a vision of nature, and a consideration of the different possibilities for the truth about nature, should so rarely be made a theme in present-day philosophy. Nature underlies all art, including technology, as Aristotle perceived. Furthermore, it is a truth implicit in the environmental movement that nature remains the basic condition of human existence and has the power to reassert itself in a negative way when the purposes to which we would turn nature outrun nature's capacity to serve these purposes. If nothing else, one would think that ordinary curiosity about human nature would occasion a consideration of the human subject in relation to other living things and inanimate nature. There are undoubtedly a number of reasons for this neglect of philosophy of nature, one of which derives from the American commitment to analytic philosophy. It was the belief of Frege and the other founders of logicism that the only necessity philosophy can address is logical necessity. Wittgenstein, for instance, believed throughout all changes in his other views that what happens by nature is contingent.[10] There is no natural necessity and so nothing about nature to discuss. Even for philosophers of science willing to entertain the notions of natural necessity and causality, the emphasis was on properly conceived statements about natural occurrences, not on what things are.[11]

American pragmatism contrasted to European traditions, see Cornel West, *The American Evasion of Philosophy: A Genealogy of Pragmatism* (Madison: University of Wisconsin Press, 1989), and Vincent Colapietro, "Entangling Alliances and Critical Traditions: Reclaiming the Possibilities of Critique," *Journal of Speculative Philosophy* 12 n.s., no. 2 (1998): 114–33.

10. "A necessity for one thing to happen because another has happened does not exist. There is only *logical* necessity. At the basis of the whole modern view of the world lies the illusion that the so-called laws of nature are the explanations of natural phenomena." *Tractatus Logico-Philosophicus,* trans. C. K. Ogden (London: Routledge, 1922), 6.37–6.371. Compare *Philosophical Investigations* 89: "[Logic] takes its rise, not from an interest in the facts of nature (Tatsachen des Naturgeschehens), nor from a need to grasp causal connexions: but from an urge to understand the basis, or essence, of everything empirical. Not, however, as if to this end we had to hunt out new facts; it is, rather of the essence of our investigation that we do not seek to learn anything *new* by it" (trans. G. E. M. Anscombe, Oxford: Blackwell, 1958). See also *PI* 372.

11. Seminal examples of the reformulation of philosophical questions about nature

It is important to realize, however, that some reasons for the neglect of nature belong specifically to the intellectual history of American thought. In spite of the neglect of classical American philosophy, its premises still influenced American thinkers. One distinctively American reason for the occlusion of nature in philosophical inquiry was the embrace of Darwinism as a model for scientific disinterestedness and honesty. This was a distinctively American phenomenon to the extent that it took place in a context of combat with religious orthodoxy in the American universities.[12] It was important for the proponents of science to overcome religious influence in the universities so as to achieve excellence and emerge from the shadow of European intellectual life. In the United States, Darwinism brought in its wake a concern with scientific method and then later a commitment to a simple materialist ideology.[13] The grafting of a reductionist conception of the human organism onto the scientific prestige of Darwin has foreclosed further discussion of nature.

Another American reason for the neglect of nature is the idealism evident in Emerson's treatment of nature. If nature is what it is only through the vision of a human being, then nature is subordinate to individual aspiration and appears as fully pliable to manipulation. Transcendentalism is, as Peirce described it, something like a virus that he suspected he had never fully expelled in himself.[14] Much later, Stanley Cavell similarly paid tribute to the power of Emersonian idealism in describing it as a youthful remnant in the mature philosopher.[15] These

in logical terms are A. J. Ayer "What Is a Law of Nature?" first published in *Revue Internationale de Philosophie* 36 (1956): 144–65; R. B. Braithwaite's *Scientific Explanation: A Study of the Function of Theory, Probability and Law in Science* (Cambridge: Cambridge University Press, 1953), which illustrates the combination of a logical formulation of scientific explanation with a Humean approach to nature; and Carl Hempel's "Methods of Concept Formation," in *International Encyclopedia of Unified Science* (Chicago: University of Chicago Press, 1953), 23–38.

12. On the intellectual combat between science, especially Darwinism, and Protestant natural theology at Harvard, see Bruce Kuklick, *The Rise of American Philosophy* (New Haven: Yale University Press, 1977), Part I. See also Kuklick's *A History of Philosophy in America, 1720–2000* (Oxford: Oxford University Press, 2002).

13. Chauncey Wright initiated the theme of scientific method as a central part of the American reception of Darwin. See Philip Wiener, "Chauncey Wright, Darwin and Scientific Neutrality," *Journal of the History of Ideas* 6 (1945): 19–45. For a treatment of the influence of science and its methodology on American philosophy, see Daniel Wilson, *Science, Community, and the Transformation.* A recent statement of reductive materialism as a philosophy of nature is Edward O. Wilson, *Consilience: The Unity of Knowledge* (New York: Knopf, 1998).

14. See Peirce's third *Monist* essay, "The Law of Mind," reprinted in *Charles S. Peirce: The Essential Writings*, ed. E. C. Moore (Amherst, N.Y.: Prometheus Press, 1998), 191.

15. Commenting on another philosopher's rejection of Emerson, Cavell says: "But I think I know by now what the man of fifty finds distasteful that made the boy of sixteen or

flashes of honest self-assessment bear witness to the fact that Transcendentalism became a kind of underground river in American intellectual life. From the standpoint of Transcendentalism, nature is another avenue of self-expression. The strong claims presently made for a sociological analysis of science may reflect this influence. Philosophically, the idea that nature or scientific knowledge is socially constructed is a "community-based" idealism.[16]

Against this background, the robust concept of nature typical of Aristotelian or Thomistic philosophy has more in common with the American love of science than with Transcendentalism. Aristotle said that nature is an internal principle of change. He meant that individual things, as instances of kinds, have distinctive powers and characteristic ways of behaving that mark their essential natures. The practicing scientist is a realist and this is a realist philosophy: natures are given in experience and remain the same, though our knowledge of them may change and may, in fact, never reach completion.[17] In general, the long Aristotelian tradition developing a realist conception of *natures* resident in things, as opposed to a Kantian conception of nature as a regulative idea, provides a different perspective on nature than is found in the American traditions of Transcendentalism, scientism, or even pragmatism.

The papers in this volume illustrate the themes of nature and community in American philosophy but also place these themes in a rich context of the authors' own expertise and interests. Some illustrate the cultural influences on the American philosophers, and others concentrate on the particular philosophical contributions and originality of these philosophers. Some interpret the American philosophers in the

seventeen ecstatic. It is an idea that Emerson and any romantic would be lost without, that the world could be—or could have been—so remade, or I in it, that I could *want* it, as it would be, or I in it. In time the idea is apt to become maddening if kept green (certainly it makes one's grown-up acquaintances impatient), a continuous rebuke to the way we live" (*In Quest of the Ordinary* [note 8], 35).

16. For social constructivist accounts of scientific knowledge, see David Bloor, *Knowledge and Social Imagery*, 2d ed. (Chicago: University of Chicago Press, 1991), and Bruno Latour, *Pandora's Hope: Essays on the Reality of Science Studies* (Cambridge, Mass.: Harvard University Press, 1999). On social constructivism as a type of idealism, see Robert Klee, *Introduction to the Philosophy of Science: Cutting Nature at Its Seams* (Oxford: Oxford University Press, 1997), 157–80.

17. For a treatment of the subject of investigation in science in relation to the Aristotelian concept of nature, see Benedict Ashley, "Does Natural Science Attain Nature or Only the Phenomena?" in *The Philosophy of Physics*, ed. Vincent E. Smith (Jamaica, N.Y.: St. John's University Press, 1961), 63–82. For the Thomistic approach to science in general, see other articles in this volume, also Charles De Koninck, *The Hollow Universe* (London: Oxford University Press, 1960), and William A. Wallace, *The Modeling of Nature* (Washington, D.C.: Catholic University of America Press, 1996).

context of contemporary philosophical debates. The particular way in which American thought assimilated German idealism is displayed in the first paper of the series, Russell B. Goodman's "The Colors of the Spirit: Emerson and Thoreau on Nature and the Self."

Goodman's thesis is that, for Emerson and Thoreau, nature "is always mediated by, or entangled with, the human being." He demonstrates that they do not simply state this entanglement as a fact, as William James later did, but they record or show within their texts the deep involvement of nature with language and feeling. I would comment that this is *how* and *why* Transcendentalism came to be the underground river of American intellect, constitutive of American attitudes toward nature and many other things. In a literary way, these essayists *performed* for Americans an amalgamation of nature and the human. Goodman uses James's analogy of cooking: "I want to say that Emerson and Thoreau search nature for something raw and wild, a reality independent of human thinking, but that they succeed mostly in showing a nature already cooked or peptonized." Goodman illustrates his thesis in terms consistent with his subject, through Emerson and Thoreau's recourse to the expression of moods to describe nature. Nature is not understood by being analyzed, but at the same time it does not remain clothed in any single kind of attire. In nature, we come to our senses, partly because of the succession of moods that lends perspective on the human. Goodman points to the metaphysical implications of these reflections in Emerson's treatment of rest, motion, and unity, and in Thoreau's ownership of the landscape from his seat in the woods. He comments, "So [Thoreau] is an active observer who, as Coleridge said, 'receives but what he gives.' Thoreau has nature to himself, but it is a nature *for* himself."

The importance of idealism in American interpretation of nature is shown again in John Clendenning's "The World Beyond Our Mountains: Nature in the Philosophy of Josiah Royce." Unlike Emerson or Thoreau, Royce was a professional philosopher. Nevertheless, a personal response to nature is deeply engrained in his philosophical outlook. Clendenning traces the connection of nature and the personal to Royce's earliest desire to explore the world beyond the Sacramento Valley, his home. This 'world beyond' is the world of culture, science, and achievement that contrasts with his limited cultural environment in pioneer California. Through references to Royce's intellectual development, Clendenning connects this desire to Royce's "longing to know an ideal reality that transcends materialism." Royce was one of the American thinkers for whom evolution constituted an intellectual challenge. Clendenning lays out the construction of Royce's philosophy of nature from *The Spirit of Modern Philosophy* to *The World and the Individual.* Whereas Emerson said nature must be sought in solitude when social additions to the individual are shed, Royce believed that an individual's knowledge of nature depends on social consciousness. A central tenet of this point of view is the idea of continuity. Every human being, acting and thinking, is bound in innumerable small ways to the whole cosmos. Even our recognition of the existence of our fellows depends on this intimate association with non-human nature. Clendenning points out that by the mid-1880s Royce had forged a philosophy of nature meant to answer materialism and transcend dualism, an objective idealism different from his better-known metaphysics of Absolute Idealism. Clendenning describes also the philosophy of nature found in *The World and the Individual,* Royce's last definitive statement of Absolute Idealism. A central tenet of Royce's philosophy of nature in this work is the intermediary, betweenness, and the triad. Physical reality is the mediating term in the triad. As Royce said, "My fellow and Myself, with Nature between us."

In Royce's philosophy, we see an interweaving of the themes of nature and community expressed in a sophisticated philosophical way. The theme of community is present in a different way in the philosophy of C. S. Peirce, i.e., in the idea of a *consensus* of a community of scientific researchers, a consensus that functions as the arbiter of the truth of a proposition. In his paper "Sense-Critical Realism: a Transcendental-Pragmatic Interpretation of C. S. Peirce's Theory of Reality and Truth," Karl-Otto Apel treats this topic in relation to a fundamental problem of critical idealism, the conditions of the possibility of objectively valid knowledge. His paper is an example of the recent turn toward American pragmatism in European philosophy, and he places his topic within the contemporary discussion of an "epistemic or discourse-pragmatic explication of the meaning of truth." Peirce replaced Kant's forms of intuition and *a priori* principles with common sense beliefs or instinctive presuppositions of scientific cognition. In this context, the problem for a notion of truth is fallibility. Apel's particular concern is to understand how Peirce's idea of an 'ultimate opinion' to be reached by a community of researchers preserves the concept of truth without presupposing unknowable things-in-themselves. The problem is the gap between the factual result of consensus-formation and the absolute concept of truth. Apel surveys the problems and also the answers offered in the present debate on this topic. He sees Peirce's concept of 'Thirdness' as serving the purposes of Kant's idea of a regulative principle. As regulative ideas did, thirdness distinguishes true principles from Platonic hypostatizations and from mere generalizations of data. Kant had called his regulative ideas 'as if' principles, however. Peirce avoids this fictionalization of the criteria for truth through his own characterization of 'thirdness' as the continuity of sign-interpretation. Apel sees Peirce as offering a unique philosophical solution within the tradition of critical idealism. His paper offers one account of why Peirce is regarded now as the greatest American philosopher.

Jean De Groot's paper "Homegrown Positivism: Charles Darwin and Chauncey Wright," treats the dual influences of Darwinism and scientific positivism in shaping a current of American philosophy that would, in the twentieth century, overwhelm the American idealist tradition. She argues that there was a European tradition of scientific positivism, expressed by Auguste Comte and Ernst Mach, different from the more familiar logical positivism of the twentieth century. According to this nineteenth-century positivism, science is endoxic, grounded in ordinary life, non-axiomatic, and realist in temper. Chauncey Wright took this positivism, so allied in his own mind with utilitarianism, as the interpretive model for his understanding of Darwinian evolution. Wright's understanding of evolution is not reductionist though he recognizes the laws of physics and chemistry as one kind of cause for which natural selection is the "mode of operation." Explanation in Darwinism is in accordance with the all-pervasive principle of utility. Neither in ethics nor in biology is utility a principle consciously applied. Rather, this principle in biology operates something like the laws of political economy. Wright's insistence on a rigorous minimalism in scientific explanation made him a tireless critic of what he understood as metaphysics, a type of philosophy that he believed always had a hidden religious motivation. Yet, he believed that every scientist is an Aristotelian, and he affirmed Aristotle's understanding of induction as well as some aspects of the Aristotelian idea of final cause. His attack was relentless, however, on any doctrine he believed harbored an idea of divine design in nature. Wright's admirable honesty in scientific investigation, the elegance of his own thought about science, and his delight in philosophical discourse and discussion made him a potent influence on a generation of young American intellectuals, among them C. S. Peirce, William James, and Oliver Wendell Holmes.

During Wright's short career teaching at Harvard, he lectured in 1870 on the psychology of Wilhelm Wundt, the German physiological psychologist. Wright understood that Wundt's research was promising to liberate psychology at last from philosophy of soul and give it a biological base. The importance of nineteenth-century German psychology in determining the character of American naturalism is the subject of Stefano Poggi's paper, "William James and German Naturalism."

Poggi sketches the debate in Germany in the second half of the nineteenth century about psychology as a science. Citing Fechner and Wundt, Poggi says that the greatest strides were made in the psychology of sensation, by experimentation involving the organs of sense. The physiology of optics and acoustics were the areas developed. This left the nervous system as a whole still the subject of philosophical treatment, however. Perhaps for this reason, psychology did not avoid being influenced by romanticism and idealism. This influence was most manifest in references in German psychology to a "dynamic inwardness," which is at the base of the whole life of the soul. James was greatly interested, Poggi says, in the consequences for the development of German philosophy of the scientific approach to mental life. Lotze's views on the foundations of a new anthropology were taken most to heart by James in this regard. Lotze influenced James's recourse to the data of psychological inquiry as James sought to lay the foundations for a science of psychology. James hoped by this empirical approach to provide a more realistic philosophical attitude to the human subject. James criticized Lotze's monism, however, and believed Fechner's psychophysics provided the best antidote to an absolutist system. Poggi treats also the influence of Mach, who shared with Fechner a belief in the inaccessibility of the inwardness of the psyche and who focused instead on manifest psychological activity. Poggi points to the continual opposition but inevitable interplay of the empirical and the idealist, the scientific and romantic, in German psychology. He suggests that James by no means entirely rejected the idealist and romantic strains in German psychology, pointing to the difference between Mach's biological reductionism and James's theory of pure experience. Poggi's paper confirms how enthusiastically Americans embraced scientific naturalism in philosophy. His research lays alongside the influence of Darwinism in this regard a second source, namely German developments in psychology.

The papers by De Groot and Poggi show the influence of scientific studies in shaping a critical approach both to religion and to the European philosophical tradition. C. S. Peirce was passionately devoted to science and, by his own account, "intensely curious about Cosmology and Psychology." In "C. S. Peirce's Reclamation of Teleology," Vincent Colapietro shows that it was Peirce's aim to reconcile evolution, psychology, and idealism in a refutation of materialist mechanism. Colapietro says that Peirce identified evolution with natural growth and associated the idea of growth with Aristotle. He says, "Peirce's guess at the riddle of the universe was animated by a concern to explain, rather than explain away, the reality of growth." Peirce's explanation and reinterpretation of teleology is, in its turn, a central part of his reclamation of Aristotelian metaphysics. He compares Peirce to both Emerson and James on the subject of nature, showing that, although a pragmatist like James, Peirce identified himself more with Emerson. Emerson's idealism is egocentric, however, and he speaks in a poetical voice foreign to Peirce's scientific and philosophical temperament. Peirce concurs in James's rejection of the idolatry of Emerson's nature worship, but he is himself more concerned to expose the "idols of the theatre such as mechanism and determinism." In this connection, Colapietro discusses Peirce's original and insightful analysis of nominalism in modern thought. Rejecting nominalism, Peirce endorses the contention of idealism about nature, that ultimate explanatory principles are psychical laws. By this, Peirce does depart from Aristotle in a modern way. Peirce's teleology is also different from Aristotle's in that Peirce posits historically emergent and mutable forms as constituting natural processes. Nature is a cosmos that has evolved out of a primordial chaos. Colapietro observes that Peirce represents a different approach to philosophical tradition than the dominant Cartesian "anti-traditionalism." Peirce's apology for both scholastic philosophy and common sense contributes to an original philosophy that reconciles the apparently conflicting American traditions of idealism and enthusiasm for science.

Although Alexis de Tocqueville was not a philosopher, his *Democracy in America* has been very influential in shaping the American intellect. In *Democracy in America,* nature figures in at least two ways. There is an underlying concept of nature and human nature expressed through his writing. This concept reflects the influence of Enlightenment science and Tocqueville's own appropriation of Christian and classical ideas. There are also reflections upon how human nature expresses itself in the emerging civilization of the New World. Harvey C. Mansfield treats both Tocqueville's European interpretation of nature and his reflections on human nature in American society in his "Nature and Fact in Tocqueville's *Democracy in America.*" He says that, unlike Aristotle, for whom the natural implicates motion toward an end, for Tocqueville nature is what is spontaneous. Tocqueville's liberal political orientation makes him prefer a nature that "generates freely" to a nature that might "control or curb" freedom. Nevertheless, he wants to avoid both the unbridled individualism and the complete determination by nature that can follow from spontaneity. The guide that nature constituted in classical philosophy is replaced in Tocqueville's thought by the "providential fact" of democracy. There is no best regime for him; democracy simply has replaced aristocracy and now serves as the constraining fact to which peoples and states must adapt. Tocqueville believed that democracy began in Christianity but then turned its back on Christianity. He states that without Jesus Christ the equality of all men would not have been understood. Where equality is concerned, though, nature can still show itself in what is in "accordance with nature." Tocqueville notes, for instance, the negative effects of slavery on the masters as much as on the slaves, when he contrasts the slave state of Kentucky to the free state of Ohio. Tocqueville systematically relies on what he understands as facts to correct theories. He idealizes some facts—his pictures of the New England township, and of American women—but by doing so, he provides the guide to conduct that substitutes for a natural order. Mansfield says that Tocqueville's analysis of America reveals man's political nature better than the liberal political philosophers on whom Americans most lately depend. Although democracy aims at "rational tranquility," in reality it is intractable. The result is that Americans "consider all authority with the eye of a malcontent."

In the political philosophy of Oliver Wendell Holmes Jr., a contrast of nature and fact also figures prominently. Values, Holmes said, are merely "generalizations emotionally expressed." This means they are matters of fact, conventions, perhaps to be respected but worthy of no special regard as judgments of right and wrong. As Robert P. George explains in "Holmes on Natural Law," values are the subject of positive science. We may be able to explore psychological or sociological reasons for their existence, but there is no transcendental sanction for them. This means also that man has no nature that provides a criterion for distinguishing the fitting or noble from the unfitting and base. Values express themselves in social conventions, which are arbitrary but which nevertheless have a legitimate claim to make for observance. Social conventions enable the goals of an individual or group to be achieved. In his discussion of the relation of positive to natural law, Thomas Aquinas concurred in this evaluation of social conventions. For Aquinas, George says, some positive laws are derived from the natural law by a process akin to deduction of conclusions from premises. Others are not derived so directly. These exist for the sake of the common good, but comprise only one scheme of laws, chosen in whatever way from among different possible schemes. Holmes's moral skepticism prevents his seeing compliance with law as ever being anything more than a hypothetical imperative. Holmes believed the only meaning of a 'transcendental basis' for behavior is the simple fact that some conditions must be fulfilled for us to live. Such necessities are absolute but do not thereby constitute *a priori* duties. George points out that this view constitutes a philosophical claim just as much as any non-skeptical claim about the basis of law and inquires what its basis might be. For this reason, he says that Holmes's philosophy faces the problem of retorsion with its threat of self-refutation.

Holmes's philosophical outlook, with its rejection of transcendent norms, could be regarded now as a formulation of relativism. In "Dewey's Metaphysics of Existence," Joseph Margolis offers an interpretation of Dewey in which the claim of relativism is grounded in the flux of nature. Margolis contends that, more so than Peirce or James, Dewey achieved the definitive formulation of pragmatism, a formulation that truly succeeds in eliminating what he calls Cartesian realism. He holds that the pragmatic realism of Putnam and the relativism of Rorty are both still in dialogue with Cartesian realism, the view that knowledge copies the world and portrays natural necessities epistemically. On the one hand, Putnam's plural ontologies cannot show themselves as divergent descriptions of the *same world.* On the other hand, Rorty, the postmodernist, can do no more than declare his triumph at the futility of the realist program, something that had already been demonstrated by Kant, Hegel, and Dewey. Dewey, however, recognized that realism must be 'biologized.' Experience is pre-cognitive, and all cognitive knowledge is relative to human aims and goals. Knowledge develops out of a "problematic situation," an indeterminate experience that produces a practical impasse for the human subject. In Margolis's interpretation, pragmatism declares that the real world is flux, and all metaphysical and epistemological questions must be relativized to the pre-cognitive indeterminacies of the existential impasse. The metaphysics of existence, then, is the "deep contingency of nature." Dewey's thought is *naturalistic* because it prefers to be guided by the sciences rather than by philosophical concepts, but it is not *naturalizing,* like the thought of Davidson or Rorty, because Dewey does not believe that explanation is ultimately causal. Unlike the postmodernist, Margolis believes that metaphysical discussion appropriately continues. "But Dewey's example confirms the reasonableness and coherence of carrying the issue further in the pragmatist's direction. Beyond that, we cannot but fall back to the usual dialectical scuffles among competitors."

In the final paper of the series, "Perspectives on Nature in American Thought," Nicholas Rescher catalogues different concepts of nature in Western thought, and in American culture in particular, to display different thinkers' commitments with respect to the relation of nature and technology, and nature and soul. Nature conceived in contrast to artifice is the Aristotelian conception. Nature has been conceived as physical reality and human artifice taken together, however, and this in either a positive, a neutral, or a negative light. In a positive light, this combination was the spiritualized nature of Emerson. Taken in a neutral way, it is scientific naturalism. Taken negatively, it is the nihilistic naturalism prominent in continental philosophy of the early twentieth century. Rescher conceives a third category—comprehensively holistic nature—in which physical reality and human artifice are "conjoined into a coordinated whole under the aegis of a 'spiritual'—that is, value-governed standpoint." In this conception, nature does not contrast parts of reality but rather what is real versus what is unreal or fictional. Rescher shows how this catalogue of perspectives on nature gives insight on the development of American culture, illustrating each view with examples from American art.

His third category is an important one for his analysis of contemporary views of nature. He believes that there has been a counter-revolution against scientific naturalism and nihilistic naturalism in favor of the integration of the work of man and nature. This development has occurred alongside a new rapprochement between science and religion, based on developments in science such as big bang cosmology, dematerialization of matter in quantum theory, and intelligent design theory in evolutionary biology. Rescher believes that the philosophical outlook that should accompany these positive developments in the conception of nature is a renovated pragmatism. He laments the "tragedy" of current interpretations of pragmatism as normlessness, since he regards pragmatism as a "doctrine designed to provide a simple and sensible way of validating norms." Authentic pragmatism also is open to a variety of intellectual cultures. Hence, the philosophy of pragmatism as originally developed by Americans appropriately promotes life-affirming values and fosters positive aspirations.

Rescher's taxonomy could well be taken to organize the American thinkers treated in this series and also the interpretive points of view offered here. His hope for what would issue from a return to authentic pragmatism echoes the values always promoted by Professor Jude P. Dougherty as Dean of the School of Philosophy at Catholic University. As Dean, Prof. Dougherty was a dedicated advocate of the value of Aristotèlian philosophy in revealing the limitations of twentieth-century Anglo-American philosophy. His view was that the logical approach is incomplete without metaphysics and philosophy of nature. Yet, he also promoted the rapprochement between medieval philosophy and contemporary methods in philosophy, particularly in philosophy of science. The range of points of view presented in this series is a fitting tribute to Prof. Dougherty's engagement in contemporary philosophical discussion, regardless of its claims, and his belief that truth is present in a variety of philosophical traditions.

NATURE IN AMERICAN PHILOSOPHY

1 The Colors of the Spirit: Emerson and Thoreau on Nature and the Self

RUSSELL B. GOODMAN

Nature as portrayed in Emerson's and Thoreau's writings is always mediated by, or entangled with, the human being. I do not mean this simply in the sense that these writers are human beings writing about nature, so that their portrayals, their texts, are human products. Rather, for all their interest in nature as it is, and for all their valuing of nature precisely for its separation from the human, they still record, advert to, or show within their texts ways in which the nature about which they care so deeply is tied up with human language, thought, feeling, and action.

I begin, however, with a figure of the later American philosophical tradition, with William James, and specifically, that strand of James's pragmatism that he calls "humanism." In the chapter on "Pragmatism and Humanism" in his book *Pragmatism,* James states that "the trail of the human serpent is over everything," and he defines what he calls his "humanistic principle": "you can't weed out the human contribution." "When we talk of reality 'independent' of human thinking," James continues,

> it seems a thing very hard to find. It reduces to the notion of what is just entering into experience and yet to be named, or else to some imagined aboriginal presence in experience, before any belief about the presence had arisen, before any human conception had been applied. It is what is absolutely dumb and evanescent, the merely ideal limit of our minds. We may glimpse it, but we never grasp it; what we grasp is always some substitute for it which previous human thinking has peptonized and cooked for our consumption.[1]

James writes as a realist, for he does not deny the existence of a reality independent of human experience: it may be "very hard to find," yet

1. William James, *Pragmatism* (Cambridge, Mass., and London: Harvard University Press, 1975), 119–20.

it is there. James's cooking metaphor also suggests realism, even as it asserts our alteration of that which we taste: for cooking requires something that is to be cooked, the raw food. Using James's terms, I want to say that Emerson and Thoreau search nature for something raw and wild, a reality independent of human thinking, but that they succeed mostly in showing a nature already cooked or peptonized.[2] Moreover, for all their interest in nature as it is in itself, and for all their confidence that they can read or understand nature, their interest is not so much in nature *simpliciter,* as it is in the proper human relation to nature.

Consider the quintessential American text on nature, Emerson's sky-blue book of 1836 entitled *Nature.* By its very title this book raises nature to a position as a centrally important subject for thought and action. Certainly nature has been a central topic of Western and non-Western philosophy for thousands of years, from the Presocratics onward, and Emerson draws specifically on such immediate predecessors as Wordsworth and Coleridge, who see nature as a scene of quasi-divine instruction. Yet beginning with Emerson's *Nature* and then continuing with Thoreau's *Walden,* a newly intense, concrete, and appreciative focus on nature appears in America, something Lawrence Buell identifies as an environmental imagination.[3] The texts examined here are the beginnings of this American tradition.[4]

The task here is to consider the degree to which Emerson's book is about nature as entangled with the human being, which brings us to the remark from which this paper draws its title: "Nature always wears the colors of the spirit" (39). Notice the universal, or eternal, form of Emerson's claim, marked by the term "always." Emerson is talking about the *necessity* of understanding nature through our own spiritual colorings, and so this is one of the many places where Emerson's thought has a Kantian ring to it. Nature wears the colors of the human

2. James understands the "aboriginal presence in experience," which may be glimpsed but not grasped, as existing "before any human conception had been applied," leaving it open whether any other sort of conception is there. In contrast, Emerson and Thoreau (and James himself in his metaphor of the client whose case is always interpreted by his lawyer, *Pragmatism,* 18–19) tend to see the wild as conceptually structured.

3. Lawrence Buell, *The Environmental Imagination: Thoreau, Nature Writing and the Foundation of American Culture* (Cambridge, Mass.: Belknap Press of Harvard University Press, 1995).

4. References to Emerson's works are incorporated into the text as follows: page numbers refer to Ralph Waldo Emerson, *Selected Essays,* ed. Larzer Ziff (New York: Penguin Books, 1982). References of the form *CW* 2:22 refer to volumes of *The Collected Works of Ralph Waldo Emerson,* ed. Robert Spiller (Cambridge, Mass.: Harvard University Press, 1971–).

spirit, as for Kant nature is a construct of things as they appear to us, organized by our human faculties of understanding and sensibility.

Emerson's claim occurs near the end of his first chapter. What sorts of colorings does he have in mind? Certainly Emerson looks back to the ecstatic moments in nature with which the chapter opens, of which perhaps the best known is the following:

> In the woods, we return to reason and faith. There I feel that nothing can befall me in life,—no disgrace, no calamity . . . which nature cannot repair. Standing on the bare ground,—my head bathed by the blithe air and uplifted into infinite space,—all mean egotism vanishes. I become a transparent eyeball; I am nothing; I see all; the currents of the Universal Being circulate through me; I am part or parcel of God. The name of the nearest friend sounds then foreign and accidental. (39)

The woods are the site for an epiphany, in which the individual human Emerson all but disappears in the "currents of the Universal Being." Nature is the place where the currents of Being are allowed to repair the tears in the fabric of life. There is no suggestion here that nature is clothed in anything, spiritual or material. In nature we come to our senses; we wake from a dream, and we know, or achieve, "all."

Yet a few paragraphs later, just before the remark about nature wearing the colors of the spirit, Emerson writes: "For nature is not always tricked in holiday attire, but the same scene which yesterday breathed perfume and glittered as for the frolic of the nymphs is overspread with melancholy today" (39). At this point, Emerson sees the earlier scene of nature and the transparent eyeball as a kind of trick, and he finds nature overspread with melancholy. How so? This question is answered in the immediately succeeding lines, with which Emerson's chapter concludes: "there is a kind of contempt of the landscape felt by him who has just lost by death a dear friend. The sky is less grand as it shuts down over less worth in the population" (39–40). These awkward but heartfelt words express a note easy to miss amongst Emerson's more appreciated words of elation in the presence of nature.[5] Emerson knew what he was talking about. By the time *Nature* was published, he had lost three dear friends to tuberculosis: his nineteen-year-old wife, Ellen, and his two younger brothers, Charles and Edward.

The expression "tricked in holiday attire" is itself tricky, for it takes a stance toward the other more inspiring and comforting colorings of na-

5. On Emerson's sense of evil, particularly in his later philosophy, see Michael Lopez, "*The Conduct of Life:* Emerson's Anatomy of Power," in *The Cambridge Companion to Emerson,* ed. Joel Porte and Saundra Morris (Cambridge: Cambridge University Press, 1999), pp. 243–66.

ture with which Emerson's chapter opens. At the beginning of the chapter, Emerson finds no trick in his joyful and elevated perceptions of nature, but here at the end of the chapter, from the perspective of a universe "less grand," tricked is how they appear. These stances toward nature are material for what Stanley Cavell has called Emerson's "epistemology . . . of moods."[6] For Emerson is in a different mood at the end of his first chapter of *Nature* than he is at the beginning. From the perspective of that later mood, nature as encountered in the early, more expansive sections of the chapter has an illusory cast to it—it is *tricked* in holiday attire. But from the perspective of the opening of the chapter, such melancholy and skepticism is itself a false view of nature. From that perspective he is not *in* a mood, but in the circulating currents of the Real. Standing back from the play of these perspectives, Emerson writes: "Our moods do not believe in each other" (*CW* 2:182).

Notice then that Emerson's chapter on "Nature"—in his book on *Nature*—is a record of nature as apprehended by a fluctuating, moody human being. In fact, Emerson begins his chapter not with nature but with "man." "To go into solitude," Emerson opens the chapter by writing, "a man needs to retire as much from his chamber as from society. I am not solitary whilst I read and write, though nobody is with me. But if a man would be alone, let him look at the stars." From the start, then, nature is discussed as a place of significance for "a man." As the chapter proceeds, Emerson enacts his philosophy of flux, as the epiphany in the woods is succeeded by the "contempt of the landscape" felt by one who has lost a dear friend.

If Emerson records our various moods with nature, his emphasis is not so much on these descriptions as on reform. "Few adult persons," he complains, "can see nature. Most persons do not see the sun. At least they have a very superficial seeing. The sun illuminates only the eye of the man, but shines into the eye and the heart of the child" (38). Emerson here propounds the characteristically Romantic themes of the child and the heart. His claim is about seeing or understanding, said to be better accomplished by a child than by an adult, and by the heart and an involved eye than by a mere surface of sensation. Emerson follows the poet William Wordsworth, who spoke in his "Immortality Ode" of the child as "the best Philosopher" and whose scenes with nature are suffused with feeling. In "Tintern Abbey," for example, Wordsworth writes: "I have learned / To look on nature, not as in the

6. Stanley Cavell, "Thinking of Emerson," in *The Senses of Walden: An Expanded Edition* (San Francisco: North Point Press, 1981), 126.

hour / Of thoughtless youth; but hearing oftentimes / The still, sad music of humanity." Nature for Wordsworth, as for Emerson, is appreciated within a human context. The problem in seeing it lies within us, for the nature we seek is, in fact, ordinarily, commonly available: "The invariable mark of wisdom," Emerson writes in the "Prospects" chapter with which *Nature* closes, "is to see the miraculous in the common" (78).

Emerson thinks of himself as a poet in *Nature,* one who properly understands and opens up the landscape for others:

> The charming landscape which I saw this morning is indubitably made up of some twenty or thirty farms. Miller owns this field, Locke that, and Manning the woodland beyond. But none of them owns the landscape. There is a property in the horizon which no man has but he whose eye can integrate all the parts, that is, the poet.

The poet-hero sees the property in the horizon that is obscured by our daily commerce and by our falsely reified conceptions of property. Is the "property in the horizon" really there, or is it projected by the poet? Emerson answers: "the power to produce this delight does not reside in nature, but in man, or in a harmony of both" (39).

The text examined so far, mostly from the first chapter of *Nature,* is part of Emerson's only attempt at an integrated work of poetic philosophy. The form at which he was soon to arrive for the presentation of his views was the essay, which by its definition is a trial or test, not a completed or final project. It is in his essays that Emerson achieves a distinctive, controlled voice—or a set of voices one might say, corresponding to his varying moods. The masterpieces of the *Essays, First Series* of 1841 include "Self-Reliance," "Circles," and "The Over-Soul," and of the *Essays, Second Series* of 1844, "Experience" and "The Poet." The *Second Series* includes a less appreciated essay entitled "Nature," to which I now turn.

"Nature" opens with some fine appreciations of the natural world: the woods and the river outside the city; and the stars, beyond the human environment altogether. Yet nature is our home, Emerson asserts, so that the encounter with nature is at the same time a discovery and a return to a familiar and comforting place:

> the mind loves its old home: as water to our thirst, so is the rock, the ground, to our eyes, and hands, and feet. . . . Cities give not the human senses room enough. We go out daily and nightly to feed the eyes on the horizon, and require so much scope, just as we need water for our bath. . . . We nestle in nature, and draw our living as parasites from her roots and grains and we receive

glances from the heavenly bodies, which call us to solitude and foretell the remotest future. The blue zenith is the point in which romance and reality meet. (*CW* 3:100)

Emerson's nature is here both robustly material—in its rocks and roots—and animistic—in the glances we are said to receive from the stars. It is also the place romance meets reality: where our senses expand, and we see the miraculous in the common. Emerson's subject is not nature in itself, but nature as the proper human home.

Although Emerson stresses the connection between solitude and the appreciation of nature, it is a solitude that may admit a friend. "My house stands in low land, with limited outlook," he writes. "But I go with my friend to the shore of our little river, and with one stroke of the paddle, I leave the village politics and personalities, yes, and the world of villages and personalities behind, and pass into a delicate realm of sunset and moonlight. . . . I am taught the poorness of our invention, the ugliness of towns and palaces. . . . Henceforth I shall be hard to please" (*CW* 3:101). This passage illustrates not only the ever-present "I" in Emerson's depictions of nature ("I am taught," "I shall be hard to please") but also the nearness, even the ordinariness, of nature. We do not have to travel far to escape our limited outlooks, for in "every landscape, the point of astonishment is the meeting of the sky and the earth, and that is seen from the first hillock as well as from the top of the Alleghanies." The key once again is not so much the landscape as the person who observes it: "The difference between landscape and landscape is small, but there is great difference in the beholders" (*CW* 3:103).

So far, so good. But now comes the first of several transitions in Emerson's essay, reversals of tone and conclusion that bring to mind the reversals of mood we observed in Emerson's book *Nature.* Emerson begins by acknowledging that people get tired of hearing nature praised, no matter how beautifully: "it is very easy to outrun the sympathy of readers on this topic," he avers. It is almost as bad as trying to talk to them about religion. Yet Emerson defends his praise for nature, once again not in terms of nature as it is in itself but of nature as it is for us:

Nature is loved by what is best in us. . . . And the beauty of nature must always seem unreal and mocking, until the landscape has human figures, that are as good as itself. If there were good men, there would never be this rapture in nature. If the king is in the palace, nobody looks at the walls. . . . [O]ur hunting of the picturesque is inseparable from our protest against false society. Man is fallen; nature is erect, and serves as a differential thermometer, detecting the presence or absence of the divine sentiment in man. By fault of our dulness and selfishness, we are looking up to nature, but when we are convalescent, nature will look up to us. (*CW* 3:104)

In this passage Emerson's central concern is with what he calls "Man" or "the king." The king is—as he had said eight years earlier in *Nature,* a "dwarf of himself,"[7] whereas nature reveals a self-sufficient and unapologetic life. In this passage, as in many others in Emerson's writing, one finds a motive for leaving town, for getting in the canoe or going out to Walden: a desire for a companionship or "society" not available in our ordinary "fallen" circumstances.

Although Emerson thus returns to his defense and praise of nature, there has been a change of tone: a new assertiveness or urgency prevails, as if he has been dislodged from the contented and celebratory mood in which the essay opens. Emerson marks the difference as one of subject matter, however. The first part of the essay has been concerned with "*natura naturata,* or nature passive" (*CW* 3:103), whereas the second part will concern "the Efficient Nature, *natura naturans,* the quick cause, before which all forms flee as the driven snows" (*CW* 3:104). In short, the first part of the essay has been concerned with Rest, and the second will consider Motion.[8]

These versions of nature are in turn forms of a central tension in Emerson's thought, between the One (sometimes thought of as the Over-soul) and the Many, the flux, or as he puts it in "Experience," "the newness" (*CW* 3:40). In my opinion, Emerson holds both views—Rest and Motion, the One and the Many—to be deeply right, even though they conflict; and he arrives at his epistemology of moods and what he calls a "Two Faced" metaphysics as ways of understanding both.

Before returning briefly to these metaphysical questions, I want to continue with Emerson's discussion of nature as flux, *natura naturans.* With flux, he holds, comes a tendency to "exaggeration":

Nature sends no creature, no man into the world, without adding a small excess of his proper quality. . . . to every creature nature added a little violence of direction in its proper path, a shove to put it on its way; in every instance, a slight generosity, a drop too much. Without electricity the air would rot, and

7. Emerson, *Selected Essays,* 77.

8. Samuel Taylor Coleridge, one of Emerson's sources for these terms, takes *natura naturata* to be "the finished products of nature, natural objects," and *natura naturans* to be "nature as a collection of active forces and processes." See Robert J. Richardson, Jr., "Emerson and Nature," in *The Cambridge Companion to Emerson,* 101.

without this violence of direction, which men and women have, without a spice of bigot and fanatic, no excitement, no efficiency. We aim above the mark, to hit the mark. (*CW* 3:107)

Emerson now portrays a violent and excessive rather than a balanced, gentle, and contented nature—and a correspondingly different human being, more in keeping with such essays as "Fate" and "Power" and "Gifts."[9] Vegetables send off not one or two, but "a prodigality of seeds" in order finally to arrive at a successor or two; animals have an excess of fear that in the few cases where fear is justified helps protect them. In the human realm, we find excess even in the character of our geniuses: "No man is quite sane; each has a vein of folly in his composition, a slight determination of blood to the head, to make sure of holding him hard to some one point which nature had taken to heart" (108–9). Nature's way of preserving and continuing itself lies through this excess. As for the writer, "no man can write anything, who does not think that what he writes is for the time the history of the world" (*CW* 3:110).

These reflections on human life now lead Emerson back to the natural world. The turbulent motion of Nature Efficient appears no longer as a scene of fulfillment, nor even of promise. It is now a scene of absence:

There is throughout nature something mocking, something that leads us on and on, but arrives nowhere, keeps no faith with us. . . . There is in woods and waters a certain enticement and flattery, together with a failure to yield a present satisfaction. This disappointment is felt in every landscape. . . . Nature is still elsewhere. This or this is but outskirt and far-off reflection and echo of the triumph that has passed by, and is now at its glancing splendor and heyday, perchance in the neighboring fields, or, if you stand in the field, then in the adjacent woods. The present object shall give you this sense of stillness that follows a pageant which has just gone by. What splendid distance, what recesses of ineffable pomp and loveliness in the sunset! But who can go where they are, or lay his hand or plant his foot thereon? Off they fall from the round world forever and ever. It is the same among the men and women, as among the silent trees; always a referred existence, an absence, never a presence and satisfaction. (*CW* 3:110–12)

As in his book *Nature,* Emerson here looks at the world through the lenses of different moods. Both the book and the essay "Nature" begin in a mood of expansive satisfaction with and in nature, and both proceed to moods of regret, oppression, or lamentation, in which nature is "overspread with melancholy," or becomes "an absence, never a pres-

9. For a discussion of gifts in relation to excess, see Gary Shapiro, "'Give Me a Break!' Emerson on Fruit and Flowers," *Journal of Speculative Philosophy* 13, no. 2 (1999): 98–113.

ence and satisfaction." The long passage quoted just above, from late in the "Nature" essay, is a lament for a nature that seems to have passed by, and the report of a "referred existence" that characterizes "men and women" as well as the "silent trees." With this mood of lament in mind, consider the differences in Emerson's moody prose by going back to the essay's opening, to a wonderfully contented, even lolling, sentence that has not yet been cited, with which Emerson's essay "Nature" begins:

> There are days which occur in this climate, at almost any season of the year, wherein the world reaches its perfection, when the air, the heavenly bodies, and the earth, make a harmony, as if nature would indulge her offspring; when, in these bleak upper sides of the planet, nothing is to desire that we have heard of the happiest latitudes, and we bask in the shining hours of Florida and Cuba; when everything that has life gives sign of satisfaction, and the cattle that lie on the ground seem to have great and tranquil thoughts. (*CW* 3:99)

No such cattle, and no such days, are discernable in the nature Emerson finds near the end of his essay. In the terms of the essay's end, this first sentence records nature present, not nature deferred or absent. But there is a hint of things to come even in the first three words of the essay: "There are days." For if there are days like this, there may be other sorts of days.

In his essay, then, Emerson enacts as well as describes two views of nature, each of which is colored by the human being who takes them. There is the Emerson of Rest or stability, and the Emerson of change or Motion. There is nature present and full, and nature absent or empty. Will the real Emerson, or the real Nature, please stand up? Like the Daoist yin-yang, each of Emerson's positions contains a hint of the other deep within itself: for Rest knows that there are other days, and Motion knows that the flux includes states of satisfaction and presence, as well as states of absence.

Noting the transformations of mood and doctrine in Emerson's essay, one may want to say that Motion is fundamental, for the essay *moves*—from the contented cattle to the referred men and women. However, since our moods don't believe in each other, from the perspective of the self-sufficient, entirely present nature recorded in some of Emerson's self-sufficient, entirely present sentences, there is a kind of stability and satisfaction that cannot be disturbed by other possible views, moments, or moods. A full treatment of Emerson's position must also take into account the fact that in most of his essays Emerson associates stability with conformity—hence with something degrading, and transition with originality or newness, hence with something elevating.

In "Experience," for example, Emerson seeks a "balance of power and form," and finds that the way of wisdom is to "finish the moment, to find the journey's end in every step of the road, to live the greatest number of good hours" (*CW* 3:35).

In any case, Emerson's essay "Nature" makes one more move as it draws to its conclusion. Just as he seems to be giving up on nature—the scene of a parade gone by—he recovers: "One look at the face of heaven and earth lays all petulence at rest, and soothes us to wiser convictions. To the intelligent, nature converts itself into a vast promise, and will not be rashly explained. Her secret is untold" (*CW* 3:112). That promise can be fulfilled through a conversion or harnessing of the flux.

The essay's last paragraph accordingly presents a vision of *mystical flux,* of "divine circulations [which] never rest nor linger." But at the same time it offers a vision—with strong Neoplatonic overtones—of a *unity* embracing both "mind" and "world." Here is that final paragraph:

> The world is mind precipitated, and the volatile essence is forever escaping again into the state of free thought. Hence the virtue and pungency of the influence on the mind, of natural objects, whether inorganic or organized. . . . That power which does not respect quantity, which makes the whole and the particle its equal channel, delegates its smile to the morning, and distils its essence into every drop of rain. Every moment instructs, and every object: for wisdom is infused into every form. It has been poured into us as blood; it convulsed us as pain; it slid into us as pleasure; it enveloped us in dull melancholy days, or in days of cheerful labor; we did not guess its essence, until after a long time. (*CW* 3:113–14)

So Emerson ends the essay "Nature," with a passage that, although it mentions the morning and the rain, presents a vision in which the special place of nature is overcome. "*Every* moment instructs, and *every* object." One may feel, therefore, that by the end of the essay nature itself has disappeared into the general instruction, and that a writer about nature might search for a more directly responsive mode of address to the natural world. Such a writer was Emerson's friend and tenant Henry David Thoreau, and it is to his writings about nature that I now turn.

Consider two passages from *Walden,* Thoreau's masterpiece published in 1853. The first, from the chapter on "Solitude," offers an account of a bout of loneliness, and its cure by a new sense of Thoreau's relation to the natural world:

> I have never felt lonesome, or in the least oppressed by a sense of solitude, but once, and that was a few weeks after I came to the woods, when, for an hour, I

doubted if the near neighborhood of man was not essential to a serene and healthy life. To be alone was something unpleasant. But I was at the same time conscious of a slight insanity in my mood, and seemed to foresee my recovery. In the midst of a gentle rain while these thoughts prevailed, I was suddenly sensible of such sweet and beneficent society in Nature, in the very pattering of the drops, and in every sound and sight around my house, an infinite and unaccountable friendliness all at once like an atmosphere sustaining me, as made the fancied advantages of human neighborhood insignificant, and I have never thought of them since. Every little pine needle expanded and swelled with sympathy and befriended me.[10]

Nature wears several colors of Thoreau's spirit here. In what he describes as a slightly insane "mood," nature seems oppressive in its foreignness and unfamiliarity—without anything resembling human friendliness or recognition. Thoreau's mood then changes suddenly, with nature assuming a friendlier aspect, the pine needles expanding and swelling with sympathy and so on. And this is more than a mood, for it becomes a perspective on nature that, according to his testimony here, Thoreau does not subsequently lose. Nature comes to constitute for him a "sweet and beneficent society," a substitute for the society of men he finds cheap and false. What Thoreau departs from, then, as he enters the society of nature, is not the human as such, but the concerns of human society. *Walden* shows us the life-world in nature of a mostly solitary human being.

The second passage from *Walden* to be considered occurs near the opening of its second chapter, entitled "Where I Lived and What I Lived For." Thoreau begins not with the idea of nature, but with that of a house, yet it is a house that is designed for the contemplation of nature, so that what is essential to it is not its roof or its walls, but the perspective it offers the seated viewer:

Wherever I sat, there I might live, and the landscape radiated from me accordingly. What is a house but a *sedes*, a seat?—better if a country seat. . . . [T]here I might live, I said; and there I did live, for an hour, a summer and winter life; saw how I could let the years run off, buffet the winter through, and see the spring come in. The future inhabitants of this region, wherever they may place their houses, may be sure they have been anticipated. An afternoon sufficed to lay out the land into orchard woodlot and pasture, and to decide what fine oaks or pines should be left to stand before the door, and whence each blasted tree could be seen to the best advantage; and then I let it lie, fallow perchance, for a man is rich in proportion to the number of things which he can afford to let alone. (*W* 81–2)

10. Henry David Thoreau, *Walden* (Princeton: Princeton University Press, 1989), 131–32. Henceforth, this source will be cited parenthetically in the text as *W*.

Thoreau depicts an afternoon of rest or contemplation, and suggests a rhythm of walking and sitting. Where he sits, there he lives, in the way one lives in a house—which offers its own perspective on things. Thoreau imaginatively molds the nature he sees, cutting trees and forming pastures; but then he releases nature—for in his economy he "can afford to let [it] alone." He is alive, now, enjoying the view and the lay of the land as if he lived there more or less permanently—but without having to worry about paying a mortgage or keeping the pasture mowed. The owner of such property cannot afford to leave it alone, concerned as he is with protecting it, and making it useful. Thoreau possesses—has the use of—the place precisely because he can afford to leave it alone.

In these two scenes from *Walden*—that of the friendly pine needles, and that of the house as a seat—we find not nature *simpliciter* but nature beheld by a human observer. The observer is a poet in Emerson's sense, someone who by integrating the parts of the horizon, "owns the landscape" in a way that the legal owners do not. The observer is the center from which the landscape radiates, and he is a grateful participant in the "sweet and encouraging" society he finds in the woods. So he is an active observer who, as Coleridge said, "receive[s] but what he give[s]."[11] Thoreau has nature to himself, but it is a nature *for* himself. The pine needles are not sweet to each other, but to him.

Walden is certainly one of the great and influential contributions to human thinking about nature. But even as Thoreau had a mostly finished manuscript of his book, he was writing in his *Journal:* "I do not know where to find in any literature whether ancient or modern—any adequate account of that Nature with which I am acquainted. Mythology comes nearest to it of any."[12] Both Thoreau and Emerson kept journals for decades, drawing on them for their published work. In the early 1850s, however, a thought occurred to Thoreau that never occurred to Emerson, that his journal, rather than some more composed work such as *Walden,* was the best expression for his literary and philosophical project of producing an "adequate account of that Nature with which I am acquainted."

The *Journal* came to be Thoreau's modern form of mythology—a twenty-four-year odyssey with no final return (though many moments of homecoming). Thoreau saw the *Journal* as the ideal vehicle for

11. Samuel Taylor Coleridge, "Dejection: An Ode," in *The Portable Coleridge,* ed. I. A. Richards (New York: Penguin, 1978), 170.

12. Henry David Thoreau, *A Year in Thoreau's Journal: 1851* (New York Penhuin, 1993), 14. Hereafter cited in text as *J.*

recording the concrete particularities of nature. The *Journal* was to be a way of making his words present to nature; of having his words determined by what Emerson calls "the potluck of the day" (*CW* 3:36). Thoreau states his aspirations for the *Journal* in another passage from 1851:

> No one to my knowledge has observed the minute differences in the seasons—Hardly two nights are alike—The rocks do not feel warm tonight for the air is warmest—nor does the sand particularly. A Book of the seasons—each page of which should be written in its own season & out of doors or in its own locality wherever it may be— (*J* 67)

The term "journal" contains the Old French *jour* or *jur;* a journal is a daybook.[13] Thoreau has the idea of a daybook (or season-book) that would be written *at the time and in the place* of the events it records. A journal has a sequence, but it may have no order, since it is constructed largely by the events of the writer's life as he meets the life of nature, rather than by the logic of a plot or narrative. *Walden,* in contrast, has the structure of its chapters on "Reading," "Solitude," "Economy," "Winter," "Spring," where Thoreau distills his experience into essays. The journal will have entries, lists, disquisitions, but no essays or chapters. In her book *Writing Nature,* Sharon Cameron argues that because of these differences in structure, the *Journal* is a more perfect embodiment of Thoreau's project than is *Walden.*[14] One need not agree with this conclusion to agree that the *Journal* is a formidable accomplishment, and that the experience of reading it—as one may do in the Penguin edition of the *Journal* for the year 1851—is quite different from the experience of reading *Walden.* While teaching it one fall, I found that after a while Thoreau's dutiful attentiveness spilled into my own life, as I formed new habits of attention to the daily differences in the plants, light, and weather.

So let us consider the *Journal.* Something Thoreau has in mind for the *Journal* is a presentness to the phenomena, what Emerson had called setting up "the strong present tense." Thoreau's figure for this in *Walden* is "improv[ing] the nick of time, and notch[ing] it on my stick." The *Journal* is a set of such notches, a set of responses to this day and then the next and the next, including records of the state of mind of the writer.

As Thoreau compiles his daily record, the pattern of the seasons emerges not only in his explicit comments about seasonal changes, but

13. *The Oxford English Dictionary,* 2nd edition (Oxford: Clarendon Press, 1989), s.v. "journal," 8:279–80.

14. Sharon Cameron, *Writing Nature* (New York: Oxford University Press, 1985).

in the shortness and paucity of the entries for the frozen months of January, February, and March, as contrasted with the easy expansiveness of the entries for August or September. There is no entry at all, for example, in the time between February 27 and March 19, and what entries there are tend to be quite short. The entry for March 27, for example consists, in its entirety, of two sentences: "Walden is ⅔ broken up[.] It will probably be quite open by to-morrow night" (*J* 26).

Three days later, the mood is more relaxed and the entry longer: "March 30th Spring is already upon us. I see the tortoises or rather I hear them drop from the bank into the brooks at my approach—The catkins of the alders have blossomed. . . . The Pewee is heard & the lark (*J* 26)." The writer is waking up too, and the entry goes on for pages more. By July and August, Thoreau is writing in the *Journal* on most days, often for three or four pages in the printed version. Counting the pages of the Penguin edition, we find that the first five months of the year—through the end of May—occupy 58 pages; the next three months, June, July, and August, occupy 128 pages. September alone takes 60 pages, more than the first five months of the year put together. Then the year closes out with 29 pages for October and November, and 23 for the reflective and somewhat bitter month of December. These trends of verbal outflow and reticence reflect the seasons. When the birds are singing, so is Henry Thoreau; when the muskrat hibernates, or emerges from its den every fortnight, the writer in nature slows and stays mostly in his den too, by the fire.

Some of the most beautiful passages in the *Journal* were written during Thoreau's moonlit summer walks, accounts of which can go on for four or five pages. They contain descriptions of a silvery-white world, and the thoughts of a philosopher. For example:

> Sep 9th 2 AM
>
> The moon not quite full. To Conantum via road. There is a low vapor in the meadows beyond the depot—dense & white though scarcely higher than a man's head—concealing the stems of the trees. I see that the oaks which are so dark & distinctly outlined, are illumined by the moon on the opposite side. This as I go up the back road. A few thin ineffectual clouds in the sky. I come out thus into the moon-lit night—where men are not, as if into a scenery anciently deserted by men . . . (*J* 212)

Into such settings walks the writer, who sometimes depicts himself writing by moonlight, sometimes just searching for a pencil in the darkness. Later in his 2 A.M. moonlight walk, he reports: "The eastern horizon is now grown dun colored. . . . Some bird flies over making a noise like the barking of a puppy. It is yet so dark that I have dropt my pencil and cannot find it" (*J* 214). Writing by moonlight has its technical problems.

Another passage, this time from early August, depicts the writer working more comfortably:

> The mosquitoes hum about me. I distinguish the modest moon light on my paper[.] As the twilight deepens and the moonlight is more & more bright—I begin to distinguish myself who I am & where—as my walls contract I become more collected & composed & sensible of my own existence . . . (*J* 145)

The writer is the part of nature that records its phenomena, and that takes them as suggestions for thought. The writer—like the Emersonian poet—finds in nature a site for his own composition and self-consciousness.

Thoreau's *Journal* is often repetitive and unstructured, random. Yet over the weeks and months, his attention to detail allows seasonally evolving nature to show through, as the changing profusions of words on his page reflect the changing composition of the meadows, woods, and rivers through which he journeys. It is difficult to get a feeling for this profusion, repetition, and randomness in a short time. As Cameron writes: "When we train observation on single passages . . . we appear to see the work too close-up."[15] Stepping back would require more space than this article permits: it would require quoting long passages from the *Journal*. Of course, the expanse of time needed to see Thoreau's *Journal* at the proper distance is part of the *point* of his *Journal*, which comes to its present moments—whether seemingly random or part of some larger coherency—after pages and pages of exquisitely rendered detail.

Keeping in mind the difficulties of reading only a slice of the journal, let us nevertheless at least *dip* into the *Journal*'s profusions, by considering a passage from August 21, 1851. It begins with a list, but soon moves to the sort of random observations that fill the *Journal:*

> The prevailing conspicuous flowers at present are. The early golden-rods-Tansy—The Life-everlastings—fleabane though not for its flower Yarrow (rather dry)—hardhack & meadow sweet (both getting dry also may-weed) Eupatorium purpureum—Scabish—Clethra (—really a fine sweet scented and this year particularly fair & fresh flower—some unexpanded buds at top tinged with red)—Rhexia Virginica—Thoroughwort—Polygala sangunea—Prunella and Dogsbane—(getting stale) &c &c. . . .
>
> In some fields fresh clover heads appear. This is certainly better than fields of lodged & withered grass.

15. Ibid., 9.

> I find ground nuts by the RR causeway ¾ inch long by ⅓ inch. The epilobium still. (*J* 172)

Notice that Thoreau is in the picture, not only as a writer in two languages, but as one who interposes his evaluative comment about the fine sweet scent of the Clethra, about how good the fresh clover heads appear, and about finding nuts. The journal here depicts nature and a man.

But notice also how Thoreau's entry for the day is dictated by the nature he encounters. Consider especially the sentence: "I find ground nuts by the RR causeway ¾ inch long by ⅓ inch." Thoreau had no plan to write about these nuts; they are not part of any scheme, such as a list of presently observable flowers. Whereas the measurements indicate Thoreau's own activity, the verb—*find*—tells us that Thoreau is guided by something, call it Nature. He measures and writes about the nuts on this day because he happens to "find" them on his walk. They drop into his journal as they drop from an unnamed tree: contingently, on this day and not another. These nut-descriptions—not just of any nuts, but of the ones Thoreau found on his walk on September 7, 1851—are one way the *Journal* gets closer to raw nature than *Walden,* the chapters of which are distillations of many days rather than responses to particular days. Of course, William James would point out that even here we find the trail of the human serpent, for it is Thoreau's *selection* of these nuts, rather than, for example, of the tree that produced them that the passage records.

I have been discussing ways in which Thoreau succeeds in his *Journal* in being present to nature as an observer, recorder, or knower. I want next to consider what the *Journal* has to say, not about the epistemology, but about the metaphysics of the human being's relation to nature. Thoreau often stresses the naturalness—even the animality—of human beings. With our voices and our peculiar ways of living in houses and our farm animals, we are parts of nature too, and Thoreau records situations in which groups of human beings seem to belong in or to nature, rather than existing apart from it. In a passage from September 4, 1851, Thoreau considers two natural creatures he has observed, a farmer and the ox who pulls his plow:

> The farmer acts on the ox & the ox reacts on the farmer—They do not meet half way it is true—but they do meet at a distance from the centre of each—proportionate to each one[']s intellectual power. The farmer is oxlike in his thought in his walk—in his strength, in his trustworthiness—in his taste. (*J* 195)

The farmer and the ox do not meet halfway because the farmer's intellectual power allows him to exert a greater pull on his oxen than they on him. For instance, he breeds them, feeds them, yokes them, and makes them do his work. And in his memories, his ambitions and his language the farmer is far from the animal world. But in his patient, placid trudging in the fields behind his ox, he acts not only in a common project with his ox, but like his ox. They share a major activity of the day.

Elsewhere in the *Journal,* human beings appear without their animals, but as if they are themselves another species of animals. From a walk on September 7, 1851, Thoreau records this incident:

> Going up the road. . . . I smell burnt land somewhere. At Tupelo Cliff I hear the sound of singers on the river young men & women—which is unusual here—returning from their row. Man's voice thus uttered fits well the spaces—It fills Nature. And after all the singing of men is something far grander than any natural sound. . . . I bathe at the north side [of] the cliff while the moon shines round the end of the rock— (*J* 208)

Nature for the solitary bather contains the human rowers and singers, as it contains the farmer and his ox, the moonlit writer, and the men and women gathered in cities and towns. Our singing is "far grander than any natural sound," and it "fills Nature." In this sense, Thoreau glimpses here the state Emerson anticipates, in which we cast off our dullness and selfishness, no longer look up to nature, and find—if not that "nature will look up to us" that we belong in this nature in which we play, sing, and work.

Although Thoreau does not particularly like town life, he is a keen observer of the townspeople's activities, especially if they approach his favored regions of the woods and rivers. The entry for June 7, 1851, reads, in part:

> One of those gentle straight down rainy days—when the rain begins by spotting the cultivated fields as if shaken from a pepper box—a fishing day—when I see one neighbor after another—having donned his oil cloth suit walking or riding past with a fish-pole—having struck work—a day & an employment to make philosophers of them all. (*J* 61)

The neighbors gather for the fishing ritual, on a warm June day when the rain makes field work impossible. Thoreau records their seasonal activity in the same tone as he records the migration of the geese or the gathering of sparrows, as they set off "one . . . after the other." Thoreau's neighbors are said not to be philosophers. Yet the day—one of "those gentle straight down rainy days"—and the employment—"fishing"—are said to be suited for making them philosophers. What is it to be a philosopher? It is, in the terms of this June 7 entry, to have a distinct sense of the possibilities of the future. "In our sanest moments," Thoreau writes, "we find ourselves naturally expecting far greater changes than any which we have experienced within the period of distinct memory" (*J* 61). Thoreau's fishing neighbors, knocking off work for the day *en masse* like a herd of animals, nevertheless have the chance—each one of them—to achieve a kind of creative sanity with, or against the background of, the river, the rain, and the fish. From such states of sanity, a society of philosophers might begin to make sense.

In conclusion, Emerson and Thoreau find in nature a subject worthy of their lifelong attention. For both, nature is a teacher, a companion in one's solitude, and a home for human beings. Emerson discovers that nature is clothed in the colors of the human spirit. As he was to generalize the point in "Experience," life "is a train of moods like a string of beads, and, as we pass through them, they prove to be many-colored lenses which paint the world their own hue" (*CW* 3:30). Thoreau depicts nature as clothed in the human spirit, but also as including human beings as its proper parts. And he searches more intensely than Emerson did for the wildness of the natural world: the whiff of its aboriginal being, as William James might have put it. Thoreau is after all the philosopher who speaks in *Walden* of sucking all the marrow out of life, and of savoring even the taste of a woodchuck for its wildness.

Where, then, do these inquiries leave us? Where, as Emerson asked, at the beginning of "Experience," do we now find ourselves? An answer: within Nature at Rest and in Motion, contented like a cow or exaggerated like the seeds of the dandelion; among the Fogs, butterflies, asters, Irish moss, Poke and Indigo Weed, Hoary Cinquefoil, and Scarlet tanagers of Thoreau's *Journal*. When originally giving the material presented here as a lecture in the autumn at Catholic University in Washington, D.C., I applied the lessons of Thoreau's *Journal* to my listeners' circumstances by adding, "within the Beltway, near the Potomac, in the clearing air of early fall, among the greens and trees of the college campus, under the bright sky, among the attentive people." May you, the reader, make your own application of these lessons to your present circumstances.

2 The World Beyond Our Mountains: Nature in the Philosophy of Josiah Royce

JOHN CLENDENNING

A few months before he died in 1916, Josiah Royce sketched a brief autobiography, and in these remarks, as he searched for the central theme of his philosophy, he wrote the following insightful observation:

> When I review this whole process, I strongly feel that my deepest motives and problems have centered about the Idea of the Community, although this idea has only come gradually to my clear consciousness. This was what I was intensely feeling in the days when my sisters and I looked across the Sacramento Valley, and wondered about the great world beyond our mountains.[1]

The meaning of Royce's mountains and the world beyond them resonates at several levels. At the literal level, he was certainly thinking of a physical reality, the Sierra Nevada, the great mountain system that contained the very limited world into which he was born. To the west, across California's Central Valley, he could see the peaks of the Coast Range, and beyond, he imagined, the Pacific Ocean. It was also a world of cities and cultures, of languages and customs, of books and learning, of imagination and speculation. Psychologically, the mountains were the personal limits he hoped to overcome—shyness, loneliness, uncertainty, provinciality. As a metaphor for Royce's philosophy, the "mountains" denote the doctrines of mechanism, materialism, necessitarianism—theories of nature that dominated late nineteenth-century American thought, which he would first briefly espouse, then permanently reject. The world beyond these mountains expresses his longing to know an ideal reality that transcends materialism. Eventually Royce would insist that what is real is our whole purposive meaning that we seek beyond ourselves, an Absolute Meaning that is abundantly present in nature, but that we never fully know in any flickering moment of consciousness.

1. Josiah Royce, *The Hope of the Great Community* (New York: Macmillan, 1916), 129.

In these pages I will explore several versions of Royce's philosophy of nature. I will consider three distinct phases of the theory, each one an idealistic construction, opposed to materialistic reductionism and mechanistic necessitarianism.

BACKGROUND

Two persistent influences on Royce's mind must, at the outset, be recognized. The first of these, evangelical Christianity, was a family inheritance. Both parents were Protestant fundamentalists. The Bible, they believed, was the literal and indisputable record of cosmic history. Josiah Royce Sr. and Sarah Eleanor Bayliss were intensely devout, and they tried to indoctrinate their only son with their religious zeal. They had spent their early adult years in Rochester, New York, the heart of the famous "burnt-over district," where they were exposed to a number of rather bizarre religious cults. The elder Royce was a bit more than eccentric. A fruit peddler in San Francisco, he ruined his business by delivering extemporaneous sermons on street corners. City urchins, believing him insane, constantly harassed him. Mrs. Royce's faith was more rational. She was a school teacher and gifted writer, but she too was firm in her beliefs, a mystic who believed that every event in nature is directed by divine providence. It is not surprising, therefore, that Royce's introduction to the philosophy of nature was through the book of Revelation, which in childhood he read in the family Bible. His early acquaintance with Scripture and the teaching he received at home were deeply rooted influences.

Second in time, but perhaps equal in importance, was the influence of Romanticism. As an undergraduate at the University of California, Royce soaked up the poetry of the English Romantics, especially Blake, Wordsworth, Coleridge, Byron, and Shelley, and as soon as he learned to read German, he made extensive researches into the works of Herder, Goethe, Schiller, Novalis, Tieck, and Heinrich von Kleist. In fact, one of the first university courses that Royce taught at Johns Hopkins in 1878, when he was twenty-two years old, was a series of lectures on "The Poetry of the German Romantic School."[2] To the Romantics, he explained, nature was not a system of universal laws, but an intense experience:

> Not what the world is to another, or to himself at another time, but what it is to him now and here, this the poet seeks to give you. The condition of his mind at the time is to be made the measure of all things.[3]

2. Royce Papers, Harvard University Archives, vols. 56–57.
3. Ibid., vol. 56.

The following year, while teaching English at the University of California, Royce revised and expanded these lectures to include the English Romantics. Although he wrote his doctoral dissertation on the epistemological foundations of science, Royce might have pursued a career as a literary scholar. Indeed, throughout his life, he never renounced these poets or their vision. He knew them by heart and quoted them effortlessly. Of the later Romantics, he was especially drawn to Tennyson, Browning, Rossetti, and Swinburne, and among the American Romantics, he was influenced chiefly by Emerson. "Nature," Emerson proclaimed, "always wears the colors of the spirit."[4] The spirit resides in nature's core, it speaks in symbols, and a kindred human spirit may learn its message:

> The moral law lies at the centre of nature and radiates to the circumference. It is the pith and marrow of every substance, every relation, and every process. All things with which we deal, preach to us. What is a farm but a mute gospel? . . . Nor can it be doubted that this moral sentiment which thus scents the air, and grows in the grain, and impregnates the waters of the world, is caught by man and sinks into his soul.[5]

Royce did not quarrel with this transcendental vision, but he did note, somewhat ruefully, its failure to prevail. It lacked the intellectual and theoretical strength to face the challenge of materialism. The popularity of evolutionary thought, with its seemingly superior reasoning, caused Romantic earnestness to lapse and decay.[6] Royce lamented the spiritual void left by this decay, and it may be argued that his philosophy of nature was an attempt to restore some remnant of Romantic faith to nature, not alone by faith, however, or by writing diatribes against science, but by rigorous thought. The task he set for himself was to devise new philosophical paradigms that could answer materialism and breathe life back into nature.

Science and the theory of evolution that dominated thought in the late nineteenth century reduced young Josiah's world to doubt. Evolution not only challenged his Romantic tendencies, it also unsettled his religious beliefs. The Biblical cosmology that underpinned his family's credo was rocked by the new thought that Josiah met when he enrolled as a freshman at the University of California in 1871. He wrote a few years later:

4. Ralph Waldo Emerson, *The Collected Works of Ralph Waldo Emerson,* vol. 1, ed. Alfred R. Ferguson (Cambridge, Mass.: Harvard University Press, 1971), 10.

5. Ibid., 26.

6. Josiah Royce, *Fugitive Essays,* ed. Jacob Loewenberg (Cambridge, Mass.: Harvard University Press, 1920), 319–20.

> I remember the failing at heart when I first had to throw overboard my little old creed, and felt that I must for example accept the modern theory of evolution as the real truth of nature, against which a poor mortal with his blind hope of immortality might struggle in vain. The individual withered, and natural selection was more and more.[7]

Royce was fortunate in receiving his introduction to evolutionary thought from the great naturalist Joseph Le Conte. During his final three undergraduate years, Royce regularly attended Le Conte's lectures in botany, zoology, and geology. For Le Conte, evolution was more than a hypothesis, it was a proven and indispensable law of nature. He saw evolution documented in the observable facts in the solar system, in the earth, in the organic kingdom, in man and human society. Nature, as taught by Le Conte, was truly a Heraclitean world of flux.

And yet Le Conte was not a religious skeptic or agnostic. Exhaustively scientific in his observations of nature, Le Conte still remained emphatically theistic. The world, he maintained, is God's plan gradually unfolding. Le Conte rejected the old design argument, with its deity as the architect of a static universe; instead, his dynamic new God of evolution is rational, benevolent, futuristic, and resident in nature.

Aside from Le Conte, the principal evolutionist to influence Royce in his youth was Herbert Spencer. Like William James, Royce was at first an enthusiastic disciple of Spencer's bold speculative system. To the college junior in 1874, Spencer was "the greatest thinker now living . . . [the] expounder of Evolution, the far-reaching grasper of scientific truth under every form."[8] To Royce, even in the 1890s, Spencer was the Prometheus of his age, one who had undertaken the task of a Titan, to bring the fire of evolutionary truth into a splendid synthesis for all mankind, forever. His universal formula, his law of evolution, was to explain everything in the knowable world: the solar system and the space beyond, the history of the earth, its life, both plant and animal, including human beings—their bodies, thoughts, cultures, politics, morals—all mechanistically determined by strict necessity. And yet beyond this march of relentless materialism, Spencer insisted, there exists an ultimate mystery, the Unknowable, a real world that forever escapes scientific discovery. Thus Spencer hoped to reconcile religion and science. But what was it, this Unknowable? Spencer did not hesitate to name it the "First Cause," the "Infinite and Absolute."[9] And yet, this mystery could never be revealed and metaphysically expounded.

7. *The Letters of Josiah Royce,* ed. John Clendenning (Chicago: University of Chicago Press, 1970), 104.

8. "Mill and Spencer," Royce Papers, vol. 53.

9. Herbert Spencer, *First Principles of a New System of Philosophy* (New York: Appleton, 1881), 38.

For Royce, the task of addressing Spencerian issues and overturning Spencer's system continued throughout the years of his early adulthood, the 1880s and 1890s. He finally settled his scores with Spencer in 1904 with an extended essay on the subject, included in a short book, *Herbert Spencer.*[10] Early in the 1880s, as a young instructor in Berkeley, we find him challenging a few of Spencer's fundamental principles, but at Harvard the dispute was earnest and persistent. From 1885 to 1896, Royce taught a popular undergraduate course on "Philosophy of Nature" or "Cosmology." Spencer's *First Principles* was the central text, and according to the *Harvard University Catalogue,* the "modern doctrine of evolution" was always a central topic in the course.[11]

PHASE ONE: 1892–1898

The construction of Royce's philosophy of nature principally belongs to a period of approximately ten years, from *The Spirit of Modern Philosophy* (1892) to the second volume of *The World and the Individual* (1901). The progress was slow and the work, painstaking. Indeed, Royce twice missed self-imposed deadlines. An article promised to the *Philosophical Review* was delayed for more than three years.[12]

Fundamental to Royce's theory is the claim that nature may be known by either of two distinct modes of thought: appreciation or description.[13] Appreciations are inherently subjective, affective, and private. Say, I report a series of symptoms to my doctor: headache, malaise, insomnia. These thoughts about my body belong, according to Royce, to the World of Appreciation. By contrast, the World of Description consists of public knowledge, measurable entities—my blood pressure, for example. One can describe a hat by its certain size, weight, and molecular composition. But when I find my hat by its "feel" in a dark cloakroom, it belongs to the World of Appreciation. Neither is more "real" than the other; the difference is in the degree to which a thought can be shared, for the hallmark of description is universal, unambiguous communicability. But appreciations, as such, are "essentially dumb."[14] A poet in love may declare:

10. Josiah Royce, *Herbert Spencer: An Estimate and Review* (New York: Fox, Duffield, 1904).

11. *Harvard University Catalogue, 1885–86* through *1895–96,* Harvard University Archives. In 1893–94 and 1894–95, William James taught this course.

12. *Letters of Josiah Royce,* 264, 292–93.

13. Josiah Royce, *The Spirit of Modern Philosophy: An Essay in the Form of Lectures* (Boston: Houghton, Mifflin, 1892), 381–434.

14. Ibid., 389.

"My love is a red, red rose"

Or ask:

"Shall I compare thee to a summer's day?"

By expressing their feelings in tropes, the poets share their thoughts with readers and other lovers; thus objectified, their appreciations are made to seem more like descriptions. The important point is that the World of Description, unlike the inner, private World of Appreciation, is a world of socially bonded minds. Individuals are entitled to their private appreciations, but descriptions are public property. A description of nature requires a validation from the community of beings whose perceptions resonate with one's own—including perceptions of red roses and summer days. If, in fact, one's descriptions differed radically from the social norm, one might—or someone might—begin to question one's sanity.

In 1894 and 1895 Royce published two seminal and sequential essays in *The Philosophical Review*. Here we find his first truly original thoughts about nature.

In Romantic poetry, one's relation to nature is a direct, face-to-face encounter, whereas socially derived thoughts about nature are considered secondhand and therefore less real. To know nature truly, Emerson repeatedly preached, one must seek her in solitude, shed one's social skin, and "enjoy an original relation to the universe."[15] However, Royce implicitly renounced this belief and concluded that one's knowledge of nature is socially determined. Nature arises in and remains always a part of social consciousness. The keenest and most patient observer of the external world, he observed, comes into contact with only an infinitesimal part of a plethora of facts whose existence is rarely seriously doubted. If one actually believed only what he has exclusively verified, and doubted all socially revealed data, one could not read a daily newspaper or step across one's threshold with confidence. Elections, obituaries, market prices, theater openings—who would claim that these are less real than the toast and coffee we ate at breakfast today? Having never visited the Galápagos Islands, I cannot personally validate their existence, but I am certain that these islands exist, for I have seen maps and photographs and I have read about them in the writings of Charles Darwin, Herman Melville, and others whom I trust and admire. My certainty about the Galápagos Islands is based on my assurance that they are real for countless others, and are in fact part of that broad world we call the social consciousness.

15. Emerson, *Collected Works,* vol. 1, 3.

Royce maintains that not only our knowledge of particular facts, but even the very idea of an external world, depends on social consciousness. An infant playing with its fists or trying to grasp an object is, in a sense, dealing with an external reality, but without a most important feature—the gradually evolving thought and ever-present assurance that our external world exists for other minds, minds with whom we share a social relationship. In its very essence, a world of external fact is a possible subject for description, that is, for social communication. In the case, for instance, of an object in visible space, the *conditio sine qua non* for its reality is localization. Unlike the vague aches and pains we all experience, external objects, such as the Galápagos Islands, must occupy a specific space, have definite dimensions and boundaries. Localization is not, however, a condition *in itself,* but belongs instead to a vast network of interpersonal verifications. A rainbow fails to meet this criterion because when observers move about, the rainbow also changes its location; because its location is not the same for all percipients, a rainbow cannot be an object in the external world.

What holds for localization, holds also for number and motion. Something indeterminate, such as the loose change in my pocket, may be real, *subjectively* real, something to be appreciated. Say, two romantics stare at the heavens on a starlit night. We cannot say that the experience is the same for both of them. Each is awed by a separate enjoyment of the beautiful uncounted flickerings. Compare this to the astronomer's map. Whatever may be said to exist in the external world must be determinate, and this principle is based on the social consciousness.

Self-consciousness, like the idea of nature, also has social origins. Before the 1890s, the prevailing belief regarding the development of self-consciousness was that a child learns first that he exists, then that there are objects in the external world, and finally that other beings like himself exist. Influenced by the new social psychology of his friend, James Mark Baldwin, Royce challenged this view, maintaining that before the child gets a sense of personal identity, he interacts with and imitates the fascinating beings who constitute his primal social consciousness. Through imitation, Royce maintained, self-consciousness slowly takes shape:

> In brief, . . . a child is taught to be self-conscious just as he is taught everything else, by the social order that brings him up. Could he grow up alone with lifeless nature, there is nothing to indicate that he would become as self-conscious as is now a fairly educated cat.[16]

16. Josiah Royce, *Studies of Good and Evil: A Series of Essays upon the Problems of Philosophy* (New York: Appleton, 1898), 208. Hereafter cited in text as *SGE.*

Parents and other caretakers introduce the child to the world of external objects and teach him what they mean. He learns that these objects are exclusively neither *mine* or *theirs,* but *ours.*

However, nature as social order is not a seamless harmony. Over time, we inevitably learn that the objects in our experience cannot be identical to the objects in the experience of others. Furthermore, as members of the social consciousness, we imitate, but the objects themselves never respond. They remain "silent partners," imitable beings that do not imitate.[17] Royce thus arrives at a dualism: seen one way, nature is brimming with social life; seen another way, nature is the "other," mute, unknowable, and presumably lifeless. As a philosophical idealist, Royce challenged dualism, and the result was a bold, strange, but striking type of panpsychism.

As previous noted, Royce observed that of that vastness we call nature, only an infinitesimal amount is actually presented to personal experience. He further observed that of these presentations, we are aware of only an equally infinitesimal portion of their contents. As I scan this room, I see this and that, a friendly face here and a color patch there; there are random sounds, pleasant odors, an agreeable temperature in the room, but I do not especially attend to these phenomena. In fact, an immensity escapes my grasp. I do not see the atoms with their whirling electrons, nor do I sense the slow yet steady flow of geological time.

And yet, as rational beings, despite our severely limited experience, we intuitively posit a broader context, a realm of experience that extends, through space and time, endlessly. Say, for instance, that someone is writing notes in a room where I am speaking. As she records my thoughts, I infer, by observing her expressive movements, that she and I share a common realm of social consciousness. The pencil and paper in her hand, the chair where she sits, the bones and blood in her body, the air she breathes, her whole biological ancestry, everything, in short, links this being by continuity to the whole cosmos. Royce wrote, summarizing his central thesis:

> In short, you cannot separate your phenomenal fellows from the order of phenomenal nature. The continuity between man and nature, known to us first as the absolute inseparability of the expressive movements of our fellows from the nature-process in which these movements appear to be imbedded, and of which they are phenomenally a part, has now become, in the light of our whole experience of natural phenomena, an all-embracing continuity, extending to

17. Josiah Royce, "The External World and the Social Consciousness," *Philosophical Review* 3 (1894): 543.

cerebral and to general physiological processes, and to the ancestry and evolution of the human race, so that the highest in expressive human nature is now phenomenally linked by the most intimate ties to the simplest of physical processes. If, then, one's fellow is real, the whole of the phenomenal nature from which his phenomenal presence is continuous must be real in the same general fashion. (*SGE* 228)

Though conceding the limitations of this argument from continuity, Royce nevertheless pressed forward with his thesis: "nature's inner reality . . . is, like our own experience, conscious, organic, full of clear contrasts, rational, definite" (*SGE* 230).

Royce was much encouraged and influenced by three articles that Charles Peirce published in the *Monist* in 1891–92: "The Architecture of Theories," "The Doctrine of Necessity Examined," and "The Law of Mind."[18] The second of these was aimed especially at Spencer's determinism. Siding with Epicurus against Democritus, Peirce argued that "the inexhaustible multitudinous variety of the world" cannot be attributed to mechanical law, that the variety and diversity in nature could "spring only from spontaneity."[19] He did not, however, adopt the extreme position of claiming that chance alone produces anything; instead he claimed that the world is due to an interaction between chance and regularity. In evolutionary terms, habit formation is an adaptation to the environment. Peirce held that in some such fashion, like gradually acquired habits, the laws of nature had evolved. This he called the doctrine of tychism and synechism.[20]

Without wholly agreeing with Peirce's cosmology, Royce adopted his hypothesis as a useful analogy between habits in human beings and the regularities in physical phenomena. A man with an inveterate habit will scarcely be conscious of his repetitive behavior. Novelty, on the other hand, produces nervous excitement; in fact, Royce insisted, novelty, not habit, is sign of the conscious mind. So nature, set in its habits, seems to slumber. The tides flow, the earth orbits, the seasons change without showing a trace of consciousness. And yet, considering the billions of years in the life of the universe, we know that such regularities are relatively new, and that in the billions of years to come, nature will continue to adapt to phenomenal novelties and every natural rhythm will change. The difference between the constantly altered habits of nature and those of our socially expressive fellows is time—that is, the tremen-

18. Charles Sanders Peirce, *Collected Papers of Charles Sanders Peirce,* ed. Charles Hartshorne and Paul Weiss, vol. 6 (Cambridge, Mass.: Harvard University Press, 1960), 11–27, 28–45, 86–113.

19. Ibid., 41.

20. Ibid., 86.

dously different time-scale required for nature to alter its habits. Thus, human consciousness is constricted by what Royce called "*The Limitation of our Apperceptive Span*" (italics Royce's; *SGE* 242). In our finite consciousness, changes that occur too swiftly or too slowly will escape our awareness. Since the length of the span itself is utterly arbitrary, there is no reason to suppose that one type of consciousness may not have an apperceptive span of a millionth of a second, or for another, that several billion years may not be too large to contain its experience. The physical world, therefore, endlessly continuous with our own, is a realm of life, of conscious experience, fully as real as ours, constantly adapting and evolving, but existing in a vastly larger apperceptive span.

Thus, by the mid-1890s, Royce had forged a philosophy of nature that answered materialism and transcended dualism. It was an objective idealism that complemented his better-known metaphysics of Absolute Idealism. Constructed with the most modern thought of his time, Royce's theory still preserved the essential *Weltanschauung* of Christianity and Romanticism, the two traditions that profoundly influenced this thought and with which he never broke alliance. Nature, he had argued, is a living, spiritual, and yes, a divine presence, capable even of "inner light" (*SGE* 230).

PHASE TWO: 1899–1901

In 1897 Royce was appointed to deliver the Gifford Lectures in Aberdeen in 1898–1899 and 1899–1900. The result was a two-volume comprehensive treatise, *The World and the Individual,* Royce's fullest construction of Absolute Idealism, and the work that made him the leading exponent of that philosophy in America. The central idea and guiding principle of *The World and the Individual* is what he called the "Fourth Conception of Being." For Royce the whole problem of Being comes down to the question of the relationship between "internal" and "external" meanings of ideas.[21] By "internal meaning," Royce means "purpose." It may be an Absolute purpose, and as such it constitutes God's will, or it may be an "imperfectly expressed pulsation." It may be a highly rational purpose, such as a mathematical idea, or it may be an urgent passion, such as love, hate, fear, hope. In any event, an internal meaning or purpose is an individual Self—for Royce, purpose is the defining principle of individuation—and this Self seeks fulfillment in the not-Self, the Other, the world of external meaning (*WI* 2:272–73).

21. Josiah Royce, *The World and the Individual,* 2 vols. (New York: Macmillan, 1899–1901), 32. Hereafter cited in text as *WI* followed by volume and page number.

However, this external meaning owes its reality to its continuity with internal meaning: "either . . . the external meaning is genuinely continuous with the internal meaning, and is inwardly involved in the latter, or else . . . the idea has no external meaning at all" (*WI* 1:33). The contrast between internal and external ideas runs parallel to the distinction between the World of Appreciation and the World of Description. And yet now we see that the Fourth Conception of Being—the realm of purpose—is the World of Appreciation. "The true world," Royce insists, "the World of Values or of Appreciation, as rightly viewed by an absolute insight, would be a world of Selves, forming in the unity of their systems One Self" (*WI* 2:106).

Royce concentrated the presentation of this second phase of his philosophy of nature in the second, fourth, and fifth lectures of the second volume of *The World and the Individual.*

In the second lecture, "The Linkage of Facts," we learn that although the World of Description never reveals the deepest truths, it is not be slighted, for what we know—publicly know—concerning nature is descriptive knowledge. One of the most fundamental descriptive categories is that of Likeness and Difference. In the world of facts these are never presented separately, but correlatively. Objects can differ only if they are, in some sense, alike. Two solid bodies with different contours are nevertheless bodies with contours. Joy differs from grief, but both are emotions and therefore alike. Furthermore, the facts of nature are rarely thrust upon us against our will. The perception of likeness and difference requires discrimination; comparison is an act involving "attentive Interest" (*WI* 2:48). To someone merely passing through a produce market, the uncounted variety of fruits and vegetables will be a blur, but to the discriminating shopper, the variety is most important, and the items will be attentively examined and selected for their significant differences. Comparison entails purpose; hence, there is no description without appreciation. The internal meaning of the idea directs discrimination and so organizes the world.

Royce acknowledged a debt to Alfred Bray Kempe, the British mathematician who offered a generalization of the relation of *betweenness.* Royce, who loved mathematical paradigms, was especially captivated by this one, and he greeted it as the logical basis of the World of Description. Appropriating Kempe's generalization, Royce noted that when, in an act of discrimination, two objects *a* and *b* are compared, they stand in a relation to a third object *m* that is *between* them. In other words, between *a* and *b* there is something else that keeps them apart or indicates their difference. Royce attributed enormous importance to the fact that the structure of the relationship is triadic. The intermediary between *a* and *b* is not an independent object over and above the pair, it is *in* them. The triad thus provided Royce with some new suggestions concerning the problem of the One and the Many. Two objects have one common nature, one nature with two expressions. The intermediary that separates any two objects also unites them.

This leads to the working postulate upon which, Royce claimed, all scientific description—all discrimination, comparison, and differentiation—depends: "*Between any two there is a third*" (*WI* 2:89). It follows that the chain of possible intermediaries between *a* and *b* is endless. Between *a* and *m* we find m_1 and so on. Any three contiguous members of the series will be a triad, each triad will be between two others, all the triads will be linked in a single series, *a* through *b*, and the whole series will be one continuous volitional process. Once again, it is important to remember that studies of external meanings are conducted under the supervision, as it were, of internal meanings.

With the fourth lecture, "Physical and Social Reality," Royce reiterated and amplified his theses that there is, strictly speaking, no private knowledge of nature, that such knowledge arises and is validated through social intercourse. A belief in man as a social being is thus logically prior to a belief in physical reality. When we observe the expressive gestures of others, they seem to be harmony with our own internal meanings. In Kempian terms, physical reality is the mediating *tertium quid* in the triad: "My fellow and Myself, with Nature between us" (*WI* 2:177).

Although nature is bound to the social consciousness in the World of Appreciation, in the World of Description nature may seem nothing more than swarms of lifeless atoms and molecules ruled by immutable laws. To counter this mechanistic materialism, Royce advanced a striking form of pragmatism, as pure a pragmatism, in fact, as ever was argued by Peirce, James, or Dewey. Royce's pragmatism was grounded in the Fourth Conception of Being. Nature described becomes increasingly a socially significant tool, for science is a human means of controlling the environment. To be useful in the service of social purposes, the laws of succession and causation must remain constant. Pragmatically we may need to describe exactly how certain results unavoidably follow given antecedents. In terms of the descriptive triads, the conditions of discrimination require that some features will remain invariant throughout the set of transformations in any ordered series (*WI* 2:180–89). Viewed from the perspective of pragmatic human history, physical law has gradually evolved. Whenever the vicissitudes of nature have had practical consequences, social interest has motivated the search for laws that regulate these phenomena. From the primitive industrial arts of construction and manufacturing, the sciences of physics and chemistry evolved. Early commerce, with its need for exact weights and measures, laid the foundations for all of the quantitative sciences. Agriculture and religion gave rise to the sciences of biology, geography, and astronomy. In no way were any of these discoveries due to innate ideas or first principles of reason, nor does it follow from these discoveries that the whole physical universe is held in the grip of dire necessity. Science is an evolving ideal construction that adapts to human needs and serves practical social purposes (*WI* 2:195–204).

In his idealistic "Interpretation of Nature," the fifth lecture, Royce offered an elaborate hypothesis that proposes to explain how physical reality can be rationally understood as a volitional consciousness—including, but extending far beyond, human consciousness—complete with motives, plans, purposes, and goals. It was only a hypothesis, Royce explained. Notably he excluded the continuity argument that dominated the 1895 essay. Therefore he did not claim to have proven anything or to own exclusive rights to this philosophical territory. A chief appeal of this hypothesis consists, he maintained, in the rejection of materialism that follows from the breaking up of competing dualistic hypotheses. Most important, the hypothesis dovetails into Royce's metaphysical theory. The Fourth Conception of Being envisions the universe as an Absolute Consciousness, individuated by its struggles through temporal failures and successes toward the fulfillment of ultimate and infinite purposes. Each finite conscious individual is part of the Absolute, and every deed on earth and beyond performed by any conscious individual is a deed performed by the Absolute. Clearly, anyone persuaded by Royce's metaphysics will be induced to subscribe also to his hypothetical philosophy of nature.

Here is the hypothesis in a nutshell:

> I suppose . . . that when you deal with Nature, you deal with a vast realm of finite consciousness of which your own is at once a part and an example. All this finite consciousness shares with yours the character of being full of fluent processes whose tendency is twofold,—in one direction towards the formation of relatively stable habits of repetition, in the other direction towards the irrevocable leaving of certain events, situations, and types of experience behind. I suppose that this play between the irrevocable and the repeated, between habit and novelty, between rhythm and the destruction of rhythm, is everywhere in Nature, as it is in us, something significant, something of interest, something that means a struggle for ideals. I suppose that this something constitutes a process wherein goals, ideals, are sought in a seemingly endless pursuit, and where new realms of sentient experience are constantly coming into view and into relation to former experiences. (*WI* 226–27)

The hypothesis also supposes, given the arbitrary time-span that limits human perception, that there may be other finite natural beings that reside in different and, for us, inaccessible spans. Imagine, for instance, "one fellow-creature who took, perhaps, a billion years to complete a moment of his consciousness, so that where we saw, in the signs given us of his presence, only monotonous permanence of fact, he, in his inner life, faced momentarily significant change" (*WI* 2:228). Evolution, according to this hypothesis, becomes a prolonged conscious process of goal-oriented activity, constant intercommunication, and habit formation. The stable structures of atoms and molecules would be instances of habits acquired through intercommunication, like the customs of nations or the grammars of languages (*WI* 2:229–30). Finally, the hypothesis suggests that human beings are "differentiations from a finite conscious experience of presumably a much longer time-span than our present one" (*WI* 2:233). Death, one might say, is not a return to a lifeless state, but a change into another living time-span.

A searching review of a hundred years of criticism yields almost no comment on this aspect of Royce's philosophy. A single advocate of Royce's theory was J. Ellis McTaggart, who in reviewing the volume in *Mind,* admired the hypothesis for its "great novelty and importance." McTaggart did not, however, engage Royce's claims at a critical level, but merely expressed his approval and quoted a page of text.[22]

Royce himself apparently never mentioned the hypothesis again, and his disciples, always ready to defend his philosophy, were similarly mute. Royce admitted that the hypothesis was "provisional and tentative" in its details, but as a general formulation, Royce was convinced that is must be true. He expected, in fact, that the theory would eventually be corrected and confirmed through "further testing" and "careful scrutiny," though he did not say how such tests could be conducted (*WI* 2:224, 246).

Peirce, in his review for the *Nation,* devoted the first two paragraphs to generous praise of the volume and its author. It "will stand," he said, "a prominent milestone upon the highway of philosophy," bringing metaphysics into the community of the true sciences.[23] Actually Peirce ignored almost everything in the book, and instead, devoted the remaining fourteen paragraphs of the review to a probing criticism of Royce's logic.

John Dewey had no sympathy for Royce's theories. Reviewing the

22. *Critical Responses to Josiah Royce, 1885–1916,* ed. Randall E. Auxier, vol. 2 (Bristol, UK: Thoemmes Press, 2000), 52.

23. Charles Sanders Peirce, *Collected Papers of Charles Sanders Peirce,* ed. Arthur W. Burks, vol. 8 (Cambridge, Mass.: Harvard University Press, 1958), 89.

book in the *Philosophical Review,* Dewey dismissed Royce's interpretation of nature in a stinging footnote:

> I do not . . . consider myself a competent critic here; the whole doctrine of 'nature' is too high for me; I cannot attain unto it. To be frank, I do not believe that such speculative constructions, with no further basis than certain vague analogies, . . . do anything but bring philosophy into disrepute. It is, I believe, this sort of thing which encourages in the man of science, as well as in the man of common sense, the too common notion about metaphysics.[24]

These seem to have been the last words written on the subject. A younger Royce, an avid polemicist, would probably have been challenged to launch a counterattack and press the debate relentlessly, but instead he remained strangely silent.

PHASE THREE: 1902–1914

After *The World and the Individual,* and throughout the remaining fifteen years of his life, Royce rarely addressed issues in the philosophy of nature. Instead, his work branched off into two rather diverse fields: mathematical logic and moral/religious philosophy. His approach to the latter set of topics was more experiential, inclined to fallibilism, and therefore Royce had fewer occasions to venture into cosmological speculations. He did not, however, abandon teleology. Through his graduate seminar on comparative methodology, Royce maintained close relations with the Harvard scientific community. One young man in particular, the chemist Lawrence J. Henderson, rekindled Royce's interest in teleology. With Royce's advice and patronage Henderson published *The Fitness of the Environment,* which raised questions about evolution from a new perspective: natural selection explains how organisms evolved through adaptation, but it does not explain the environment's fitness for life.[25] To the chemist, the baffling coincidences of the many unique and complex properties of carbon, hydrogen, and oxygen—and particularly the characteristics of the compounds of water and carbonic acid—could be explained neither by chance nor by any known scientific principle. Rejecting the eighteenth-century design argument as well as Bergsonian vitalism, Henderson gingerly crossed the line that separates science and philosophy, and posited a "tendency" in nature—

24. John Dewey, review of *The World and the Individual, Second Series,* by Josiah Royce, *Philosophical Review* 11 (1902): 398.

25. Lawrence J. Henderson, *The Fitness of the Environment: An Inquiry into the Biological Significance of the Properties of Matter* (New York: Macmillan, 1913). See *Letters of Josiah Royce,* 572–73.

call it design or purpose, a "preëstablished associate of mechanism," or an invisible tendency *within* the mechanical processes that could conceivably evince a biocentric universe, a universe wherein the goal of at least three chemical elements is to produce life.[26]

Near the end of his last great work, *The Problem of Christianity* (1913), Royce cited *The Fitness of the Environment* with warm approval, adding that it illustrates his thesis "that the time-process as a whole . . . possesses and includes . . . a total meaning [i.e., purpose] and a coherent interpretation."[27] Royce did not elaborate, but perhaps he meant that since communities are inherently time-bound and goal-oriented, an evolving world, even one governed by the mechanical processes that Henderson described, has the characteristics of a community of interpretation, complete with personhood and purpose. "Fitness" would thus lie *between* the environment and life, linking the pair in a triad and serving as their interpreter.

In the same pages of *The Problem of Christianity*, Royce discussed a similar instance of "fitness" in a brief passage from Peirce's essay, "A Neglected Argument for the Reality of God."[28] Noting that it is the "proper function" of birds to fly and build nests, Peirce had argued that a parallel function in human beings is to create, and that in the realm of science "man's mind must have been attuned to the truth of things in order to discover what he has discovered."[29] Royce went further. He flatly denied that this instinctive scientific aptitude, being so far removed from practical adaptations, could have resulted from natural selection. Consider also the rapid advance of the inductive sciences since the sixteenth century. Such progress could not have been attained, Royce insisted, if left to mere chance. The old teleologies had failed to understand that man the interpreter, inherently attuned to nature, is the clear sign of the divine spirit in the finite world.[30]

Partly through his friendship with Henderson and the influence of Peirce, Royce presented a paper—"The Mechanical, the Historical, and the Statistical"—to scientific colleagues at Harvard in 1914.[31] It was his last attempt at a teleological interpretation of nature. The title and methodological perspective were inspired by the distinguished Scottish

26. Henderson, *Fitness of the Environment*, 274–76, 305–12.

27. Josiah Royce, *The Problem of Christianity* (Chicago: University of Chicago Press, 1968), 400–401 n. 3.

28. Ibid., 390–98.

29. Peirce, *Collected Papers*, 6:324–25.

30. Royce, *Problem of Christianity*, 397–400.

31. Josiah Royce, *The Basic Writings of Josiah Royce*, ed. John J. McDermott, vol. 2 (Chicago: University of Chicago Press, 1969), 711–33. Hereafter cited in text as *BW* followed by volume and page number.

physicist James Clerk Maxwell. When a single, novel event occurs in nature—such as a solar eclipse—it may be considered "historical," but when invariant laws are introduced to explain or—as in the case of the eclipse—to predict the event, we are dealing with the "mechanical." Statistics, on the other hand, studies the average behavior of large aggregates and is concerned with probability, not fixed and precisely predictable phenomena. Insurance actuaries clearly illustrate the use of statistical data. If an insurance company had access to all of the mechanical factors that result in deaths and casualties, they would certainly know exactly which dire events would occur and when. Since, however, the company has no such knowledge, it hires statisticians to compute risks and premiums. The statistical method is not, however, merely a makeshift: "not the mechanical," Royce insisted, "but the statistical form is the canonical form of scientific theory" (*BW* 2:727).

Citing Peirce's *Monist* essays of 1891–92, Royce outlined the essential factors in a statistical rendering of the external world. First, we need a large aggregate composed of a wide range of diverse members. Second, such an aggregate must constitute a "definable whole." Third, it must exhibit a tendency toward increasing "mutual assimilation" (*BW* 2:729). This increase in similarities (shared fortunes or relationships) may be expressed in the statistically demonstrable "law of the fecundity of aggregation" (*BW* 2:730). Add to this some principle of selection—such as natural selection—in an always changing environment and a further tendency of the aggregate members to repeat behavior and gradually to form habits. Thus we have the foundations of a new theory of evolution, one based not on mechanical necessity, but on statistical analysis, and also one that is motivated by purpose. Royce's new theory was thus similar to his earlier panpsychic hypothesis, but it differed in two important claims. First, nature, no longer certainly conscious, shows a tendency "towards what seems to be a sort of unconscious teleology—towards a purposiveness whose precise outcome no finite being seems precisely to intend" (*BW* 2:731). Second, this teleological tendency does not clearly extend throughout the universe. "Whether the whole world is ultimately and consciously teleological or not," Royce admitted, "this view of nature would of course be unable to decide" (*BW* 2:733).

Clearly, over the years, Royce limited the range and boldness of his interpretation of nature. In 1895 he argued that the external world, being continuous with other minds, must itself be a conscious being. In 1901 he was no less convinced of this panpsychism, but he urged it only as an attractive hypothesis, appealing because it conformed to his metaphysics. In 1914 the conscious being became an unconscious teleology that may or may not extend throughout the whole world. Royce remained, however, a consistent idealist and thoroughgoing evolutionist in maintaining that the world is forever developing into new forms, and that this whole evolving process is the meaning of an indwelling purposive agent. Without attempting to psychoanalyze him, I think it is safe to say that his religious convictions and latent Romanticism were so profoundly connected to his character that Royce was simply unable to frame a human problem without bringing these depths to the surface. Of course, important objections to his philosophy will always be raised. Perhaps the appeal of Royce is primarily esthetic: we, or at least some of us, are attracted by the beauty of his ideas, by the rich, dense texture of his writing, or by our own prior and deeply felt beliefs. But who can say that esthetic factors can or should be set aside when we address the momentous questions of life?

Royce's philosophy of nature is certainly the most neglected aspect of this most neglected of American philosophers. He is remembered today primarily as a religious and moral philosopher. His ethics envisions a world of free, responsible moral agents, each guided by a personal life-plan centered on loyalty. The universal being that he sometimes calls God or the Absolute "is not in ultimate essence another being than yourself" (*SGE* 14). This being is also Nature, for the Absolute is part of the finite world, striving and suffering through all finite experience to achieve its infinite ends. The world, Royce insists, is the living process of becoming literally a self or a person, seeking paradoxically "the completeness of his eternity" (*SGE* 14). Royce's philosophy of nature, therefore, harmonizes with his metaphysics and ethics, and is furthermore a vital aspect of his comprehensive philosophy, not a part to be detached and dismissed, but a part of "the great world beyond our mountains."

3 Sense-Critical Realism: A Transcendental-Pragmatic Interpretation of C. S. Peirce's Theory of Reality and Truth

KARL-OTTO APEL

The need has arisen in Peirce studies for a systematic account of Peirce's understanding of truth. It has become important to provide such an account because of recent debate about the so-called epistemic or discourse-pragmatic explication of the meaning of truth. Both the German and the American participants in this debate have, at least implicitly, related their discussion to Peirce's theory of reality and truth.[1] But they have not always taken into account the full scope and bearing of Peirce's arguments. Quite recently the debate has culminated in a definite rejection of the Peircean or quasi-Peircean approach. Representative instances include Hilary Putnam's reassessment of his former conception of truth as "rational acceptability under ideal conditions"[2] and Jürgen Habermas's abandonment of his discourse-pragmatic explication of truth in terms of "rationally grounded consensus" under conditions of an "ideal speech situation."[3] Because of this context of recent discussion, the purpose of the present paper is not to contribute to Peirce exegesis, as I have done in former writings,[4] but to present a systematic account of Peirce's understanding of truth.

1. For a more detailed account of the debate in question see Apel, "Pragmatism as Sense-Critical Realism Based on a Regulative Idea of Truth: In Defence of a Peircean Theory of Reality and Truth," *Transactions of the Charles S. Peirce Society* 37 (2001): 443–74.

2. See H. Putnam, *Reason, Truth, and History* (New York: Cambridge University Press, 1981), 55f. He distances himself from this position in Putnam, "Pragmatism," in *Proceedings of the Aristotelian Society* 95 (1994–95): 291–306, and: "Pragmatism and Realism," *Cardozo Law Review* 18 (1996): 153–70.

3. See J. Habermas, "Wahrheitstheorien," in *Vorstudien und Ergänzungen zur Theorie des Kommunikativen Handelns* (Frankfurt: Suhrkamp, 1984), 127–86, and for his abandonment of this position, see Habermas, *Wahrheit und Rechtfertigung* (Frankfurt: Suhrkamp, 1999), 256ff.

4. Cf. K.-O. Apel, "Einführung," in Charles Peirce, *Schriften* I, ed. K.-O. Apel (Frank-

Throughout the last decades, I have elaborated a discourse-pragmatic conception of truth similar to that of Habermas, but closer to that of Charles Peirce, as I understood Peirce in my first introduction to his philosophy in 1967.[5] In that introduction, I presented Peirce's early theory of reality and truth, which preceded his pragmatism but which may also be derived from it, as an ingenious *transformation* of Kant's critical epistemology. Peirce's theory provided a response to Kant's question concerning the conditions of the possibility of objectively valid knowledge. Peirce did not presuppose, however, unknowable things-in-themselves—indeed, he showed that Kant's presupposition of unknowable things-in-themselves, being a corollary of modern nominalism, is senseless. I called the Peircean conception of reality "sense-critical" or "meaning-critical realism," and in the present situation it seems to me that this approach may be reconstructed in such a way as to answer the recent debate about the possibility of an epistemic or discourse-pragmatic explication of the meaning of truth. To try to show this will be my aim in what follows.

A TRANSCENDENTAL-PRAGMATIC INTERPRETATION OF PEIRCE'S TRANSFORMATION OF KANT'S TRANSCENDENTAL IDEALISM

Before entering upon the reconstruction of Peirce's conception of sense-critical realism, let us consider what is presupposed by a transcendental pragmatics of language or transcendental semiotics.[6] In taking up this approach as a systematic conception of philosophy—even as a paradigm of first philosophy—I was originally inspired by Peirce. Later the notion of transcendental pragmatics provided a heuristic horizon for an interpretation of Peirce's thought—that is, for my positive assess-

furt: Suhrkamp, 1976), reprinted in Apel, *Der Denkweg von Charles Peirce* (Frankfurt: Suhrkamp, 1975), part 1, ch. 3 (*Charles S. Peirce: From Pragmatism to Pragmaticism*, trans. John M. Krois [Amherst: University of Massachusetts Press, 1981; reprint, New Jersey: Humanities Press, 1995], part 1, ch. 3). Compare Apel, "Von Kant zu Peirce," in *Transformation der Philosophie* (Frankfurt: Suhrkamp, 1973), vol. 2, 157–77 (selected essays trans. Glyn Adey and David Frisby, *Towards a Transformation of Philosophy* [London: Routledge and Kegan Paul, 1980; reprint, Milwaukee: Marquette University Press, 1998], 77–92).

5. See note 1 and my papers, "C. S. Peirce and Post-Tarskian Truth," in *The Relevance of Charles Peirce*, ed. E. Freeman (La Salle, Ill.: Monist Library of Philosophy, 1983), 189–223; "Fallibilismus, Konsenstheorie der Wahrheit und Letztbegründung," in Apel, *Auseinandersetzungen in Erprobung des transzendental-pragmatischen Ansatzes* (Frankfurt: Suhrkamp, 1998), 81–194; and "Husserl, Tarski oder Peirce?," in *I forste, andre, og tredje person: festskrift til Audun Øfsti*, ed. Solveig Bøe, Bengt Molander, and Brit Strandhagen (Trondheim: Norges teknisk-naturvitenskapelige universitet, 1999), 3–94.

6. Cf. *Auseinandersetzungen* and Apel, *Selected Essays*, vol. 1, *Towards a Transcendental Semiotics*, ed. E. Mendietta (Atlantic Highlands, N.J.: Humanities Press, 1994).

ment of Peirce's version of pragmatism as contrasted to the other classical versions, for example, the pragmatism of William James and John Dewey, or the contemporary version presented by R. Rorty. What is meant by the word "transcendental" in "transcendental pragmatics" or "transcendental semiotics"[7] is one of the most fundamental aspects of this heuristic. For some, this is also the most problematic aspect. Yet, Peirce's logic of scientific inquiry—as it was first developed in the pre-pragmatic papers and finally in the classification of sciences, when he made logic of inquiry a "normative science" between "phenomenology" and "hypothetic metaphysics"[8]—is a semiotic, and therefore also sense-critical, transformation of Kant's transcendental logic. Starting in the 1860s, Peirce worked throughout his life on this transformation. But why use the term "transcendental," since it is well known that Peirce often scornfully refused "transcendentalism"?

The answer is provided by a careful reflection on what is given up and what is preserved or replaced by Peirce's transformation of Kant's transcendental logic. First it has to be recognized that Peirce's "logic of inquiry" or later "normative (or semiotic) logic" cannot be equated with pure formal logic. Peirce was a pioneer, along with Boole, de Morgan, Frege, and Schroeder,[9] in the development of formal logic into mathematical logic in the nineteenth century. For Peirce, formal logic figured in his classification of sciences after 1900 as "mathematics (of logic)." As such, it was for Peirce an abstract presupposition for the foundation of categories—a modern substitute, so to speak, for Kant's metaphysical foundation of the categories in the table of judgments.[10] But the logic of inquiry or semiotic logic was from the beginning Peirce's equivalent to Kant's transcendental logic, which had been introduced in the *Critique of Pure Reason* to account for the conditions of the possibility of objectivity, that is, of the intersubjective validity of scientific experience.

The relevance of Peirce's logic of inquiry to the Kantian transcendental logic is evident already in the "New List of Categories" of 1867. This was Peirce's first attempt, using his own three fundamental

7. Cf. my argument with Rorty in Apel, "What Is Philosophy? The Philosophical Point of View after the End of Dogmatic Metaphysics," in *What Is Philosophy?* ed. S. Heidt and C. P. Ragland (New Haven: Yale University Press, 2001).

8. Cf. Apel, "Transcendental Semiotics and Hypothetical Metaphysics of Evolution: A Peircean or quasi-Peircean Answer to a Recurrent Problem of Post-Kantian Philosophy," in *Peirce and Contemporary Thought,* ed. K. L. Ketner (New York: Fordham University Press, 1995), 366–97.

9. Cf. M. Murphy, *The Development of Peirce's Philosophy* (Cambridge, Mass.: Harvard University Press, 1961), 151ff.

10. Cf. Apel, *Charles S. Peirce: From Pragmatism to Pragmaticism,* ch. 6, sec. D (pp. 119f.).

categories (i.e., "firstness," "secondness," and "thirdness"), to replace Kant's "transcendental deduction" of the twelve categories of cognition. These categories of Kant are related to his "synthetic unity of apperception." Peirce's three categories replaced the transcendental deduction insofar as they are derived from the semiotic and epistemic unity of representation. Firstness is relation—free suchness or quality. Secondness is encounter of the *I* and non-*I*. Thirdness is mediation of firstness and secondness of perception through the generality of concepts. This transformation of the transcendental deduction of the categories was, at a later date, further elaborated by Peirce in his semiotic logic, for example by relating the three classes of signs ("icons," "indices," and "symbols") and the three types of inferences with the three fundamental categories. But if we interpret the purpose of the three categories to be the transformation of the transcendental deduction, what should we make of Peirce's insistent refusal of the transcendental *I* and its faculties as well as the Kantian principles *(Grundsätze)* or "synthetic *a priori* judgments"?

Peirce's verdict that "there is no need for transcendentalism" was possible because of his recourse to indispensable common-sense "beliefs" or vague, instinctual presuppositions. These provide the background for his rejection and replacement of Kant's apriorism of the "forms of intuition" and the Kantian principles. But there is a residue of Kant's transcendentalism, or perhaps a substitute for it, that is easily overlooked in Peirce's philosophy, especially by philosophers with an empiristic or naturalistic background. These philosophers have no sensitivity to the transcendental presuppositions of thought that may ground a philosophical outlook more profoundly than the "categorial schemes" of cognition. Nowadays, the categorial schemes are relativized as methodological presuppositions of experimental "protophysics," related to the "macrocosmos" of our immediate natural environment, to which evolution may have adapted our cognitive equipment. This relativizing of apriorism is reinforced by the rejection of "transcendental arguments" in the wake of Peter Strawson's critical reconstruction of Kantianism. Strawson's reconstruction focused on the categorial schemes of objective cognition and, to this extent, could be relativized by holistic arguments.[11] There are, however, deeper aspects of aprioristic transcen-

11. Cf. R. Rorty, "Transcendental Arguments, Self-References, and Pragmatism," in *Transcendental Arguments and Science*, ed. R-P. Horstmann (Boston: Reidel, 1979), 77–103, and D. Davidson: "On the Very Idea of a Conceptual Scheme," *Proceedings and Addresses of the American Philosophical Association* 47 (1973–74): 5–20. With reference to the whole problem of detranscendentalization, see M. Niquet, *Transzendentale Argumente: Kant, Strawson und die Aporetik der Detranszendentalisierung* (Frankfurt: Suhrkamp, 1991). This book also raises the possibility that the detranscendentalization of categorial schemes

dentalism which are uncovered by reflecting on the necessary presuppositions of argumentation. This reflection is opened up by the semiotic transformation of the logic of cognition. When he refused the categorial schemes and principles, Peirce did not abandon the Kantian question as to the condition of the possibility of intersubjectively valid arguments. This question is renewed in a modified form in his concern for the 'validity in the long run' of the forms of synthetic inference, namely induction and abduction.[12]

This possibility of a renewal of the Kantian question followed upon Peirce's ingenious assumption that all affirmative sentences or judgments—perceptual judgments as well as *Grundsätze* or *synthetical a priori judgments* in Kant's sense—can be conceived as sediments of unconscious inferences. Now, this assumption—together with the other fundamental assumption of semiotic logic, that all cognition has the character of an interpretation of signs—must shift the Kantian supposition of a highest point of the transcendental deduction of constitutive principles of cognition toward the *end* of the whole process of cognitive research in science. That is, the Peircean question of the grounds of the validity of the laws of the logic of synthetic inferences became equivalent to the question of the objective validity in the long run of scientific knowledge. And the answer to this question had to presuppose as its highest point the ultimate unity of cognitive sign interpretation, and that means, the truth about the reality of the real in general. It is not the possible truth of particular (single) objective scientific experiences that can be grounded transcendentally, as with Kant. On the contrary, the truth claims of all single judgments of science, even of Kant's so-called synthetic *a priori* judgments, are empirically related to the real insofar as it is independent of our factual cognition. Thus far, our judgments are fallible. But the truth about the reality of the real in general, according to Peirce, must be cognizable in the long run, due to a convergence of our synthetic inference and semiotic interpretation processes.

At this point we can grasp the connection between Peirce's transformation of Kant's transcendental logic and his theory of reality and truth. For we can see that Peirce, through his shift of the highest point of Kant's transcendental deduction toward the postulated end of the research process, dispensed with the Kantian distinction between unknow-

may be relativized from the standpoint of a transcendental-pragmatic reflection on the presuppositions of argumentation.

12. See C. S. Peirce, "Grounds of Validity of the Laws of Logic" (1869), in *Collected Papers* (hereafter *CP*) 5.318–5.357, and "Deduction, Induction, and Hypothesis" (1878), in *CP* 2.619ff. On this topic; see Apel, *Charles S. Peirce: From Pragmatism to Pragmaticism*, 47ff.

able things-in-themselves and mere appearances as possible objects of scientific experience. For the following difference must be acknowledged in this connection. Kant could not postulate that the transcendental conditions of an *a priori* necessary constitution of the form of experience could be *a priori* valid even for things-in-themselves. Therefore the distinction between things-in-themselves and mere appearances became a necessary corollary of Kant's constitutional transcendentalism (apriorism). This problem disappeared for Peirce, however. If the transcendental postulate of intersubjective validity of experience concerns only validity in the long run and the possibility of approximating the truth about reality in general, then there is room for relating all single judgments (and theories) of science, as fallible hypotheses, to the things as they are in themselves. In this way, the real itself becomes the natural object as the knowable in principle. However, the knowable, that is, the knowable in the long run, must be distinguished from what can be known in fact, because all conceivable factual cognitions are fallible. Hence the distinction between the knowable and the factually known replaces Kant's distinction between the knowable appearances and the unknowable things-in-themselves.

Apart from many other sense-critical arguments, this is the most important point in Peirce's critique and transformation of Kant's theory of the relationship between cognition and reality; and my aim is to show that it is also the crucial vantage-point for an appropriate understanding of Peirce's theory of truth, and, moreover, for a defense of this theory against its contemporary critics.

Before we can enter into this debate, however, we must first return to our question concerning the transcendental status of Peirce's transformation of Kant on the basis of a logic of sign-interpretation and synthetic inferences. Why must Peirce suppose all this to be possible, in particular the convergence of inference on truth about the reality of the real? This question seems to me to be crucial for the assessment of Peirce's transformation of Kant in the terms of a transcendental semiotics or pragmatics of language. Most interpreters of Peirce's philosophy, seeing it as part of American pragmatism, do not recognize the transcendental features of Peirce's logic of inquiry; and, indeed, Peirce's own statements concerning this question are ambivalent, lacking a thorough reflection on the sense-critical implications of his novel approach. Let us try, however, to answer my question by beginning with the usual objections against the view that the novel presuppositions of Peirce's logic of inquiry have these transcendental implications.

A rather trivial objection against the postulate of an "ultimate opinion" trades on the possibility that the progress of scientific inquiry could break off, for example because the human race might perish. In connection with this argument, however, a more important one was raised by Peirce himself. For a long time, he seriously supposed that the conceptual reality of the real should be dependent on our factually reaching the truth about it, and so he was compelled to equate the truth about the reality of the real with what will be factually reached as ultimate opinion in the research progress.[13] In this case, however, the principle of fallibilism, to which every factual result of our research process is subject, would already imply a refutation of the possibility of explicating the meaning of truth by recourse to the ultimate opinion of the research community. It was only in his last phase—that is, in the papers on "pragmaticism" after 1900—that Peirce clearly realized that this argument was a residual mistake based on his earlier nominalism. His error was similar to the argument, mistakenly derived from the pragmatic maxim, that a diamond was not hard as long as he could not factually show up its hardness through resisting an attempt at scratching it. Peirce finally realized that not only conceptual generality but also modality, that is, the possibility based on natural laws of showing up sensual effects in experiments, had to be supposed to be real.[14] As a consequence of this insight, Peirce went on to replace his incautious "will be" formulations with regard to the application of the pragmatic maxim, and hence also with regard to the meaning of the truth about reality, by "would be" formulations.[15] This culmination of Peirce's antinominalism or realism about universals is indeed crucial for his version of pragmatism as well as his theory of truth and its defensibility, as this paper will show.

There is another objection to the supposition that at least the possibility of reaching the truth about the reality may figure as the highest point of a transcendental deduction of the validity of our cognition in the long run. This objection appears also to be trivial *prima facie*, but

13. Thus Peirce in his first argument with J. Royce wrote, "for scepticism about the reality of things,—provided it be genuine and sincere, and not a sham,—is a healthful and growing stage of mental development. Let us suppose, then, for the sake of argument, that some questions eventually get settled, and that some others, indistinguishable from the former by any marks, never do." Thereafter, Peirce admitted that if a part of our questions cannot be answered by scientific research, "in that case" his conception of reality would be "rather a faulty one, for while there is a real so far as a question that will get settled goes, there is none for a question that will never be settled; for an unknowable reality is nonsense" (*CP* 8.43). It is clear that here Peirce, as in his earlier interpretation of the hardness of a diamond, was falling back on a nominalistic reduction of general meaning (including the meaning of real possibility) to facts of our experience. See my critical interpretation in *Charles S. Peirce: From Pragmatism to Pragmaticism,* 140ff.

14. Cf. *CP,* 5.453.

15. Cf. *CP* 8.113, 8.191, 8.216.

the answer to it belongs to the most essential aspects of Peirce's semiotic transformation of Kant's transcendental logic. The trivial objection claims that no single subject of cognition, that is, no finite human being, can possibly reach the truth about the reality of the real, whereas within the Kantian framework it makes sense to postulate for each subject of cognition the possibility of reaching the unity of apperception in his/her judgments. The non-trivial response to this objection from the point of view of Peirce's semiotic logic is the following: In principle—or transcendentally—an indefinite speech community is presupposed in order to conceive of the intersubjective validity of cognition. This presupposition holds for the component of thirdness, namely symbolic interpretation, in single judgments, in contradistinction to the firstness component of perceptual judgments. Firstness may indeed be evident for a single consciousness and its synthesis of apperception.[16] The assumption of a speech community holds *a fortiori* for the postulate of the intersubjective validity of sign interpretation in the long run, and hence of approximating the truth about reality.

This is an important aspect of Peirce's transformation of Kant that figures implicitly in his transformation of modern philosophy of consciousness from Descartes through Husserl. These modern philosophies presupposed "methodical" or "transcendental solipsism" as a pre-condition of their epistemology. From this overcoming of methodological solipsism, which was confirmed in a sense by Wittgenstein's famous argument against the possibility of a "private language," it is possible to derive a novel conception of *rationality*, a conception that presupposes the identification of the single thinker with the unlimited community of thinkers.[17] This conception can even be used for a foundation of ethics if one generalizes the question concerning the presuppositions of scientific rationality to the question concerning the rationality of argumentation in general. This use cannot be explored here.[18]

16. Cf. Apel, "Das Problem der phänomenologischen Evidenz im Lichte einer transzendentalen Semiotik," in *Die Krise der Phänomenologie und die Pragmatik des Wissenschaftsfortschritts*, ed. M. Benedikt and R. Burger (Vienna: Öesterreichische Staatsdruckerei, 1986), 78–99; and Apel, "The Pragmatic Turn and Transcendental Semiotics: The Compatibility of the Linguistic Turn and the Pragmatic Turn of Meaning Theory within the Framework of a Transcendental Semiotics," in Apel, *Selected Essays*, vol. 1, 132–74.

17. Cf. *CP* 5.354ff. and 2.684.

18. Cf. Apel, "Das Apriori der Kommunikationsgemeinschaft und die Grundlagen der Ethik," in *Transformation der Philosophie*, vol. 2, trans. *Towards a Transformation*, 225–300. However, in discourse involving ethical generalizations the self-surrender that is demanded by Peirce is considerably changed. It no longer pertains to all individual interests as such, as Peirce suggests, but to the contrary: all individual interests of human beings ought to be taken into account, as long as they can be defended through arguments as validity claims manifesting their universal acceptability for all affected persons. Thus the

Instead, let us consider how the Peircean conception of rationality that presupposes one's identification with an unlimited community issues in a possible application of the pragmatic maxim to the meaning of truth.

It is important to see that in applying the pragmatic maxim of the explication of meaning to the meaning of truth, there is both a similarity and a radical difference between the Peircean approach and that of James (and now of Rorty). We can suppose that all pragmatists ask the following question: What can we do in order to find out what the predicate "is true" that is ascribed to a proposition or opinion should mean? James, in his characteristic line of thought, proposes to try to believe in the opinion, that is, to act on it, and then see whether it will pay off or prove to be satisfactory for one's life praxis. That it prove satisfactory is what we must expect when we consider an opinion to be true. Thus, James thinks primarily of testing beliefs through their application to one's individual life praxis, especially in situations crucial to life or survival. It is from this standpoint that he also defends the practical relevance of religious beliefs.[19] Rorty relates the pragmatic testing of opinions called true primarily to rhetorical attempts to "persuade" a particular audience. This persuasion, renewed from one occasion to the next, is achieved by means of suggesting that it is "good to believe" in the pertinent opinion.[20]

Peirce, on the other hand, in order to test the truth of opinions, recommends experiments that have the structure of *if . . . , then . . .* conditionals, hypotheticals consisting of possible actions and experiences expected to result. He presupposes from the outset, however, that truth is the same as unrestricted universal validity and therefore can be inductively tested in the long run only by an indefinite and unlimited community of researchers. Thus it is clear that Peirce cannot concede that the decisive test for the practical expediency of a belief in propositions called true would lie in the fulfillment of vitally important interests of individuals, or even particular communities. Rather all searchers for the truth have to bracket their individual interests in the paying off of a

moral self-surrender consists only in everyone's subjection to the procedural rules of argumentative discourse. This would be my reply to Putnam' s assessment of the relationship between Peirce and discourse ethics in his Frankfurt address of 1999.

19. See in particular W. James, "The Will to Believe" (1897), in *Pragmatism and Other Writings* (New York: Penguin Books, 2000), 191–218.

20. See especially R. Rorty, "Pragmatism, Davidson and Truth" and "Representation, Social Practise, and Truth," in *Objectivism, Relativism, and Truth* (Cambridge: Cambridge University Press, 1991), 126–161, and Rorty, "Is Truth a Goal of Enquiry? Davidson versus Wright," *Philosophical Quarterly* 45 (1995): 281–300. For a critique, see J. Habermas, "Rortys Pragmatische Wende," *Deutsche Zeitschrift für Philosophie* 5 (1996): 715–42, and Apel, "What Is Philosophy?"

belief, even a religious one, in favor of their identification with the long-term enterprise of the unlimited community of scientific investigators. Peirce later makes it clear that in matters vitally important to personal life, acting on instinctual or traditional beliefs has its claim to make, but this "will to believe" (James) has nothing to do with a *rational* testing or explication of the meaning of truth.

It is only on the presupposition of the specific idealizations in the rational procedures of the unlimited community of researchers—that is, on the presupposition of applying the three types of inferences, later supplemented with regard to the normative direction of the progress of sign interpretation by the regulative idea of the "ultimate logical interpretant"—that Peirce could propose his explication of the meaning of reality and truth. This explication is presented authoritatively as an application of the pragmatic maxim in the 1878 paper "How to Make Our Ideas Clear." Peirce writes, "The opinion which is fated to be ultimately agreed to by all who investigate, is what we mean by the truth, and the object represented in this opinion is the real."[21]

ARGUMENTS IN DEFENSE OF PEIRCE'S THEORY OF REALITY AND TRUTH AGAINST RECENT QUESTIONINGS

With the exception of Rorty, all participants in the recent debate about the possibility of a pragmatist explication of the meaning of truth have, like Peirce, recognized the need for idealizations. Putnam, for example in his 1981 explication of truth, spoke simply of "rational acceptability under ideal conditions." Habermas emphasized the ideal conditions of communication.[22] As I have pointed out, however, these conditions are necessary but not sufficient, since the fulfillment of ideal experience conditions is needed for us to be entitled to conceive of a consensus about all potentially available truth-criteria—for example, empirical evidence, coherence, simplicity.[23]

Nevertheless, why should we from the outset suppose along with Peirce that the truth about reality in general "is *fated* to be ultimately agreed to by all who investigate" [my emphasis]? We have already made clear that the reality of the real is not dependant on our factually reaching the truth about it. The factual reaching of the ultimate opinion about most questions can, according to most passages in Peirce's work, only be an object of hope. By admitting this reservation, however, we

21. *CP* 5.407.
22. See note 3.
23. See notes 4 and 5.

have not denied the necessity of the supposition that, under ideal conditions, the ultimate consensus *would* be reached. It is tenable that this is the meaning of Peirce's phrase "is fated to be ultimately agreed to." But why is this a necessary presupposition of our explication of the meaning of the truth about reality?

This question implicates two subsidiary questions. One pertains to the general question we touched upon in the preceding: whether the presuppositions of the semiotic logic of cognition are necessary in a transcendental sense. Nowadays, many philosophers argue that necessary presuppositions of the logic of cognition may, as assumptions, be indispensable but nevertheless need not be true.[24] Peirce sometimes seems to share this opinion. Nevertheless, this argument makes no sense; for we cannot by arguments deny or question indispensable and so far necessary presuppositions of argumentation without committing a performative self-contradiction. This is because argumentation is non-circumventible. This point provides the sense-critical basis of a transcendental-pragmatic, and it can even be used in an explorative test to identify the transcendental presuppositions of argumentation.[25]

This transcendental-pragmatic argument also applies to the ultimate presuppositions of Peirce's logic, for example to the presupposition that in all our argumentation we propose a truth-claim—as a claim to universal intersubjective validity—to be redeemed in principle by a consensus of all possible partners of discourse.[26] If one denies such truth-claims in a philosophical discussion, as Rorty in fact does, one immediately shows up a performative self-contradiction of one's argument. In fact, denying one's truth-claim either cancels serious argumentation or attempts to immunize it against possible criticism. The intention to succeed in persuading a particular audience, be it as large as possible, cannot replace a criticizable truth claim, since "solidarity" without a measure of objectivity, or ideal intersubjective validity, may rest on deception or illusion.

Peirce postulates approximating a consensus of the unlimited community of researchers in the long run through an indefinite continuation of discourse. This postulate follows from the indispensable presup-

24. See e.g. B. Stroud, "Transcendental Arguments," *Journal of Philosophy* 65 (1968): 241–56.

25. Cf. Apel, "The Problem of Philosophical Foundations in Light of a Transcendental Pragmatics of Language," in *After Philosophy: End or Transformation?* ed. K. Baynes, J. Bohman, and T. McCarthy (Cambridge, Mass.: MIT Press, 1987), 250–90, reprinted in Apel, *Collected Essays,* vol. 2: *Ethics and the Theory of Rationality* (New Jersey: Humanities Press, 1996), 68–102.

26. See Apel, "Fallibilismus, Konsenstheorie der Wahrheit und Letztbegründung," in Apel, *Auseinandersetzungen,* 81–194.

positions of all argumentation. It follows if ideal conditions of a continuous research and discourse process are supposed. This whole presupposition constitutes the advantage of Putnam's undifferentiated definition of truth as rational acceptability under ideal circumstances. A claim of truth and the supposition in principle of its possible redemption by arguments belong to the transcendentally necessary presuppositions of a logic of research.

However, at this point in the contemporary discussion the second subsidiary question arises, concerning the appropriateness of the epistemic explication of the meaning of truth. Is it not possible that a factual consensus, reached under ideal communicative and epistemic conditions, may still be different from the truth about reality, simply because the truth is an absolute concept, so to speak, that is, a concept that is not qualified by a more or less, whereas a factual consensus of argumentation, even if it has so far been reached under ideal conditions, is only a stage in a process of rational justification, that is, a result of argumentation that can be corrected. This argument seems indeed to have played a crucial role in inducing Habermas to abandon his former consensus theory of truth and his conceiving of truth as "transcending all possible justifications."[27] Now, a first answer to this argument could be the following. Of course, a difference between the truth and a factual consensus—any factual consensus of a finite community—is not only possible but must be supposed, because of the principle of fallibilism. But this has been taken into account by Peirce from the beginning. It is reflected in the most radical distinction of his transformation of Kant, the distinction between the real as the knowable and anything known.

A difficulty remains, however. If there is in principle a difference between the truth and any factual consensus, how then is it possible to postulate along with Peirce that the truth is "the opinion which is *fated* to be ultimately agreed to . . ."? Even the very distinction between the real as what is knowable in the long run and anything known seems to be paradoxical; for *prima facie* it seems to mean that the real must be the unknowable, since it can never be known. But this would amount to a restoration of the Kantian supposition of unknowable things-in-themselves, which Peirce wanted to replace by his novel distinction. The crucial difference here is this: Whereas Kant had to suppose a divine perspective, a "god's eye view," to follow Putnam,[28] in order to speak about the things-in-themselves, which cannot be meaningfully conceived by us, the Peircean distinction can be always verified by us,

27. See Habermas, *Wahrheit und Rechtfertigung*, ch. 5.
28. Cf. Putnam, *Reason, Truth, and History*.

namely from the "internal" perspective of the research progress. We can indeed ascertain, on each occasion after having reached a fallible result of our research, that the real always remains in front of us in the future, not as the unknowable, but as the 'still knowable,' that is, the object of further research. Thus Peirce's distinction fits the postulate of Putnam's "internal realism," namely that we should not make use of a "God's eye view" in talking about the real.

A problem remains, however, namely that an infinite task is anticipated counterfactually. How could we be entitled, by a definition of the meaning of truth in epistemic terms, to anticipate counterfactually the ultimate opinion as a possible result of a potentially infinite research project of an indefinite community of investigators? This problem may perhaps be elucidated in the following way: On the one hand, there is the absolute concept of truth, which is not itself relevant as a criterion in the manner of the pragmatic maxim, because the concept of truth does not tell us what we could do and subsequently expect as a possible consequence of our praxis. The absolute concept of truth could be metaphysically explicated only with the aid of a strong equation theory of truth, which supposes a God's eye view. Otherwise, the absolute concept of truth must have recourse to Tarski's logico-semantical explication of truth, which is empty as a criterion and cannot even show that the redundancy theory of truth is insufficient.[29] On the other hand, there is the possibility of explicating the meaning of truth in epistemic or discourse-pragmatic terms, that is, redeeming or justifying truth-claims by consensus formation in the community of discourse. But this way of explication seems always to reach a limit because of the gap between every factual result of consensus-formation and the *absolute* concept of truth. Now, how could an idealization strategy be applied to the method of epistemic explication that would bridge the gap?

Donald Davidson has formulated a dilemma with regard to our problem. He has suggested that either the idealizations are not strong enough to do justice to the "absolute" concept of truth or they would be too strong, that is, so strong that the conceivable connection with our normal procedures of research would be lost.[30] The difficulty obviously hinges upon the concept of the infinite, or the transition to the limit of an infinite process. To cope with this problem was precisely what was meant by Kant's conception of "ideas of reason" or "regulative principles." This conception, together with the conception of a coun-

29. Cf. Apel, "Husserl, Tarski oder Peirce?"

30. See D. Davidson, "The Structure and Content of Truth," *Journal of Philosophy* 87 (1990): 279–328, in particular 307.

terfactual anticipation, can be used to explicate the notion of an ideal consensus and to understand ideal consensus as part of the necessary transcendental presuppositions of the logic of argumentation. This solution to the problem has its intricacies. But let us try to explicate and defend it.

First, the counterfactual anticipation of the universal validity and hence of the ideal consensus of all communication partners can be traced back below the reflective level of philosophy. It is a characteristic property of the truth claim of any serious statement in ordinary speech and thus far can be called "pragmatic" or "performative idealisation," as A. Wellmer has proposed.[31] But the reflective awareness of one's own performative truth claim and its implications in a philosophical discourse are present alongside the truth-claims of discourse partners, claims that may be based on other reasons (i.e., truth-criteria) and hence may possibly deviate from one's own claims. This opens up a free space of acknowledgment of fallibility with regard to the performative idealization of one's own truth-claim. It is possible then for a critical scientist to utter a truth-claim without connecting it with a certainty claim, as the followers of Karl Popper have rightly pointed out.[32] Now, taking into account the principle of fallibilism, on the philosophical level of reflecting on truth-claims in general and not on the pre-reflective level of the "idealization" of one's own truth-claims, one must raise the question, what would be a redemption of truth-claims that would take into account all possible counterarguments that could be brought forward in an unlimited discourse? This question is based on the recognition that it would be senseless to suppose that a positive response to it, that is, to its fulfillment conditions, could still be different from the truth. Thus far the question shows up the internal relation between our "absolute" concept of truth and the fulfillment of ideal conditions of argumentative discourse.

Now the response to the last question, I suggest, is provided by the Kantian conception of a "regulative principle," or perhaps rather by the transformation of this conception in Peirce's category of "thirdness,"

31. See A. Wellmer, "Wahrheit, Kontingenz, Moderne," in *Endspiele* (Frankfurt: Suhrkamp, 1993), 157–77, especially 163, and "Der Streit um die Wahrheit. Pragmatismus ohne regulative Ideen," in *Die Renaissance des Pragmatismus*, ed. M. Sandbothe (Weilerswist: Velbrück, 2000), 253–69.

32. I acknowledged this in my argument with the Popperian Hans Albert (see my paper quoted in note 26), but I also had recourse there to the Wittgensteinian argument that no functioning language game of doubting is possible without presupposing *paradigmatic certainties*. This insight I used to restrict the scope of the *fallibilism* principle in favor of the undeniable transcendental-pragmatic presuppositions of philosophical discourse, e.g., the presupposition of the truth-claim and its redeemability in principle.

conceived of as continuity of sign-interpretation. Let us first elucidate the Kantian conception. For Kant, "regulative ideas" serve as complements to the "constitutive" conditions of possible experience—that is, they serve as conditions of our conceiving of the completeness of experience, which is postulated by reason. According to Kant, they have to be distinguished in two respects: on the one hand, by contrasting them to transcendent-metaphysical ideas, and on the other hand, by contrasting them to all empirical suppositions. In the first respect, Kant distinguished "regulative ideas," understood as conditions for completeness of experience, from Platonic hypostatizations of ideas, understood as transcendent entities. In the second respect, he distinguished them as "ideas of reason" from all possible data of experience. Data of experience, Kant says, can never completely correspond to ideas of reason, if the latter are to fulfill their regulative function.

Kant has sometimes characterised the function of regulative ideas by calling them "as if" *("als ob")* principles, with regard to the completeness of experience. This has inspired the Neo-Kantian Vaihinger, who was influenced by Nietzsche, to write his famous book *Philosophie des Als-ob* ("Philosophy of the As If"). But it seems clear that this "fictionalistic" interpretation cannot be accepted by a Peircean approach, for it presupposes the Kantian distinction between unknowable things-in-themselves and mere appearances. By contrast, using the conception of regulative ideas in a Peircean sense, one may avoid fictionalism as a form of nominalism and still properly distinguish the twofold Kantian distinction of regulative ideas from Platonism and from empiricism.

Now, Peirce's distinction between the categories of thirdness and secondness, and especially his illustration of thirdness through the continuity of possible experience, can fulfill the conditions of a legitimate use of regulative ideas. This paper seeks to show this by a conclusive defense of the Peircean theory of reality and truth against the present critique of this kind of theory. This critique, which at last has induced Habermas to give up the consensus-theory of truth, has been brought forward by Albrecht Wellmer, especially against my own use of "regulative ideas."[33] He first supposed that by the epistemic and discourse-pragmatic concepts of an ultimate consensus, we commit ourselves to imagining a certain state of the human community, namely that of an "ideal communication community" that would have settled all problems of communication so that no further use of language and performance of communication would be necessary. Now, to imagine such a state as factually existing, be it in a metaphysical realm beyond human experience or be it within the

33. A. Wellmer (note 31).

sphere of experience in space and time, would indeed be absurd; but, as pointed out in the preceding, such an imagination has already been excluded from the conception of regulative ideas by Kant. I would use the conception of an "ideal communication community." This conception highlights the morally relevant preconditions of serious discourse only as a regulative idea, in the sense of a counterfactual anticipation. The same specifications of the conception apply to an "ideal consensus" of the "ideal communication community" to be reached under ideal epistemic conditions.

In our having recourse to Kant our problem is nevertheless not yet settled. For the remaining question is whether it makes sense to use regulative ideas if they do not permit imagining our having actually reached the aim of all research. If we are to follow a regulative principle that we know leads beyond any imaginable state of factual consensus to be reached in the course of our research, this seems to commit us to striving for something that would be identical with the "end of human history" (thus Wellmer and Habermas). This suggestion is misleading, however, since we can only approximate the aim of inquiry. Why should we not move in the direction that is pointed to by the regulative idea without caring for an imagined factual state of the end of our potentially infinite progress? In any case, abandoning the epistemic and discourse-pragmatic conception of explicating the meaning of truth by declaring that truth is "something that transcends all possible justification,"[34] something that can be explained only by its relation to the real, would have much less satisfactory consequences than sticking to the conception of regulative ideas. It would dissolve the internal relation between the "absolute" concept of truth and the rational concept of justifying truth-claims; and this would make it impossible to apply the pragmatic maxim of meaning-explication to the concept of truth. Thus we could no longer know what to expect with regard to redeeming the claim to a universal truth of opinions. In that case, if the applicability of the pragmatic maxim is the criterion for distinguishing sense from nonsense or senselessness, as Peirce suggested, then this would mean that the concept of truth is senseless. This is as much the result in Rorty's "deflationism" as it is in supposing the truth is something beyond all possible justification and as such related to unknowable things-in-themselves. Thus the sense-critical realism grounded by Peirce would have to be replaced by one of two alternatives: a return to transcendent metaphysical realism or the giving up of philosophy altogether—say, by replacing it with "edifying conversation."

34. Habermas (note 3), 284f.

4 Homegrown Positivism: Charles Darwin and Chauncey Wright

JEAN DE GROOT

In the middle of the nineteenth century, European positivism began to have the same broad and varied influence on American thought as German idealism had exerted during the preceding fifty years. Assessments of positivism's influence on American philosophy usually focus on the maxim of verification, phenomenalism in the interpretation of sense experience, and the rejection of metaphysics and theology as nonsense. From this standpoint, positivism assured the independence of science and ushered in a new enlightenment of logic.[1] There are, however, deeper currents that positivism initiated in American philosophy. To understand them, we must look beyond the two great positivist doctrines of the twentieth century, utilitarianism and logical positivism, and focus on a more agile and fluent scientific positivism of the nineteenth century. This earlier form of positivism was pioneered by Auguste Comte in his *Cours de philosophie positive,* published from 1830 to 1842, but was best expressed in Ernst Mach's work of 1883, *Die Mechanik in ihrer Entwicklung.*[2] Key aspects of this scientific positivism

1. An important and influential statement of this theme is Philip Wiener's in *Evolution and the Founders of Pragmatism* (Cambridge, Mass.: Harvard University Press, 1949). Wiener's view is particularly clearly stated in "Chauncey Wright, Darwin and Scientific Neutrality," *Journal of the History of Ideas* 6 (1945): 19–45. For a treatment of this theme from an historical standpoint, see Kuklick, *Rise of American Philosophy,* parts 1 and 2.

2. See August Comte, *Cours de philosophie positive,* 6 vols. (Paris: Bachelier, 1830–42), and Ernst Mach, *Die Mechanik in ihrer Entwicklung; historisch-kritisch dargestellt* (Leipzig: F. A. Brockhaus, 1883, 2nd ed. 1889). In this paper, reference will be made to Mach's book by its English title, *Science of Mechanics.* It is important to recognize that there are traits of the scientific positivism of the nineteenth century that distinguish it from twentieth-century versions of positivism. One important difference is the use, by Comte and Mach, of a critical historical approach to analyze philosophy and science. Twentieth-century logical positivism tended to disregard the history of philosophy. The rejection of philosophical realism is usually taken as a key tenet of positivism. The thesis of the present paper is that Wright articulated a version of scientific realism that was *not* incompatible with positivism of the nineteenth century. Distinctions within the positivist movement are only beginning

were elaborated in an original American form by the philosopher of science, Chauncey Wright.

By the tenets of this scientific positivism, science is endoxic, grounded in ordinary life, non-axiomatic, and, for Wright, also realist in temper.[3] Because of Wright's elaboration of it, this positivism was allied with Darwinism when Darwin's theory of evolution was introduced into this country. For Wright, understanding evolution as a positive science unites evolutionary thought with the most intimate and practical of human concerns. As he says, natural selection is simply the most general formulation of the principle of utility that also governs human choice.[4] Because this interpretation of natural selection was not necessarily allied with a reductive materialism, it made evolution in the natural world a fit subject for speculation by the two most metaphysical of American philosophers, C. S. Peirce and Josiah Royce. Paradoxically, then, in its first introduction into this country, positivism encouraged metaphysical speculation. Most importantly, however, it offered an interpretation of Darwin's evolution that continues to be revealing of the nature of that science.

A cautionary note is in order. Although Darwinism, in this interpretation, does not implicate material reductionism, it would be a mistake to understand it as *anti*-reductionist. Wright accepts that underlying natural law governs all occurrences and processes. These laws govern at a level below the operation of natural selection. By denying that these underlying natural laws are first principles in explanation, Wright's interpretation of Darwinism as a positive science focuses attention on large-scale, multi-caused events, actions, and entities. These features of nature, so well-proportioned to human perception itself, derive their

to be treated in detail. See Robert C. Scharff, *Comte after Positivism* (Cambridge: Cambridge University Press, 1995). For a clarification of the range of positivist views between realism and instrumentalism, see Jerzy Giedymin, "Antipositivism in Contemporary Philosophy of Social Science and Humanities," *British Journal for the Philosophy of Science* 26 (1975): 275–301.

3. For the character of Wright's realism treated in relation to positivism and verificationism, see Robert Giuffrida, "Chauncey Wright's Theory of Meaning," *Journal of the History of Philosophy* 16 (1978): 313–24. The best book-length treatment placing Wright's thought in relation to pragmatism and twentieth-century empiricism is Edward Madden's *Chauncey Wright and the Foundations of Pragmatism* (Seattle: University of Washington Press, 1963).

4. Chauncey Wright, *Philosophical Discussions* (New York: Burt Franklin, 1877, repr. 1971), 101, 161 (hereafter cited in text as *PD*). See also *Letters of Chauncey Wright with Some Account of His Life,* ed. James Bradley Thayer (privately published 1878; reprint, American Biography Series), 222 (hereafter cited in text as *L*). Most of Wright's writings are collected in these two sources, *Philosophical Discussions* and *Letters*. A few of his articles published in periodicals are still available only in those original sources, in particular in *Nation.*

intelligibility from a sort of nominal teleology expressed by the idea of utility. In actual fact, it seems that Darwinism's reliance on utility contributes both to the wide applicability of the theory (explanatory power) and to its irrefutability (non-falsifiability). We shall examine these characteristics of the theory in Wright's understanding of it and also his treatment of the relation of utility to final causality.

A central commitment of scientific positivism was its belief that not only the methods of science but also the very concepts of science incorporate and refine ordinary ways of organizing experience and solving problems. For instance, Comte says that gravitation is a "general fact" that is itself "a mere extension of [a fact] which is perfectly familiar to us, and which we therefore say that we know;—the weight of bodies on the surface of the earth."[5] This understanding of science as extending ordinary experience reflects the influence of classical mechanics on the self-conception of science in the eighteenth and nineteenth centuries.

Mechanics originated with practical problems of weighing bodies and designing simple machines to move heavy bodies. Mechanics became the generalized treatment of locomotion only with Newton's *Principia,* and even then, the idea of efficacy or practical consequences continued to define mechanical concepts. In Aristotle's dynamics, *rhopê* was the excess of weight or lightness responsible for initiation of movement or differences in speed. In Galileo's dynamics, moment was a potential for displacement of a body produced by a coalition of heterogeneous influences, including the weight and position of the body.[6] Both the Aristotelian and Galilean conceptions take as their model for defining force the movement of a balance and departure from equilibrium. Later on, for Newton, inertia was measured by its opposite, the force required to overcome it, that overcoming being again the initiation of movement. Similarly, the continuing application of force is defined and measured by acceleration, that is, measurable increase in speed.[7] Generalizing on these facts of the history of mechanics, Mach says that just

5. Comte, *The Positive Philosophy of Auguste Comte, freely translated and condensed* (London: J. Chapman, 1853), 28–29 (hereafter cited in text as *Comte*). This translation of Comte is by Harriet Martineau and was likely available to Wright.

6. In Aristotle, see for instance *Physics* IV.8, 216a12–21. Edward Hussey treats the different senses of *rhopê* in "Aristotle's Mathematical Physics," in *Aristotle's* Physics*: A Collection of Essays,* ed. L. Judson (Oxford: Clarendon Press, 1991), 229. For Galileo's concept of moment, see his *Mechanics:* "Moment is that impetus to go downward composed of heaviness, position, and of anything else by which this tendency may be caused." I. E. Drabkin and S. Drake, *Galileo Galilei: On Motion and On Mechanics* (Madison: University of Wisconsin Press, 1960), 151.

7. Isaac Newton, *Mathematical Principles of Natural Philosophy and His System of the World,* trans. Florian Cajori, vol. 1 (Berkeley: University of California Press, 1966), Definitions 3 and 4 and the Second Axiom. For an interpretation of inertia and acceleration in the

as force in mechanics is defined by the effect it produces, in general any scientific principle is to be matched to an observable effect and to extend no further than its accounting of the effect. Thus, Mach says that our knowledge of the conditions of a phenomenon is sufficient when the conditions determine the phenomenon precisely and uniquely.[8] The unique determination of a phenomenon is conceived in terms of economy.

The lesson we should draw from this brief survey of mechanics is that the principle of verification associated with nineteenth-century positivism was not primarily a philosophical commitment to minimalistic empiricism. Rather, it was recognized that (1) the content of mechanics was defined in terms of effects, and (2) this definition gave mechanics a particular logical form, not a single set of axioms.[9]

Mach saw that, in its content, this most sophisticated science, mechanics, is allied with the simple goal-orientation of covering a distance or displacing an obstacle. The meaning of the scientific concept of force thus depends on ordinary practical experience. Force is not a fundamental physical reality but an anthropomorphizing expedient to accurate prediction or achievement of an end. Generalizing this feature of mechanics, Mach believed that, in any positive science, the concepts will be understood as instrumental and will be conceived as far as possible only in terms of the logic of their goals. It is a valuable rule for understanding Darwin's evolution that the best science would be the one that, at its very inception, limited its concepts to their strategic significance. The principle of natural selection is limited in just this way. It is non-causal, descriptive, and defined in terms of accomplished fact. In evolution as in mechanics, the content and logical characteristics of the theory are not readily distinguishable. This is regarded as a virtue of the theory.[10]

---

spirit of Mach, see Robert B. Lindsay and Henry Margenau, *Foundations of Physics* (New York: John Wiley and Sons, 1936), 85–98.

8. Ernst Mach, *The Science of Mechanics: a critical and historical account of its development*, 6th ed., trans. Thomas J. McCormack (LaSalle, Ill.: Open Court, 1960), 15 (hereafter cited in text as *M*).

9. This feature of explanation in mechanics figured importantly also in C. S. Peirce's understanding of the science. In "How to Make Our Ideas Clear," Peirce says, "According to our rule, we must begin by asking what is the immediate use of thinking about force; and the answer is, that we thus account for changes of motion." *Peirce on Signs*, ed. James Hooper (Chapel Hill: University of North Carolina Press, 1991), 171–74. See also "A Guess at the Riddle" (Hooper, 190–91, 196). Peirce associates positivism with this characterizing of concepts in terms of effects. He describes pragmatism as a *prope-positivism* in the context of presenting his pragmatic maxim: the meaning of any conception is the consequences or practical bearing of the conception. See his "Pragmaticism," in *Charles S. Peirce: The Essential Writings*, ed. E. C. Moore (Amherst, N.Y.: Prometheus Books, 1998), 271–74.

10. Robert Wesson touches on this characteristic of Darwinism and its similarity to

Positivism is often understood to belong to philosophical skepticism because it implies, though it does not necessitate, a denial of the reality of the theoretical entities named in scientific theories. It also lends itself to conventionalism or even idealism, since it is mind that identifies goals, whether real or nominal, and devises strategies. Indeed, science may be understood as both subjective and voluntarist from this standpoint. Robert Musil, however, in his 1908 dissertation on Mach, points out that there is another 'indifferent' interpretation of Mach's insights about scientific concepts. He says, "[I]t is possible to agree with these stimulating observations without either holding that the tasks of epistemology are thereby disposed of or, perhaps, that they are even remotely involved."[11] On this interpretation, Musil says, the positivist understanding of concepts has nothing to do with how laws and concepts should be constructed or with their status or adequacy in philosophical terms. Musil only mentions this interpretation of Mach's positivism and does not adopt it himself. There is no question, however, that the insights of positivism were often taken by the nineteenth-century American philosophers, and Wright in particular, according to this interpretation of indifference, as unencumbered by prior or consequent commitments to skepticism or conventionalism.

Wright holds that positivism is not a philosophy but "a system of universal methods, hypotheses, and principles" founded on the sciences (*L* 141). Its aim is the clarification of the logic of the sciences. Wright expresses the belief, a main tenet of Comte's positivism, that this clarification brings in its wake the revelation of scientific principles of ever greater universality. Wright thinks that beyond the method of science there are only beliefs, not philosophy. Positivism "allows large latitude for beliefs" that inevitably will vary because of differences in intelligence and character. Positivism comes into play only where belief is a matter of *evidence*. The circumstances constituting evidence Wright characterizes in this way:

> All observers not laboring under hallucinations of the senses are agreed, or can be made to agree, about facts of sensible experience, through evidence toward which the intellect is merely passive, and over which the individual will and character have no control. (*L* 96)

---

classical mechanics in *Beyond Natural Selection* (Cambridge, Mass.: MIT Press, 1991), 35–36. For an account of the logical structure of explanation by natural selection, see Elliott Sober, *The Nature of Selection* (Chicago: University of Chicago Press, 1984), ch. 5.

11. Robert Musil, *On Mach's Theories,* trans. Kevin Mulligan (Washington, D.C.: Catholic University of America Press, 1982), 24–25. Musil also describes the skeptical and conventionalist interpretations in these pages.

Although such circumstances of evidence are not the only ones that produce belief, the positivist maintains, Wright says, that only evidence gained in this way should issue in a high degree of conviction.

Though his criteria for evidence are strictly empirical, they are in the service of what we would now call scientific realism. He insists that terms be marks of things or of other distinctions that have real value in classification (*PD* 370). His statement of this point bears such a close affinity in sense and example to a passage in Comte as to merit quoting the two authors together:

Wright

Botanists, zoölogists, and chemists have made it evident that a distinction, however clearly defined, is not of value in classification unless it is something more than a distinction. It must coincide with and be of use as a sign of other distinctions—that is, be a mark of the things distinguished by it, in order to have real value in classification. (*PD* 370)

Comte

We must derive encouragement from the example set by recent botanists and zoologists, whose philosophical labors have exhibited the true principle of classification; viz., that the classification must proceed from the study of the things to be classified, and must by no means be determined by *a priori* considerations. The real affinities and natural connections presented by objects being allowed to determine their order, the classification itself becomes the expression of the most general fact. And thus does the positive method apply to the question of classification itself, as well as to the objects included under it. (*Comte* 39)

Apart from being evidence of Wright's reading, this comparison of passages locates a central theme of positivism, namely that science is properly taxonomic and that, however much we must decry the misleading theoretical elaboration of the names given to regularities and relations, the differences and order discerned by science are present in nature. Wright says that distinctions are marks of things, taken individually or as classes. In this way, the distinction becomes, as Comte says, an expression of a fact. Distinctions, by their duality, function as signs of difference. In Wright's positive science, it appears that such a sign is indexical—it necessarily implicates its reference—but transparent. No extra entity is to mediate understanding. It is for this reason that the positive method applies to the question of classification as well as to what is classified. Here we see an instance of the interconnection of concept and logic that is typical of mechanics in Mach's interpretation.

Classification reflects differences in effect. We could say that, in Wright's conception, the positivist is the staunchest realist of all because he has only the minimal conceptions persistently recommended to him by an intransigent nature to sustain his entire method.

Wright's realism is, however, limited to the concepts of science. Because of the taxonomic economy of science, Wright believes that every scientist within his own province is both a positivist and a realist:

> Investigators in modern science not especially distinguished for philosophical acumen yet often have the skill to exert toward the objects of their pursuit the logical function of giving valid names, or tying things together in new bundles. This skill, so far as it goes, gives to the scientific empiricist in practice a power which is shown in the higher philosophy only by the most original thinkers. (*PD* 363)

Although he says every scientist is "more or less of a realist unconsciously, if not avowedly," he regards realism as a "vice of thought" just like transcendentalism. It is a vice because it supposes that "the empirical attributes connoted by the name are collected around a central and essential, but transcendental, condition of their co-existence, that brings them all together." The metaphysical impulse consists in the effort to seize upon this condition, but nothing more is gained in the metaphysical move than was already present in the empirical taxonomic phase of investigation. Wright admired Aristotle, but he says that while Aristotle was a positivist in logic and astutely rejected the transcendentalism of Plato, he was not free of realism (*PD* 363).

An important aspect of the positivism of both Mach and Wright is their common view on the sources of scientific principles. In his *Science of Mechanics,* Mach says that the principles of a science are sufficient for explanation long before the logic of the science is fully consistent. When Newton had finished his work, the principles of the science sufficed to explain every mechanical phenomenon (*M* 356–57). By the time of Mach's writing, mechanics had long been in the last stage of logical refinement. Much of his book, however, is concerned with what constitutes the sufficiency of mechanical principles in the first stage of their development, when the efficacy of the principles is clear. Accordingly, positivism as it emerges from Mach's analysis of mechanics is not concerned with science as an axiomatic system but with principles still rough-hewn that are nevertheless both effective and sufficient to account for motion. In illustration, let us consider the simplest example Mach gives from the history of mechanics.

In his treatment of Archimedes' deduction of the law of equilibrium and the law of the lever, Mach shows that the requirement for determining the phenomenon precisely and uniquely is satisfied by original assumptions that incorporate a great deal of unanalyzed perception and complex previous experience.[12] Archimedes' assumptions are two and both concern equal weights suspended from a balance. The first assumption is that equal weights acting at equal distances are in equilibrium. The second is that of equal weights at different distances from the fulcrum, the one more distant from the fulcrum descends. Mach says that this first assumption follows from an instinctive perception determined by the symmetry of our own bodies. Mach contends, nevertheless, that these assumptions are not self-evident or simple:

> But we forget, in this, that a great multitude of negative and positive experiences is implicitly contained in our assumption; the negative, for instance, that dissimilar colors of the lever-arms, the position of the spectator, an occurrence in the vicinity, and the like, exercise no influence; the positive, on the other hand, (as it appears in the second assumption,) that not only the weights but also their distances from the supporting point are decisive factors in the disturbance of equilibrium, that they also are circumstances determinative of motion. By the aid of these experiences we do indeed perceive that rest (no motion) is the only motion which can be uniquely determined, or defined, by the determinative conditions of the case. (*M* 15)

Mach speaks here not of abstraction to simple initial propositions or hypotheses but of the separation of positive and negative experiences. The assumptions taken to found the law of the balance are not different in kind from the aspects of experience they leave out. They are rather ordinary perceptions that succeed in determining the result to be explained. Mach shows that "instinctive elements of our perception of [phenomena]" also determine Galileo's treatment of the balance as well as other achievements in mechanics. He points out that it is impossible to deduce many of these scientists' results from their assumptions without understanding what we now call statical moment as tacitly introduced by them all (*M* 18–19). In other words, from the standpoint of axiomatic deduction, in which everything must follow explicitly from axioms, their principles are confused or incomplete. This detracts in no way from their achievement, however. Mach says: "Assuming the facts of experience referred to, that the weights and their distances *alone* are decisive, the first proposition of Archimedes really possesses a

12. *Mechanics*, 15, 18. The words Mach uses to describe this familiar knowledge are "instinktive Einsicht" and "instinktiven Erkenntniselemente" (*Die Mechanik* [note 2], 11, 13). He says, for example, "Stellt sich der Beschauer selbst in die Symmetrieebene der betreffenden Vorrichtung, so zeigt sich der Satz 1 [von Archimedes] auch als eine sehr zwingende instinktive Einsicht, was durch die Symmetrie unseres eigenen Körpers bedingt ist" (11).

high degree of evidence and is eminently qualified to be made the foundation of further investigations" (*M* 15).

It does not matter that the principles are perceptions imbedded in experience, a mix of sensation and generalization with no discernible point of origin as grounding. The object of Archimedes and his successors, says Mach, was "to reduce the more complicated case of the lever to the simpler and apparently self-evident case, to *discern* the simpler in the more complicated, or *vice versa.* In fact, we regard a phenomenon as explained, when we discover in it known simpler phenomena" (*M* 19). Certainly, one thing Mach is saying is that the logical character of explanation in mechanics does not take its point of departure from the model of mathematical deduction that was so important to Descartes. Explanation is discerning simpler experiences within more complex experiences. Accordingly, deduction in science may involve a movement from simpler to more complex, but it is always movement from one experience to another, and both experiences rely on unexpressed tacit knowledge to be intelligible.

Concerning this tacit knowledge, Mach says: "Everything which we observe in nature imprints itself *uncomprehended* and *unanalyzed* in our percepts and ideas, which, then, in their turn, mimic the processes of nature in their most general and most striking features" (*M* 36). This knowledge, which is unanalyzed, has parts and is as much constituted by relations as by single impressions. Interestingly, he says that instinctive knowledge is "predominantly of a negative nature": "We cannot so well say what must happen as we can what cannot happen, since the latter alone stands in glaring contrast to the obscure mass of experience in us in which single characters are not distinguished" (*M* 36). Thus, we have some understanding of what is excluded from possible experience, and from this exclusion can be gleaned the principles to organize actual experiences. Explaining one experience by another imbedded within it does mean that knowledge is in one sense circular. Mach says that familiar knowledge, like our understanding of how the balance will not move given equal weights distributed at equal distances, leads to a principle that accounts for that knowledge, the law of the lever. But the discovered principle, itself a fact, is corroborated by the existence of the familiar instinctive knowledge from which it originated. The principle can be so corroborated because this original knowledge is a separate fact. Still, the two—principle and its more immediate and prior experience—support and reinforce one another.

That mechanics has this feature of circularity in explanation emerged, Mach believes, through efforts over two centuries to refine the deductive rigor of Newtonian mechanics and to address conceptual difficulties, such as the anthropomorphic aspects of the force concept and the circularity and indistinctness of the concept of mass. Mach says, "Newton's sense of *what* fundamental concepts and principles were required in mechanics was admirable" (*M* 245). Yet, the *form* of his enunciations left something to be desired. Thus, the later history of classical mechanics was a reworking of the principles initially delivered by Newton. *Explanans* and *explanandum,* both being experiences, were not irrevocably prior and posterior but could be interchanged or reformulated so as to achieve a more consistent logical form for mechanics.[13]

There are present in Mach's treatment of mechanics many of the characteristics of philosophy of science promoted by August Comte in his *Cours de philosophie positive.* Comte had said that science is the connecting of phenomena with one another "by the natural relations of succession and resemblance" (*Comte* 28). For both Comte and Mach, this interpretation of science as the connecting of facts, whether taken as axioms or as results, entailed that considerations of what gravitation or attraction is are futile. As Mach says, "We signalize by the term attraction merely an actually existing *resemblance* between events determined by conditions of motion and the results of our volitional impulses" (*M* 307). Considerations within a science of what its concepts really mean were evidence, for Comte, of the science's still laboring in an immature metaphysical stage of thought. The need to frustrate the speculative impulse is, however, compensated by the palpable connection between science and common sense. The anthropomorphic aspects of a concept such as force need not be shunned but can be understood as the connection between the empirical in science and the practical in life.

Comte makes clear, however, that he does not intend to render each of the natural sciences a positive science, since this is beyond his or perhaps anyone's competence. His aim is positive philosophy. He says, "We have only to consider each fundamental science in its relation to the whole positive system, and to the spirit which characterizes it; that is, with regard to its methods and its chief results" (*Comte* 31). Positive philosophy would discover the laws governing all phenomena—physical, psychical, and social—and reduce these laws to the smallest possible number. As we turn to the positivism of Chauncey Wright, we shall see that Wright uses many formulations of Comte and also of John Stuart Mill. Wright especially takes to heart Mill's call for a clarification of the

13. For an extended treatment of this characteristic of classical mechanics, see Heinrich Hertz's introduction to his *Principles of Mechanics Presented in a New Form,* trans. D. E. Jones and J. T. Walley (London: Macmillian, 1899). A short account of the main issues is given by Lindsay and Margenau in *Foundations of Physics,* 102–3, 118.

logic of science. In the great work of his life, however, the American reception of Darwin, he was attempting to do for this newly minted science what Mach had done for mechanics in its long history, that is, interpret it as a positive science.

Wright's view of the origin of scientific principles is similar to Mach's though he approaches the issue explicitly in terms of induction. He holds that all evidence to be brought to bear in forming knowledge is empirical. Inevitably, he says, non-empirical thinkers will try to broaden this conception of evidence to include within it intuition. When they do, he says,

> Intuition is held to be another and an independent form of experience. This adoption of the word "experience" is in accordance with the time-honored practice in metaphysics of annexing troublesome neighbors, giving a vague and metaphysical expansion to the meanings of hostile words, and thus destroying their critical powers. (*PD* 371)

The strategy is to redefine intuition as experience while leaving induction to conscious operations over the driest empirical data. Wright attributes this strategy to its advocates' having an impoverished understanding of induction. As it was used, he says, by both Aristotle and the best of England's thinkers in the past, induction is properly the basis for both the intuitive and the discursive functions of thought (*PD* 372).

Wright defines intuition as "rapid, instinctive judgment, whether in the objective sensible perception of relatively concrete matters, or in the most abstract" (*PD* 372). He says intuition is different from conscious inference, whether inductive or deductive. He insists, however, that "there is no contrast or alternative between intuition and induction in reference to ultimate grounds of belief." (*PD* 373). Induction is involved "in sensible perception and in reflective intuitions, or in rapid, habitual, and instinctive judgment generally, quite as essentially as in formal and consciously guarded or tested generalization" (*PD* 371). He says that the greatest misunderstanding of 'induction' and 'inductive' is not to realize these terms refer directly to evidence and not to any special procedure for generalizing from evidence. He shows considerable perspicacity in making this distinction, since a major problem in the interpretation of Aristotle on induction has been to suppose *epagôgê* is either a conscious method or an unconscious process by which we *gain* conceptions. In either case, the supposition is that the workings of induction are to be detailed. A point of contact between scientific positivism and Aristotelian science is that both take for granted the formation of evidential judgments from a variety of empirical sources and at more than one level of investigation. Wright understands Aristotle's doctrine of induction to be that "axioms are based upon inductions, although they are not the results of a formal and consciously guarded procedure in accordance with the canons of inductive logic" (*PD* 372). Like Mach, he regarded the deductive form of science as secondary to its explanatory sufficiency:

> But all that is really implied in the name [axiom] is that truths when *called* axioms are *used* for the deductive proof of other truths, and that their own proof is not involved in the process. This does not deny, however, that they may be, as truths, the conclusions of other processes; to wit, the inductions of experience. If they are, then the only ultimate truths are the particulars of concrete experience, and no postulate or general assumption is inherent in science until its proceedings become systematic, or the truths already reached give direction to further research.[14]

Although an axiom may be capable of being expressed with clarity and simplicity, it was originally a habitual and rapid interpretation of experience, no different from many other ascriptions of meaning to experience that are later overthrown by subsequent experience. An axiom is an interpretation that survives, is strengthened, and becomes habitual. In such a way, it becomes a conception as well as a belief (*PD* 372). Wright makes clear that the power of evidential judgments comes from their being criticized and often altered as a result (*PD* 340). Thus, induction is a doctrine about the source of knowing, not its method. Wright seems to agree with Mach's point that axioms are simply facts that by their universality and ubiquity have established themselves in our minds as key to the order nature itself has. Accordingly, he says this of theory and facts:

> Theories, if true, are facts,—a particular class of facts indeed, generally complex ones, but still facts. Facts, on the other hand, even in the narrowest signification of the word, if they be at all complex, and if a logical connection subsists between their constituents, have all the positive attributes of theories. (*PD* 44)

In spite of the strong logical character of Wright's pronouncements on scientific method, for him as for Mach, a positive science is not foremost an axiomatic system on the mathematical model, nor is it the kind of system that relies upon atomism, whether logical or naturalistic. Science is an organization of the facts of experience, an organization that is fruitful because it sorts and relates simple and complex facts so as to lend coherence and predictability to a subject matter.

Wright applies this interpretation of science to the principle of natu-

14. *Letters,* 109. See also 126.

ral selection when he insists that natural selection cannot submit to requirements of demonstration or axiomatic deduction. He writes, "In determining the limits of the action of Natural Selection, and its sufficiency within these limits, the same demonstrative adequacy should not, for obvious reasons, be demanded as conditions of asserting to its highly probable truth, that Newton proved for his speculation" (*PD* 137). He says that natural selection must be compared to gravitation or other physical principles not as these principles appear in the laboratory or in the relatively simple terms of celestial mechanics but rather as these principles are actually working "in the concrete courses of outward nature, in meteorology and physical geology." He continues:

> Still better, perhaps, at least for the purposes of illustration, we may compare the principle of Natural Selection to the fundamental laws of political economy, demonstrated and actually at work in the production of the values and the prices in the market of the wealth which human needs and efforts demand and supply. (*PD* 137)

He describes natural selection as a process in which three different classes of cause are involved. The first class comprises the external conditions of an animal's or plant's life. Secondly, there are the laws of mechanics, optics, and acoustics that Wright calls "the general principles of the fitness of means to ends, or of supplies to needs." The third class of causes includes the phenomena of variation and their relation to the laws of inheritance (*PD* 142). He speaks of natural selection as depending upon these causes, but he says that utility in conjunction with the laws of inheritance determines the path of development of a species (*PD* 143). In the course of his criticism of Herbert Spencer's Law of Evolution, he says, "Strictly speaking, Natural Selection is not a cause at all, but is the mode of operation of a certain quite limited class of causes" (*PD* 108). He continues that within this class, the efficient causes all act through the principle of utility.

Natural selection illustrates how "the principles of utility and adaptation are all-pervasive laws in the organic world." The fact that humans anticipate wants and advantages by their mental actions is simply one illustration of this general principle (*PD* 102). Similarly, in moral matters, utility is not to be understood as a motive. Rather, utilitarian morality is best illustrated in the moral agent who thinks steadily and with clarity while under the influence of strong feeling. In him, conscience displays the utilitarian principle (*L* 223–24). Along similar lines, Wright addresses, in a letter to Darwin, the problem of human choice in changes that a language undergoes. He says that if the question were how men might become better inventors rather than how these inventions have actually arisen and been adopted by others, there might be some point in insisting on the significance of choice in language change. But it is the *adoption* of some change by several speakers that concerns natural selection (*L* 243). Whatever are the motives for adoption, whether authority or ease of pronunciation or distinctness from other utterances, adoption of changes, says Wright, corresponds to what Darwin calls "unconscious selection" (*L* 244). In nature, variations are not themselves the direct causes of change in species or structures or habits. Similarly, for changes in language, an account in terms of utility makes some variation in language the opportunity or condition for selection by some agency.[15] Accordingly, natural selection is a complex general fact of which utility is the organizing principle.

The closest Wright comes to a definition of utility appears in a long letter to Miss Grace Norton on the utility of color perceptions for animals. He says: "Let the questions of the uses of life, then, be put in this shape: To what ascertainable form or phase of life is this or that other form or phase of life valuable or serviceable?" (*L* 274–75). Giving an example of serviceability, he says that Nature invented colors "to avoid the confusing effects of dispersion" and "to produce definition by *limits in sensibility*" (*L* 279). Concerning the delight engendered by color perception, he says: "Beauty is *our* motive to exercises, the natural ends of which we discover only by philosophy,—by that philosophy which is founded on a study of physics and natural history" (*L* 281).

Wright says that, to avoid misunderstanding, utilitarianism needs to be supplemented by a philosophy of habit. Every habit, he says, "is its own motive, its own 'excuse for being'" (*L* 282). He continues:

> The pains of disconcerted or frustrated habits, and the inherent pleasure there is in following them, are motives which nature has put into our wills without generally caring to inform us why; and she sometimes decrees, indeed, that her reasons shall not be ours. So that, practically, we find ourselves acting the more reasonably and more for the real ends of nature, in proportion as these are not our immediate motives, but give place to more completely devoted, single-purposed, and therefore effective powers, or to instincts and habits.

This quote illustrates again the separation of three things: (1) the conditions militating toward habit, (2) the agency that selects habit, and

15. Wright here accurately locates perhaps the main achievement of Darwin's theory. As Richard Lewontin puts it, "The process of variation is causally independent of the conditions of selection." *The Triple Helix* (Cambridge, Mass.: Harvard University Press, 2000), 42. This amounted to an "alienation of the outside from the inside" that was essential to the development of modern biology (47). In Wright's thought, it becomes clear how this distinction made it possible for utilitarianism to found a research program in biology.

(3) the principle of selection itself, utility. For us, it is the habits that we live and that we come to through discipline or choice. Nevertheless, utility governs their formation and makes habits and forms of life intelligible. What Wright said of utility in ethics, he could also say of natural selection in biology: it "sits in permanent judgment over all law-*making*" (*L* 291).

There are several important observations to make about Wright's comments on natural selection and utility. In the first place, natural selection is descriptive and accounts for change in those medium-sized objects (neither microscopic nor stellar) directly observable by ordinary perception. Just as in classical mechanics, it does not matter what sort the object is—whether a simple organism, a population of insects, or a human reasoner. Following the analogy to mechanics, we can see that utility in Darwinism has the role played by initiation of movement, acceleration, or covering a distance in mechanics. That is, utility casts all explanation within the science in a particular logical form. Thus, natural selection is, as much as anything else, a criterion of what constitutes an acceptable explanation.

On this aspect of positive science, Ludwig Wittgenstein, an admirer of Mach, is famously eloquent. Wittgenstein described classical mechanics as a net whose mesh could be of any fineness or shape.[16] At least part of what he meant by this is that the exact characterization of the axioms of mechanics is less important than the general picture of the world provided by mechanics. As the history of mechanics had shown, the system of mechanics yields a logical picture, not a physical picture. Wittgenstein said: "It thus supplies the bricks for building the edifice of science, and it says, 'Any building that you want to erect, whatever it may be, must somehow be constructed with these bricks, and with these alone'" (*Tractatus* 6.341). There is a similar desideratum for evolutionary science. *Which* explanation by natural selection is advanced to explain a feature of life or a structure of an organism is less important than the general form of explanation by utility. In correspondence with Darwin, Wright says:

> The inquiry as to which of several real uses in the *one* through which natural selection has acted for the development of any faculty or organ, or stands and has stood in the first rank of essential importance to an animal's welfare in the struggle for life, has for several years seemed to me a somewhat less important question than it seemed formerly and still appears to most thinkers on the subject. (*L* 335)

16. Wittgenstein, *Tractatus*, 6.341.

Wright then introduces the notion of a plurality of uses for the same feature, sometimes succeeding one another in the course of evolution of a species and sometimes contemporaneous with some uses secondary to others. He continues:

> The value of a plurality of coexisting uses in making the principles of natural selection and that of the inherited effect of habit co-operate in a larger number of cases and to a greater degree than could otherwise happen, ought to raise the principle from the rank of a scholium to that of a main theorem in the development doctrine. . . . It is, no doubt, a very interesting inquiry how any given organ or faculty is specially related to essential conditions of an animal's existence; but it is not so important to the theory of natural selection as it would be if the efficacy of this process depended solely or generally on a single or permanent relation of this sort. (*L* 336)

In introducing his own contribution to evolutionary biology, his paper "The Use and Origin of the Arrangements of Leaves in Plants," Wright says that his principal object of discussion is not the origin of these arrangements but their uses. He says that the value of natural selection as a hypothesis is the light it sheds on physiological questions and the way it enables the scientist to make connections between simpler and more complex forms of plant life (*PD* 296). That is, it provides a template of explanation according to which it is possible to establish other kinds of connections at lower levels.

The comments of Wittgenstein and Wright on their respective sciences highlight why a positive science is low in theoretical content and high in taxonomic structure. It is not just the rejection of metaphysical ideas and theoretical conceptions of nature and matter. It is because the main principle(s) of the science set the form of explanation even more than they fill out the content of explanation. It is this characteristic of Darwinism that leads to the charge that explanation by natural selection is tautologous.[17] But this charge does not take into account the aim of the theory to be a comprehensive logical template for explanation and not a particular causal account.

In a letter to Miss Grace Norton, Wright says that the understanding of utility in nature that comes out of Darwinism is consistent with Aristotle's definition of final cause in nature. He says:

> The Final Cause of any thing is that very thing, when it is or can be considered as conserved or reproduced by that essential part of its action or effects which perpetuates the life of which it is a part. Is it not singular that this definition has

17. Concerning natural selection or the fitness criterion as tautologous, see Sober, *Nature of Selection*, ch. 2.

just reminded me of what I read long ago about Aristotle's definition of Final Causes? I never quite understood that, and find, on turning to the Encyclopaedia, that it is in these words: "The *final* cause of the thing is that very thing in its completeness; as a statue when made." (*L* 286)

Wright is drawing on one meaning of final cause in Aristotle's *Physics*—the entity that is the product of change. His own formulation draws upon what Aristotle takes as evidence of formal and final cause in *Physics* II—the fact that the organism is produced as the culmination of action that conserves and perpetuates the life of the species. Wright says that the phrase from the Encyclopaedia, "the very thing in its completeness," does not distinguish well enough between formal and final cause. He means by formal cause the type of the thing. The idea of completeness involves final causality, he thinks:

Should we not say, rather, that the properties of any thing by which it is the agent, though indirectly, of its own production or of the production of its sort, belong to and define it as an end or final cause? The "completeness" meant is, perhaps, in the round of its self-restoring or self-preserving agency as a species. (*L* 286–87)

Wright appears to mean that what makes us recognize final cause are the stages of development or useful functions of parts of the organism (the properties by which it is the agent of its own production) that point to the entity-organism as their culmination. Final cause is involved in the particular development of an individual of the type and is not just the type of the organism. So much is highly consistent with Aristotle's mode of arguing from evidence in *Physics* II.8 to final cause in the case of individual developmental change. Since in evolutionary theory, however, survival and reproduction is the purpose of all self-conserving action of an organism, all ordering of action and features of the organism must be considered in relation to perpetuation of the species. This is one reason Wright focuses on the *round* of agency, meaning the full course of development, achievement of mature form, and reproduction. This focus is interesting since, for Aristotle too, to recognize *nature* as an internal principle requires the whole course of change involving the organism. Given Wright's other commitments, his understanding of final cause would have to remain without implications for the priority of form in any metaphysical sense. As he says elsewhere, "Nothing justifies the development of abstract principles in science but their utility in enlarging our concrete knowledge of nature" (*PD* 56). His remarks about final cause do show, however, that by utility alone, the scientist may recognize compartments of change and culmination governed by an internal ordering. There are coherent stretches of change in which, by whatever agency, some actions or organs have come to serve *now* as genuine means to particular ends.

Wright's partial concordance with Aristotle on this issue is not entirely coincidental. Wright regarded every scientist to be an Aristotelian type of mind, by which he means:

> it still cannot look upon the intricate system of adaptations, peculiar to the organic world (which illustrates what Cuvier calls "the principle of *the conditions of existence,* vulgarly called the principle of *final causes*"),—it cannot look upon this as an arbitrary system, or as composed of facts independent of all ulterior facts (like the axioms of mechanics or arithmetic or geometry), so long as any explanation, not tantamount to arbitrariness itself, has any probability in the order of nature. (*PD* 100)

The Aristotelian mind looks for causes and explanations and does not attribute facts to spontaneity or causes of a non-natural order. This he regarded as wholly compatible with Darwinism, since natural selection acts on variations that are 'accidental' only in the sense that we do not know their causes (*PD* 141–42). Although Wright does not make a theme of the Aristotelian idea of nature as an internal principle, he has grasped the implication of that concept, which is that change within the cosmos is explained by regular and recurrent causes almost all of which are features, members, or parts of the same cosmos.

Positivism in the interpretation of science is often seen as a retreat from the robust claims for scientific knowledge typical of both classical science and the Scientific Revolution. Some commentators deplore this lowering of expectations for science, while others embrace it as a welcome liberation from what they see as science's desiccated naturalism about the human being. An investigation of scientific positivism in the nineteenth century, particularly the positivism of Mach, presents a more complicated picture, however. In this picture, positivism is integral to the development of Western thinking about science in ways that continue aspects of the classical tradition of science. In the first place, scientific knowledge, when attained, is to be formulated in such a way that it is permanent and incorporates only what remains true. Secondly, scientific ideas originate in experience and are not different in kind from ordinary understanding. Explanation even has aspects of the classical conception of demonstration, insofar as explanation is finding within a complex situation the simpler fact that moves and actuates it.[18] For scientists such as Mach, Poincaré, and Hertz, who were also educated in philosophy, this refinement of the classical theory of science

18. For these characteristics of classical science, see Aristotle's *Posterior Analytics* I.1–2.

placed a premium on aesthetic values of knowledge such as economy and logical simplicity, while at the same time honoring science's connection to the ordinary.

Perhaps this synthesis of ancient and modern was too fragile to endure. One could argue that to remove from scientific explanation sophisticated concepts with long histories ensures their being replaced eventually by thoughtless ideologies such as reductionism. It would appear, however, that Chauncey Wright saw in Darwinism some of the values of this scientific positivism. Wright seized upon the logical simplicity and the potential for generality present in Darwinism. Wright's pluralistic understanding of scientific principles and causes gave him an appreciation of the logical advantages of natural selection as an organizing principle for biological explanation. His remarks are still instructive about the structure of Darwinism as a scientific theory. Darwin's achievement of minimalism in biological explanation meant that, like classical mechanics itself, his theory was bound to be successful.

Of Wright himself, we can say that his was the sort of intellect that greatly exceeds the limitations of its intellectual context by its concentration on a single idea. His single idea was his conception of what science is. He applied this idea to the defense of the new science of evolution by natural selection. In doing so, Wright taught Americans what it would mean to live in the chill clear light of a scientific ideal in which all that matters is the empirical and the mind's capacity to know the empirical.

5 William James and German Naturalism

STEFANO POGGI

I

In his last book, *A Pluralistic Universe,* published two years after *Pragmatism,* William James offers a witty critique of many aspects of the philosophical debate in Germany. His criticism is devoted above all to the professional philosophers of contemporary Germany and their followers and imitators in Britain and Scotland. James comes close to ridicule in criticizing their "monism of a devout kind" and its "great disdain for empiricism of the sensationalist sort." James gives another reason for criticizing the German approach to philosophy, however. He directs his polemic also against the lack, in his German colleagues, of "all spontaneity of thought" and "all freshness of conception." The most dramatic consequences of these limitations, he says, can be seen in America too: "The over-technicality and consequent dreariness of the younger disciples at our American universities is appalling." The Americans, he says, are captive to "professional shop-habits" borne of their own propensity to follow the German example. James's lack of regard for the German professors is unmistakable: "In Germany the forms are so professionalized that anybody, who has gained a teaching chair and written a book, however distorted and eccentric, has the legal right to figure forever in the history of the subject like a fly in amber."[1]

German philosophers too were acknowledging that "philosophy has long assumed in Germany the character of being an esoteric and occult science." James's observations correspond to those of Friedrich Paulsen about the German scene.[2] Thus, the need for improvement was felt in

1. William James, *A Pluralistic Universe: Hibbert Lectures at Manchester College on the Present Situation in Philosophy* (New York: Longmans, Green, 1909; reprint with introduction by H. S. Levinson, Lincoln: University of Nebraska Press, 1996), 7, 17.

2. James himself refers (*Pluralistic Universe,* 335) to Friedrich Paulsen's paper "Die Zukunftsaufgaben der Philosophie," in *Die Kultur der Gegenwart,* vol. I.6, *Systematische Philosophie* (Leipzig: Teubner, 1907). Among the other contributors to this volume were Dilthey, Wundt, and Ostwald.

Germany too. There was a widespread desire for a more concrete, more popular, view of the philosopher's tasks. This desire arose from the "vaster vistas" opened by the development of the natural sciences.

It is wrong, though, to consider the German scene as closed. Certainly, the "full pantheistic scheme" of the *Identitätsphilosophie* had acquired a large audience. *Identitätsphilosophie* was the doctrine that "our philosophizing is one of the ways in which the absolute is conscious of itself." At the same time, however, the appeal to an absolute unity of nature, as well as to an eternity that temporally rooted human beings are unable to attain, was being undermined by an increasing sense of the problematic character of such a unity. As James says, if the chief role of philosophy in the development of the human race is to ensure unification, one still has to bear in the mind the deep truth that "nature can have little unity for savages" and that "nature, more demonic than divine, is above all things multifarious." James emphasizes the distinction between empiricism and rationalism: "empiricism means the habit of explaining whole by parts," while "rationalism means the habit of explaining parts by whole." There could be for James no doubt that rationalism is dangerously close to the monistic claim of "imitating the All," words that James quotes from the original prospectus of the journal founded by P. Carus. Empiricism, he believed, appears to offer a much more reliable foundation for philosophical inquiry. In fact, as humans concerned in this kind of inquiry, "we are invincibly parts . . . and must always apprehend the absolute as if it were a foreign being."[3] We cannot, however, dispense with the problem presented by monism. On one side, we are confronted with the endless variety of natural facts, and on the other side, we aim both to uncover the connections between these facts and also to discern a possible underlying unity. In fact, a systematic integration between the empiricist and naturalistic standpoints seems to be not only unavoidable but even necessary. And in many respects, the German debate in the last quarter of the nineteenth century was following exactly the contours of development that James delineated in *A Pluralistic Universe.*[4]

3. James, *Pluralistic Universe,* 18, 37, 40, 21–22, 7–8, 40. James refers here to the prospectus of the *Monist.*

4. For the German context, see K. Sachs-Hombach, *Philosophische Psychologie im 19. Jahrhundert: Ihre Entstehung und Problemgeschichte* (Freiburg-Munich: Alber, 1993); Kurt Röttgers, "Romantische Psychologie," *Psychologie und Geschichte* 3 (1991): 24–64; Odo Marquardt, *Transzendentaler Idealismus, romantische Naturphilosophie, Psychoanalyse* (Cologne: Dinter, 1987); S. Koch and D. H. Leavy, eds., *A Century of Psychology as Science* (New York: McGraw-Hill, 1985); G. Verwey, *Psychiatry in an Anthropological and Biomedical Context: Philosophical Presuppositions and Implications of German Psychiatry (1820–1870)* (Boston: Reidel, 1985); M. Ash and W. Woodward, eds., *The Problematic Science: Psychology in the Nineteenth Century Thought* (New York: Praeger, 1982); Stefano Poggi, *I sistemi dell'esperienza:*

II

James was directly acquainted with the way this approach had developed in Germany through the rise of a scientific approach to psychological inquiry. This can be seen in the two volumes of his *Principles of Psychology.*[5] Before examining James's psychology, however, it is necessary to give a brief sketch of the German debate about psychology as science in the second half of the nineteenth century. To a great extent, the development of German scientific psychology started with the program of physiological psychology developed by Wundt in the 1870s.[6] Wundt's program depended, in its turn, on the analysis of the relations between physics and physiology outlined in Fechner's psychophysics.[7]

Fechner's project had a very complex genesis with two things playing particularly important roles: (1) the understanding of experimental physics achieved in the first half of the century, and (2) the profound influence of the spirit of German Romantic science. The importance of the influence of Romanticism is shown both by Fechner's interest in the dark, "nocturnal" side of natural phenomena in the living world and by his refusal of any mind-body dualism. This dualism was indeed already strongly opposed by panpsychism.[8] Nevertheless, if we consider the impact of Fechner's program on making psychological analysis scientific and also examine its essential import, we see that Fechner's psychophysics was a consistent application of some of the major arguments of Herbart's scientific psychology, which rested upon experience, mathematics, and metaphysics.[9]

Psicologia, logica e teoria della scienza da Kant a Wundt (Bologna: Il Mulino, 1977); E. G. Boring, *A History of Experimental Psychology*, 2nd ed. (New York: Appleton-Century-Crofts, 1957); E. G. Boring, *Sensation and Perception in the History of Experimental Psychology* (New York: Appleton, 1942).

5. James, *The Principles of Psychology*, 2 vols. (New York: Henry Holt and Co., 1890; reprint, New York: Dover Publications, 1950).

6. Wilhelm Wundt, *Grundzüge der physiologischen Psychologie* (Leipzig: Engelmann, 1873–74).

7. Gustav Theodor Fechner, *Elemente der Psychophysik*, 3rd ed., 2 vols. (Leipzig: Breitkopf and Härtel, 1907); *Zend-Avesta: Gedanken über die Dinge des Himmels und des Jenseits vom Standpunkte der Naturbetrachtung*, 3 vols. (Leipzig: Voss, 1851); *Über die physikalische und philosophische Atomenlehre*, 2nd ed. (Leipzig: Mendelssohn, 1864).

8. J. Brozek and H. Gundlach, eds., *G. T. Fechner and Psychology* (Passau: Passavia Universitätsverlag, 1988); M. Heidelberger, *Die innere Seite der Natur: Gustav Theodor Fechners wissenschaftlich-philosophische Weltauffassung* (Frankfurt: Klostermann, 1993).

9. Johann Friedrich Herbart, *Psychologie als Wissenschaft: Neu gegründet auf Erfahrung, Metaphysik und Mathematik*, 2 vols. (Königsberg: Unzer, 1824–25), in Herbart, *Sämtliche Werke in chronologischer Reihenfolge*, ed. K. Kehrbach and O. Flügel, 19 vols. (1887–1915; reprint, Aalen: Scientia, 1964), vols. 5 and 6. On Herbart, see F. Träger, *Herbarts realistisches Denken* (Amsterdam: Rodopi, 1982); I. Volpicelli, *Esperienza e metafisica nella psicologia*

Fechner's psychophysics aimed at discovering the "physics of the soul" and endeavored to lay the bases of the exact science of the psyche. To achieve these ends, Fechner appeals to both the mathematical and the empirical. On the one hand, he takes mathematical physics as the model of natural science, and on the other hand, he refers to the latest experimental findings regarding the physiology of sensations. The great success of Herbart's ideas among researchers in the physiology of sensations and even among psychiatrists was his adoption of a model for the "life of the soul" that was based on the relationship between representations and consciousness. Fechner holds also to the vision of the psyche as the center of representational activity, variable in intensity, as documented by the constant swinging of consciousness across the "threshold" of unconsciousness. Fechner, however, advances another step, foreseeing the possibility of assessing the products and effects of psychic processes by measuring them with exactness in quantitative terms. The use of mathematics in dealing with the intensive forces at work in the psyche is therefore directed to the evaluation of the products of drives. While acknowledging the fundamental importance of experimental data, his view involves acceptance of the metaphysical thesis of a substantial soul as the seat of a representational power subject to all sorts of gradations. At the same time, he uses mathematics to understand the psychic world in a way that is not so different from its use in investigating the physical world. In both cases scientists need to measure the effects of "unseen" forces, a point asserted by Herbart himself.[10]

Fechner takes the existence of spiritual "inwardness" as an unquestioned fact. Such "inwardness" is inaccessible in its essence, and yet it is recognized as the foundation of our understanding of reality. He makes this assumption clear in the sections of *Elemente der Psychophysik* that present the distinction between external and internal psychophysics. These sections stress the existence of two different "thresholds" that the activity of the soul must overcome to produce its effects. Although presented in the complex terms of parallel physical and psychic aspects of a single entity, Fechner's psychology does circumscribe the entire psychic domain, observing its manifestations as objects, and recognizing their absolute specificity. Fechner's psychophysics clarifies some key problems of the German debate on the characteristics of the

di J. F. Herbart (Rome: Armando, 1982); Renato Pettoello, *Introduzione a Herbart* (Rome-Bari: Laterza, 1988); W. Henckmann, "Einleitung," in Herbart, *Lehrbuch zur Einleitung in die Philosophie* [1834], ed. W. Henckmann (Hamburg: Meiner, 1993).

10. Herbart, *Über die Möglichkeit und Nothwendigkeit, Mathematik auf die Psychologie anzuwenden* [1822], in Herbart, *Sämtliche Werke,* vol. 5, 100–103.

"life of the soul" in the first half of the century. At the same time, however, it encapsulates the major obstacles that were to affect the foundation and development of the program of psychology as empirical science in the last quarter of the century.

III

During the 1870s, Wundt's scientific psychology received a systematical outline and was focused on what Wundt defined as the necessary "psychological" interpretation of the "law" of proportionality of reactions to stimuli, the so-called Weber-Fechner law. In the same period of time were active two other eminent personalities of the German debate on the nature of the psyche: Franz Brentano and Carl Stumpf. Like Wundt, they initiated fundamental lines of thinking and research. At the same time that Wundt published his *Grundzüge der physiologischen Psychologie,* Brentano and Stumpf published, respectively, the *Psychologie vom empirischen Standpunkt* (1874) and *Über den psychologischen Ursprung der Raumvorstellung* (1873). What is more, in 1873 the first volume of a work on logic and methodology was published, Sigwart's *Logik.* This work devoted considerable attention to the connection between the theory of knowledge and psychology. Ewald Hering, who had already made important contributions to the theory of vision, published a short memoir with the title *Das Gedächtnis als eine Funktion der organisirten Materie.* And finally in 1873, the second edition of Lange's *Geschichte des Materialismus* was released, providing the first interpretation of a new psychology completely rid of the "power of the soul," and defining itself as "psychology without soul." The debate about the scientific analysis of the psyche had been joined, and the main lines of its future development were already clear.[11]

The most striking element of psychological research in the 1880s is the challenge presented by Darwin's theory of evolution. Wundt had already referred to this theory in his *Vorlesungen über die Menschen und Thierseele,* published in 1863–64.[12] The influence of biological evolution is documented in the first studies on child psychology, conducted by W. Preyer. It is also evident in the widespread recourse to parameters

11. Wundt, *Grundzüge der physiologischen Psychologie;* Franz Brentano, *Psychologie vom empirischen Standpunkte* (Leipzig: Duncker and Humblot, 1874); Carl Stumpf, *Über den psychologischen Ursprung der Raumvorstellung* (Leipzig: Hirzel, 1873); Christoph Sigwart, *Logik,* 2 vols. (Freiburg: Mohr, 1873); E. Hering, *Uber das Gedächtniss als eine Funktion der organisirten Materie* (Vienna: Gerold, 1870); Friedrich Albert Lange, *Geschichte des Materialismus und Kritik seiner Bedeutung in der Gegenwart,* 2 vols. (Iserlohn: Baedeker, 1873–75).

12. Wundt, *Vorlesungen über die Meuschen-und Theirseck,* 2 vols. (Leipzig: Voss, 1863–64).

of biological evolution in the study of psychic functions, for example in Ernst Mach's early writings on the theory of knowledge, collected in his *Analyse der Empfindungen,* published in 1885. The impact of the evolutionary approach is recognizable in the fresh momentum it gave to the study of psychic and nervous pathologies. Within this field, Theodor Meynert and Carl Wernicke devoted special attention to aphasia and other complex pathologic disorders that seemed not to be clearly traceable to physiological causes. From a more strictly psychological point of view, the early 1880s saw the development of lines of research that questioned, as Brentano had done ten years before, the "scientification" of psychology on the basis of the sheer physiology of sensations. Besides the studies on memory carried out by Hermann Ebbinghaus with methodologies that did not at all refer to the physiology of sensations, the *Tonpsychologie* developed by Carl Stumpf is worth mentioning. In a renowned, and unfinished, book of 1883, Wilhelm Dilthey's *Einleitung in die Geisteswissenschaften,* Dilthey expressed unease about a psychology based on the physiology of sensations. One of the most determined innovators of experimental work in psychology, Ebbinghaus, later pointed to the "extra-scientific," almost "ideological," inspiration of Dilthey's arguments in his criticism of Dilthey's ambitious program of "descriptive and analytical psychology" in 1896.[13]

We now reach the years during which questions about the real scientific nature of psychic investigation became particularly crucial. At this time, a true rivalry between psychology and philosophy emerged, a rivalry whose terms are well known and which was destined to turn into a conflict in the first decade of the new century. A manifesto signed by a number of philosophers created a stir when it appeared in protest

13. W. Preyer, *Die Seele des Kindes: Beobachtungen über die geistige Entwicklung des Menschen in den ersten Lebensjahren* (Leipzig: Grieben, 1882); Ernst Mach, *Beiträge zur Analyse der Empfindungen* (Jena: Fischer, 1886); Mach, *Populär-wissenschaftliche Vorlesungen* (Leipzig: Barth, 1896); Carl Wernicke, *Lehrbuch der Gehirnkrankheiten für Aerzte und Studirende* (Kassel: Fischer, 1881); T. Meynert, *Psychiatrie: Klinik der Erkrankungen des Vorderhirns begründet auf dessen Bau, Leistungen und Ernährung* (Vienna: Braumüller, 1884); Hermann Ebbinghaus, *Über das Gedächtnis: Untersuchungen zur experimentellen Psychologie* (Leipzig: Hirzel, 1885); Carl Stumpf, *Tonpsychologie,* 2 vols. (Leipzig: Hirzel, 1883–90); Wilhelm Dilthey, *Einleitung in die Geisteswissenschaften* (Leipzig: Duncker and Humblot, 1883). Ebbinghaus review of Dilthey's *Einleitung,* "Über erklärende und beschreibende Psychologie," *Zeitschrift für Psychologie und Physiologie der Sinnesorgane* 9 (1896): 161–205, reprinted in *Materialien zur Philosophie Diltheys,* ed. Fritjof Rodi and H. U. Lessing (Frankfurt: Suhrkamp, 1984), 45–87. On the debate on *aphasia* see: G. H. Eggert, *Wernicke's Works on Aphasia: A Sourcebook and Review; Early Sources in Aphasia and Related Disorders* (New York: Mouton, 1977); O. Marx, "Nineteenth-Century Medical Psychology: Theoretical Problems in the Work of Griesinger, Meynert, and Wernicke," *Isis* 61 (1970): 355–70; N. Geschwind, "The Work and Influence of Wernicke," in *Selected Papers on Language and the Brain* (Boston: Reidel, 1969), 1–97.

against philosophy's being taught by psychologists in German universities.[14] When psychologists asserted the regulative role of their discipline on logic and ethics, they were accused by philosophers of being relativistic. The charge was that psychologists were unable to provide either a rigorous foundation to science or the consistency that all scientific theories require. The empirical-genetic analysis carried out by psychologists should not be confused, philosophers said, with the philosophical investigation of the "laws of thought" and must not be taken as the basis of scientific investigation.[15]

The complexity of this *Psychologismusstreit* is important to keep in mind, since to focus on the most uncompromising version of criticism against psychologism in logic and ethics obscures the many relationships that existed between psychologists and anti-psychologists. These relationships were closer and more nuanced than one might expect, particularly as they emerge with Husserl, one of the champions of antipsychologism at the beginning of the twentieth century. There was a reaction against the philosophical claims of psychology, because the early projects and programs of psychology as science had so poorly understood the powerful philosophical presuppositions that lay at their own origins. Originally, these presuppositions had been consciously assumed and explicitly formulated as assumptions by those who had undertaken to turn the study of the psyche into science, but due to the growing hope that scientific psychology might provide solutions to the "highest problems," these presuppositions came to be taken as real certainties.

IV

Let us now step back to the 1860s, to the first emergence of the project of making psychology scientific. This project, which came to genuine fruition at the beginning of the 1860s with Fechner and especially Wundt, was based on the assumption, not always explicitly formulated, of the existence of something "inward" to which we do not have access (i.e., the "soul") but whose manifestations and products can be observed and measured in the same way as the functions of the living world. Living things can be observed, examined, and described irrespective of whether or not they have some "vital force."

14. M. Ash, "Wilhelm Wundt and Oswald Külpe on the Institutional Status of Psychology," in *Wundt Studies,* ed. W. G. Bringmann and R. D. Tweney (Toronto: Hogrefe, 1980), 407–9.

15. M. Rapp, *Der Psychologismusstreit in der deutschen Philosophie* (Freiburg-Munich: Alber, 1994); M. Kusch, *Psychologism: A Case Study in the Sociology of Knowledge* (London: Routledge, 1995).

The physiology of sensations, so closely related to the physiology of the nervous system, developed during this time as an investigation confined to the functions that can make the sensations objects of direct experimentation. Accordingly, the main object of study in psychology became the behavior of the organs immediately involved in carrying out the sense functions. The remarkable progress achieved by the physiology of sensations at this time was limited to optics and acoustics. The nervous system as a whole was not accessible to systematic experimentation. A wide area of psychology was consequently left open to philosophical assumptions.

To give a physiological account of the powers of the soul in terms of the functions of a central coordinating organ was an unsolved problem during the 1860s. Psychic "inwardness" became more and more central to investigation until it became the principle that justified the coordinated unity of functions of the living world. Oversimplifying, one could say that the program of physiological psychology got underway only upon acceptance of the belief that, for the time being at least, it was impossible to treat human brain functions as an unity. To give up the study of the central nervous system, and most of all of the encephalum, appeared to be the necessary and probably also the sufficient condition for the constitution of a science of the psyche.

A number of further specifications should be made about the complex connections between Romanticism and Idealism in relation to the issues of consciousness and what makes for individuality. The blooming of classic Idealism and the Romantic movement's embrace of Idealism lent strength to the conviction that some "dynamic inwardness" was at the basis of the whole development of the "life of the soul." The existence of productive activity of a psychic kind became the postulate—the implicit but positive assumption—that was not to be questioned even by the new project of scientific psychology. There was little interest in giving this concept any intrinsic complexity. Debate about the "life of the soul" resulted from progress in the physiology of sensations and the possibility of dealing experimentally with the processes of sense and perception. This progress in dealing with particular 'soul-functions' eventually obscured the complex problem of the actual structure of individual consciousness.[16]

16. On the influence of Romanticism and Idealism on treatment of consciousness and the soul, see M. Greene, *Hegel on the Soul* (The Hague: Nijhoff, 1972); H. Drühe, *Psychologie aus dem Begriff: Hegels Persönlichkeitstheorie* (New York: De Gruyter, 1976); Dieter Henrich, ed., *Hegels philosophische Psychologie, Hegel-Studien: Beiheft 14* (Bonn: Bouvier, 1979); S. Oehler-Klein, "Die Schädellehre Franz Joseph Galls in Literatur und Kritik des 19. Jahrhunderts: Zur Rezeptionsgeschichte einer medizinisch-biologisch begründeten

V

As indicated above, it is not difficult to trace many of the views developed by James in the *Principles* to the German debate over the programs outlined and developed by Wundt and others. The chapters of James's masterpiece continually refer to the names of Wundt, Fechner, Lotze, Helmholtz, and Hering. Moreover, the German physiology of sensations, as well as the new research examining brain-functions in relation to the pathology of the nervous system, are important reference points for James. Yet, the consequences for German philosophy of the scientific approach to mental life also deeply interested James.

In this regard, the role played by R. H. Lotze[17] is fundamental, not only from the point of view of a more scientific theory of knowledge grounded on the data of psychology, but first and foremost from the point of view of the development of a whole *Weltanschauung* for psychology. The ideas concerning man and his history, and especially Lotze's views about the necessity of laying down the foundations of a new anthropology, received a wider audience during the 1870s and the 1880s, not only in Germany, the rest of Europe, and Britain, but also in the United States. Lotze's ideas appeared in competition with, or sometimes allied with, other views, such as those of Spencer's "synthetic philosophy." It is easy to discern in James the echo not only of Lotze's views about space-perception and related subjects, but also of his views about man and consciousness. This is seen in many chapters of James's *Principles of Psychology*, but also in *A Pluralistic Universe*. In the second chapter of this book, a chapter devoted to the discussion of the issues of "monistic idealism," James refers to Lotze's "proof of monism" as a typical example of the way an intellectualistic point of view, or to be more exact, the point of view of a "vicious intellectualism," should *not* be used to solve problems that demand instead an accurate scrutiny of the facts under examination.[18]

Theorie der Physiognomik und Psychologie," *Sömmerring-Forschungen*, 8 (New York: Verlag, 1990); Stefano Poggi, "Neurology and Biology in the Romantic Age in Germany: Carus, Burdach, Gall, von Baer," in *Romanticism in Science: Science in Europe (1780–1840)*, ed. Stefano Poggi and Maurizio Bossi (Boston: Kluwer, 1994): 143–60; Stefano Poggi, *Il genio e l'unità della natura: La scienza della Germania romantica (1790–1830)* (Bologna: Il Mulino, 2000).

17. R. H. Lotze, *Medicinische Psychologie oder Physiologie der Seele* (Leipzig: Weidmann, 1852). See also the new edition of selected papers by Lotze: *Kleine Schriften zur Psychologie: Eingeleitet und mit Materialien zur Rezeptionsgeschichte Versehen*, ed. R. Pester (New York: Springer, 1989). See also George Santayana, *Lotze's System of Philosophy*, ed. P. G. Kuntz (Bloomington: Indiana University Press, 1971). For a concise account of Lotze's ideas about psychology see W. Woodward's paper, "From Association to Gestalt: The Fate of Hermann Lotze's Theory of Spatial Perception, 1846–1920," *Isis* 69 (1978): 572–82.

18. James, *Pluralistic Universe*, 42–43, 55, 60.

The role played by Lotze in the development of James's philosophy is not, at this stage of James's career, negative; James was not yet critical of Lotze. Lotze represents for James a fruitful confrontation between philosophical thought and scientific inquiry, especially with regard to the physiological study of sensory processes. The new science of psychology owed to Lotze fundamental insights, especially the definition of soul and of the relationship between the physical and the psychic, the body and the mind.

During the 1930s, this aspect of the development of James's thought was examined in a series of articles published by Otto F. Kraushaar in *Psychological Review, Philosophical Review,* and *Journal of the History of Ideas.*[19] Kraushaar's outline remains definitive and valuable; the documents at our disposal are still the same, namely, the *Principles of Psychology* and the philosophical texts from the first ten years of the twentieth century.[20]

VI

Lotze greatly influenced James's project of using the data of psychological inquiry to lay the foundations of a new scientific psychology and to open the way toward a more concrete, "realistic" philosophical attitude. The way Lotze set the relations between philosophical reflection and scientific inquiry was the point of departure for James. In addition, Lotze's understanding served for James as a filter for many German views about science and nature, eliminating or setting aside many of the frankly materialistic traits of German naturalism.

Lotze, who had a propensity to monism, was not the sole influence on James, however. In fact, James found a reliable point of reference in Fechner, the other father of German scientific psychology. James's *Principles of Psychology* includes references to Fechner's psychophysics and especially to the so-called psychophysical law.[21] James was concerned

19. Otto F. Kraushaar, "Lotze's Influence on the Psychology of William James," *Psychological Review* 43 (1936): 235–57; also "What James's Philosophical Orientation Owed to Lotze," *Philosophical Review* 47 (1938): 517–26; "Lotze as a Factor in the Development of James's Radical Empiricism and Pluralism," *Philosophical Review* 48 (1939): 455–71; and "Lotze's Influence on the Pragmatism and Practical Philosophy of William James," *Journal of the History of Ideas* 1 (1940): 439–58. For an evaluation of the role played by Lotze in James's development see S. Franzese, *L'uomo indeterminato: Saggio su William James* (Rome: D'Anselmi, 2000).

20. Besides *Pluralistic Universe,* see James, *The Varieties of Religious Experience* (New York: Longmans, Green, 1902); *Pragmatism: A New Name for Some Old Ways of Thinking* (New York: Longmans, Green, 1907); *The Meaning of Truth: A Sequel to* Pragmatism (New York: Longmans, Green, 1909).

21. James, *Principles of Psychology,* vol. 1, 539–41.

not only with a scientific, "exact" examination of the relations between stimulus and sensation, but also with the new approach to the whole activity of the soul in Fechner's psychophysics. James devoted an entire chapter of the book to Fechner. Fechner's psychophysics provided James with a worldview, which "seems at first to have much in common with absolutism" but in fact "really stands at the opposite pole" from any form of monism. James was led to an appreciation of Fechner's worldview by a cautious, if not overtly polemical, attitude toward a very special version of monistic absolutism, i.e., the absolutism of McTaggart's interpretation of "Hegel's gospel." It is the "thickness" of reality, James observes, that gets lost when one assumes McTaggart's point of view. The assertion "that in every nut of experience and thought, however finite, the whole of reality" (the absolute idea, as Hegel calls it) is "implicitly present" is an assertion that eventually opens the way to mysticism. The question of mysticism in James himself, especially in the late James, remains open. James's negative remarks on mysticism, however, can easily be traced back to the fear that *logical* mysticism would end up in a crude monistic absolutism. James's appeal to Fechner's method must be seen in this perspective, namely as aiming to avoid the fatal "contrast between the abstract pretensions of rationalism and what rationalistic methods concretely can do." Attaining some metaphysical conclusiveness about reality is possible—and Fechner does draw conclusions of this sort. There are no grounds for rejecting such conclusions, as long as we avoid "abstract pretensions of rationalism." And this means the necessity of adopting a truly scientific method in this regard, that is, the method of "hypotheses, and deductions from these, controlled by sense-observations and analogies with what we know elsewhere."[22]

VII

For James, Fechner's mind represented in an exemplary fashion the "indestructible richness of the German cerebral endowment." James's admiration for the polymath Fechner stemmed from his firm belief that not only science, but also philosophy, must devote its attention to manifest facts. From this point of view, materialism has exactly the same rights as spiritualism to lay down the foundations of our worldview.[23] James was partial to Fechner's panpsychism, because Fechner portrayed nature in its actual complexity. Even though Fechner's method

22. James, *Pluralistic Universe,* 135, 141, 144, 145.
23. Ibid., 20.

seems to exemplify the use of analogy, nevertheless he was still careful to preserve any difference that the method of analogy might miss. Echoing Bain's opinion that genius has to be considered as "the power of seeing analogies," James remarks upon the fact that the number of analogies Fechner could perceive was prodigious. His analogies were, however, counterbalanced by a consistent appeal to the differences between the facts under observation. In any case, continues James, we are led to acknowledge that the "original sin . . . of both our popular and our scientific thinking, is our inveterate habit of regarding the spiritual not as the rule but as an exception in the midst of nature." James does not mind that Fechner will eventually turn out to be "a monist in his theology." What really matters to him is that "there is room in his universe for every grade of spiritual being between man and the final all-inclusive God."[24]

James was not preoccupied by the implications of Fechner's panpsychism, in particular Fechner's revival of the old conception of an "Earth-soul." What Fechner meant by "Earth-soul" is actually a metaphor, namely that "the constitution of the world is identical throughout," that "we must suppose that my consciousness of myself and yours of yourself, although in their immediacy they keep separate and know nothing of each other, are yet known and used together in a higher consciousness, that of the human race," and that "the whole human and animal kingdoms come together as conditions of consciousness of still wider scope."[25]

The "ordinary monistic idealism leaves everything intermediary out," it "recognizes only the extremes, as if, after the first rude face of the phenomenal world in all its particularity, nothing but the supreme in all its perfection could be found." Fechner, on the contrary, without confusing himself with the supporters of "materialistic science," with its infinite molecules and electrons, invites us to get hold of the "complexity in unity" of each organism living on the earth, a complexity that, however, "far exceeds that of any organism." The attitude that James promotes is one of searching for and detecting connections and interactions, by means of analogy. He admits this is a kind of "naturalistic metaphysics."[26]

24. Ibid., 151–52, 150, 153.
25. Ibid., 155.
26. Ibid., 175, 157.

VIII

In the chapter of *A Pluralistic Universe* just summarized, James showed himself highly sensitive to the views that Fechner had inherited from German Romantic science, the views sketched by Schelling and by German scientists from the first decades of the nineteenth century, such as Burdach, Treviranus, and Oken.[27] It would be interesting to look for the way James was in fact led to rediscover, through Fechner, the roots of the worldview of his father, above all the ideas of Swedenborg. This is, however, a rather complex question that cannot be dealt with here.[28] To pursue this question, one would have to begin with the German and British Romantic roots of American speculation about man and nature in the first half of the nineteenth century. This inquiry, important as it is, should not be allowed to detract from the significance of James's connection to German naturalism.

Besides Lotze, Fechner, and a long series of other German scientists and philosophers of the second half of nineteenth century, it was Ernst Mach to whom James was most indebted. Mach accepted, shared, and developed the ideas constituting the core of the foundational program of a scientific psychology, in what amounted to a systematization of the approaches proposed by Fechner, and in some respects by Lotze too. Mach's and Fechner's worldviews were not exactly the same, since Fechner's approach to the understanding of natural processes has a "spiritualistic" imprint totally uncharacteristic of Mach. Yet, Mach's approach to the relationship between the observational and experimental data of sensory physiology and what can be considered as their psychological translation or interpretation was deeply rooted in Fechner's psychophysics. Mach shared with Fechner, and perhaps derived from him, a belief in the impossibility of attaining the "inwardness" of what is observed and described as a "psychological activity." This commitment on the part of both Fechner and Mach was a reaction against the strict atomistic explanation of natural processes. In fact, Mach's well-known propensity for a dynamistic interpretation of atomism can be traced to a very similar attitude in Fechner, whose source was the "dynamic atomism" of Schelling's works on "philosophy of nature," especially *Von der Weltseele*.[29]

27. See *Romanticism and the Sciences*, ed. A. Cunningham and N. Jardine (Cambridge: Cambridge University Press, 1990); Poggi, *Il genio e l'unità della natura*.

28. On the history of James's development, see H. M. Feinstein, *Becoming William James* (Ithaca, N.Y.: Cornell University Press, 1984); G. E. Myers, *William James: His Life and Thought* (New Haven, Conn.: Yale University Press, 1986).

29. W. Swoboda, "Physics, Physiology and Psychophysics: The Origins of Ernst Mach's Empiriocriticism," *Rivista di Filosofia* 22–23 (1982): 234–74; see also Gereon Wolters's

It is important to keep in mind, however, the main difference between Fechner and Mach, which is their attitude toward Darwin's theory of evolution. Mach advocated the Darwinian point of view. While Fechner was not completely opposed to an evolutionary approach to the understanding of natural processes, he always took an anti-Darwinian stance, which was deeply rooted in his own Romantic, metaphysical background.[30]

Given the role Darwinian evolution plays in James's psychology and philosophy, we have now reached an essential point for evaluating James's relationship with what we have called "German naturalism."[31] There is a significant but problematic kinship between what Mach says about the relationship between physics, physiology, and biology, on the one hand, and James's remarks about the common ground of a scientific psychology, on the other. James's remarks are characterized by unmistakable German traits. Mach's views were grounded in a threefold approach—based on physics, physiology, and biology—to the study of natural processes and to defining the place of man therein. In other words, Mach was reducing psychology to these three sciences, a move that, if not directly opposed by James, is not one that he himself made. This is why, in James's ongoing confrontation with German naturalism, James is finally closer to Fechner than to Mach. This is so, notwithstanding his long and friendly relationship with Mach,[32] and despite James's criticism of Fechner. James says that Fechner's assumption "that conscious experiences freely compound and separate themselves" requires careful scrutiny.[33] Fechner's views about consciousness and the "life of the soul" are without doubt, from James's point of view, much more respectful of the rights of psychology than Mach's views. Compared with Fechner, Mach's views about sensation and consciousness appear very reductionist. As reported by Ralph B. Perry,[34] James noted this, in his copy of Mach's *Analyse der Empfindungen,* which was published in 1886. James refuses all reduction of psychology, via psy-

introduction to the reprint of Mach's *Analyse der Empfindungen* (Darmstadt: Wissenschaftliche Buchgesellschaft, 2000), i–xxxii.

30. On this subject, see Heidelberger, *Die innere Seite der Natur.*

31. R. J. Richards, "The Personal Equation in Science: William James's Psychological and Moral Uses of the Darwinian Theory," in *A William James Renascence: Four Essays by Young Scholars,* ed. M. R. Schwehn, *Harvard Library Bulletin* 30 (1982): 387–425; E. Taylor, "W. James on Darwin: An Evolutionary Theory of Consciousness," in *Psychology: Perspectives and Practice,* ed. S. M. Pfafflin et al., *Annals of the New York Academy of Sciences,* 1990 (no. 602): 7–33.

32. See Myers, *William James,* 569–70.

33. James, *Pluralistic Universe,* 176.

34. Ralph B. Perry, *The Thought and Character of William James,* 2 vols. (Boston: Little, Brown, 1935), quoted in Myers, *William James,* 569.

chophysics, to physics. He also emphasizes the danger of losing, due to reductionism, the specific character of psychological inquiry.[35]

The views of James about psychological inquiry are not equivalent, however, to those of Dilthey or others, who advocate a psychology more "spiritualistic" than "naturalistic." The biological background of James's psychology is still present, even in the later formulations of his philosophical point of view. This is confirmed by James's attention to Fechner's conception of an "Earth-soul." It is easy to trace this biological background both to his years spent at Harvard in the school of Louis Agassiz who, like Fechner, was a firm opponent of Darwinism,[36] and to his years spent in German universities. This time witnessed a fierce confrontation between the supporters of two different faiths in evolution: the Romantic and the Darwinian. Examining the development of James's ideas against this background is a task still outstanding in the scholarly literature. Such an examination would provide useful hints for understanding the influence exerted on James by Fechner and by other typical expressions of German Romantic *Naturphilosophie,* such as Ostwald's popular writings.[37] It would also provide a means of evaluating the problematic character of the relationship between James and Mach. Mach's reductionism is "biological," and his views concerning the way the world is built by changing aggregates of sensations is echoed in some ways in James's theory of "pure experience." More than half a century ago, Ralph B. Perry pointed out, however, that we are confronted with "the question of why, given James's conclusion that everything experienced is physiological prior to being conceptualized in terms of pure experience, he did not, like Mach and Russell, attempt to accommodate sensations into an all-embracing framework of physics rather than conceiving of them as neutral pure experience."[38] Perry's

35. On James's caution about reductionism, see W. R. Woodward, "Introduction," in James, *Essays in Psychology: The Works of William James,* ed. F. H. Burkhardt, F. Bowers, and I. K. Skrupskelis (Cambridge, Mass.: Harvard University Press, 1983), xi–xxxix; D. W. Bjork, *The Compromised Scientist: William James and the Development of American Psychology* (New York: Columbia University Press, 1983); *Reflections on the Principles of Psychology: William James after a Century,* ed. M. G. Johnson and T. B. Henley (Hillsdale, N.J.: L. Erlbaum, 1990); *The Philosophical Psychology of William James,* ed. M. H. De Armey and S. Skousgaard (Washington, D.C.: Center for Advanced Research in Phenomenology, 1986).

36. See Kuklick, *Rise of American Philosophy,* 21–23; see also what James writes on Agassiz as quoted by F. O. Matthiesen, *The James Family: Including Selections from the Writings of Henry James, Senior, William, Henry, and Alice James* (1947; New York: Vintage Books, 1980), 537–42.

37. R. B. Perry, *The Thought and Character of William James,* New paperback ed. with introduction by Charlene H. Seigfried (Nashville: Vanderbildt, 1996), 236. James (23.7.1902) writes to H. Münsterberg: "I am reading Ostwald's *Vorlesungen über Naturphilosophie* [Leipzig, 1902], and find it a most delectable book."

38. R. B. Perry, *Thought and Character* (1935), as quoted by Myers, *William James,* 569.

question remains unanswered. It is still controversial, and it is essential for the understanding of James's late philosophy. The exact debt James owed to German naturalism has yet to be ascertained. It is a task that promises discoveries about James's philosophy that are relevant not only to the historical reconstruction of James's philosophy but also to its very meaning.[39]

39. In the last two decades, the importance of the history of German psychology for understanding James's philosophy has become more widely recognized. See, for instance: P. M. Ford, *William James's Philosophy: A New Perspective* (Amherst: University of Massachusetts Press, 1982); G. Bird, *William James* (London: Routledge and Kegan Paul, 1986); J. D. Wild, *The Radical Empiricism of William James* (Garden City, N.Y.: Doubleday, 1989); C. H. Seigfried, *William James's Radical Reconstruction of Philosophy* (Albany: State University of New York Press, 1990); W. J. Gavin, *William James and the Reinstatement of the Vague* (Philadelphia: Temple University Press, 1992); D. Olin, ed., *William James. Pragmatism in Focus* (London: Routledge and Kegan Paul, 1992); M. E. Donnelly, ed., *Reinterpreting the Legacy of William James* (Washington: American Psychological Association, 1993); R. A. Putnam, ed., *The Cambridge Companion to William James* (Cambridge: Cambridge University Press, 1997); D. C. Lamberth, *William James and the Metaphysics of Experience* (Cambridge: Cambridge University Press, 1999); R. M. Gale, *The Divided Self of William James* (Cambridge: Cambridge University Press, 1999); H. Brown, *William James on Radical Empiricism and Religion* (Toronto: University of Toronto Press, 2000).

6 C. S. Peirce's Reclamation of Teleology

VINCENT COLAPIETRO

INTRODUCTION

C. S. Peirce's orientation toward nature was, at once, an innovative continuation of R. W. Emerson's vision and an equally innovative reclamation of the Aristotelian conception of natural teleology. This is, at least, my thesis. But since the emphasis of my account will ultimately fall upon Peirce's reclamation of teleology (since this is the direction in which my reflections finally tend), my title stresses this side of my thesis. My own authorial teleology does not encompass the goal of proving this claim; rather my aim is to render this thesis sufficiently definite, interesting, and plausible to encourage others to join me in exploring this topic.

The revolutionary outlook of Charles Darwin would appear to have thoroughly discredited both the Emersonian vision and the Aristotelian. Yet Peirce's own commitment to evolution did not prompt him to focus exclusively on the natural world; nor did it incline him to suppose that immanent principles are ultimately sufficient for explaining natural processes. In "A Neglected Argument for the Reality of God" (1908) and other texts, he argued that a fully receptive encounter with the natural world prompts the unprejudiced mind to suppose there is a creative divinity infinitely transcending the empirical universe. In brief, Nature points such a mind toward a Spirit from which Nature emanates and on which it depends. Moreover, Peirce's commitment to evolutionism did not involve banishing teleology from nature. For him, nature was first and foremost a realm in which growth was observable. He even tended to identify evolution with growth: "Evolution means nothing but *growth* in the widest sense of that word" (1.174).[1] But growth is not mere quantitative increase; it is rather qual-

1. "But a pseudo-evolutionism which enthrones mechanical law above the principle of growth is," in Peirce's judgment, "at once scientifically unsatisfactory, as giving no possible hint of how the universe has come about, and hostile to all hope of personal relations

itative transformation. Such transformation is rendered inexplicable by mechanism: "mechanical law out of like antecedents can only produce like consequents" (1.174).[2] The desperate attempts to fit the multifarious phenomena of genuine growth into the Procrustean bed of thoroughgoing mechanism must be exposed for what they are, illicit demands made by the theoretical imagination at the prompting of a monistic ideal of scientific explanation.[3] "So if observed facts point to real growth, they point to another agency [besides mechanism], to spontaneity" (1.174) or chance. In turn, chance secures the possibility of growth in the forms we observe in nature.

Just as Peirce tended to identify evolution with growth, he tended to associate the idea of growth with the philosophy of Aristotle (*EP* 2: 373).[4] "This idea of Aristotle's has proved marvellously fecund" (ibid.). It is arguably the most fruitful idea yet discovered for making sense out of the world of our experience. In some respects, Peirce was very much a child of his time, especially in his assessment of the century in which he was born: "Many and many a century is likely to sink in Time's flood, and be buried in the mud of Lethe, before the achievements of the nineteenth shall get matched" (ibid.). But historical consciousness allowed Peirce to grasp the extent to which the nineteenth century was in its intellectual accomplishments yet under the tutelage of Aristotle: "of all those achievements, the greatest in the eye of reason, that of bring-

to God" (6.158). In accord with the established practice of citing the *Collected Papers of Charles Sanders Peirce,* references will be made to the volume and the numbered paragraph of the text cited. Thus, "1.174" refers to volume 1, paragraph 174, of Charles Sanders Peirce, *The Collected Papers of Charles Sanders Peirce,* vols. 1–6 ed. Charles Hartshorne and Paul Weiss, vols. 7–8 ed. Arthur W. Burks (Cambridge, Mass.: Harvard University Press, 1931–1958).

2. My views regarding both teleology in general and Peirce's conception of teleology are deeply indebted to T. L. Short, "Teleology and Linguistic Change," in *The Peirce Seminar Papers,* vol. 4, ed. Michael Shapiro (New York: Berghahn Books, 1999), 111–58. There Short stresses, "Teleology is not a primitive doctrine like animism. It was explicitly introduced by Plato in his *Phaedo* . . . and in the *Timeaus,* as providing an explanation for those forms of order that the materialist and mechanist theories of the presocratic philosophers had failed to explain" (111). Peirce reclaimed this doctrine as a way of explaining those forms of order and transformation that the materialist and mechanist theories of the postmedieval philosophers rendered inexplicable.

3. Peirce confessed to "a shocking leaning toward anthropomorphic conceptions" (5.212). In response to the charge that he is guilty of projecting onto nature traits rooted in his imagination rather than nature herself, he would likely claim that the thoroughgoing mechanism to which so much of modern science is wedded can itself be seen as a projection of the theoretical imagination. The crucial issue is thus not whether anthropomorphism or mechanism is a projection of our imaginations, but what theoretical gains are secured by these rival projections.

4. "*EP* 2" refers to volume 2 of Charles Sanders Peirce, *The Essential Peirce: Selected Philosophical Writings,* ed. Nathan Houser and Christian J. W. Kloesel (Bloomington: Indiana University Press, 1992). Hereafter for this source, this system will be used.

ing to light the supremacy of the element of *Growth,* was, after all, nothing but a special application of Aristotle's pure vision" (ibid.).

For our purposes, the upshot of these considerations may be briefly summarized. In one way, nature points beyond herself; in another, she points beyond all forms of reductive mechanism for which any appeal to final causes would be dismissed as an illicit mode of scientific explanation. An appreciation of Peirce's vision of nature requires, at least, attention to both of these trajectories. Reading Peirce's position in light of two figures with whom he was historically connected and personally acquainted can illuminate the first. Moreover, reading him in conjunction with Aristotle should throw light on Peirce's efforts to reclaim something closely akin to Aristotle's teleology.[5] In my discussion of Peirce vis-à-vis James, however, I will already have occasion to consider these two philosophers' contrasting attitudes to Aristotle; hence, even before turning directly in the penultimate section of this paper to Peirce and Aristotle, I will have called attention to important facets of Peirce's appreciation of Aristotle's thought.

My first step is, thus, to formulate a twofold contrast. Ralph Waldo Emerson was one of Charles Sanders Peirce's cultural elders, and William James was one of Peirce's immediate contemporaries. At the outset, then, I would like to contrast Peirce with each of these figures. This will help us to read Peirce *into* the historical context in which his philosophical life and, in particular, his evolutionary cosmology actually took shape. The marked tendency to read American philosophers primarily, often solely, in reference to European thinkers effectively reads them *out of* their own cultural context.[6] This manner of reading is certainly legitimate and frequently quite illuminating. Considering, for example, William James and German naturalism promises to be instructive; so too does reading Peirce in light of his own creative appropriation of (for example) the Kantian notion of a regulative ideal. But the way of honoring Peirce and other thinkers in our traditions does not *always* entail relating them to Descartes or Locke, Kant or Hegel, Foucault or Derrida. Their complex relationship to more culturally proximate figures often deserves more detailed attention than it receives. So I will introduce Peirce by way of comparison and contrast, first to Emerson and then to James.

5. Cf. Short, "Teleology and Linguistic Change," 111–12.

6. Stanley Cavell is an example of this. See Douglas R. Anderson, "American Loss in Cavell's Emerson," *Transactions of the Charles S. Peirce Society* 29, no. 1 (Winter 1993): 69–89.

EMERSON'S CELEBRATION OF SPIRIT

It is appropriate here to recall that one of the most important texts in our literature is entitled simply *Nature* (1836).[7] But it is also noteworthy that in this work Ralph Waldo Emerson takes the topic of nature to be an occasion to celebrate Spirit: "the noblest ministry of nature is," in his words, "to stand as the apparition of God. It is the organ through which the universal spirit speaks to the individual, and strives to lead back the individual to it" (E 72). Emerson goes so far as to reduce nature to the status of a shadow and also that of a dream. Nature "is faithful to the cause whence it had its origin. It always speaks of Spirit. It suggests the absolute. It is a perpetual effect. It is [thus] a great shadow pointing always to the sun behind us" (E 71). This sun is of course a metaphor for Spirit. In this same essay, moreover, Emerson insists that the natural world in its apparent solidity and sufficiency "is a divine dream, from which we may awake to the glories and certainties of day" (E 72).

Emerson's monograph on Nature thus turns out to be an ode to Spirit. In addition, it is a nuanced statement of Emerson's philosophical idealism, in which the ancient lineage of this doctrine is acknowledged and its principal antagonist is identified. The doctrine can trace its roots to Plato; its enemies are those giants of the earth for whom materiality defines the limits of reality.

"To the senses and the unrenewed understanding, belongs a sort of instinctive belief in the absolute existence of nature. In their view man and nature are indissolubly joined. Things are ultimates, and they [the senses and understanding] never look beyond their sphere. The presence of Reason [however] mars this faith" (E 63). The unrenewed understanding, severely constrained by the despotism of the senses, represents a truncated rationalism: it takes the conditioned and derivative to be the unconditioned and absolute because such understanding forsakes the task of tracing reality to its self-luminous source.[8] In contrast to metaphysical materialism, Emersonian idealism asserts that "matter is a phenomenon, not a substance, . . . Idealism is a hypothesis to account for nature by other principles than those of carpentry and chem-

7. References to Emerson's work will be given in parenthetical references of the form "E 72," which cites page numbers from Ralph Waldo Emerson, *Selected Essays,* ed. Larzer Ziff (New York: Penguin Books, 1982).

8. In A. N. Whitehead, *Science and the Modern World* (New York: Macmillan, 1925; reprint, New York: Free Press, 1967), Whitehead claims: "A self-satisfied rationalism is in effect a form of anti-rationalism. It means an arbitrary halt at a particular set of abstractions. This was the case with science" (201 in reprint edition).

istry" (E 72). According nature this status does not rob her of her use or value. "Whether nature enjoy[s] a substantial existence without [i.e., an outward substantial reality], or [whether it] is only in the apocalypse of the mind, it is alike useful and alike venerable to me" (E 62–3). The utility and venerability of nature are not compromised by treating the natural world as a derivative phenomenon, rather than as an absolute substance.

To characterize nature as a dream, apparition, apocalypse, phenomenon, and shadow is, of course, a way of stressing that nature is not primordial or absolute. The emphasis on its derivative (or phenomenal) status, however, needs to be linked with Emerson's insistence on its symbolic (or sacramental) function. Nature performs the office of a sacrament, for it is an inexhaustible source of perceptible signs of the true absolute. It is, above all else, an outward, legible sign of an infinite, gracious power.

Peirce too suggested "the universe is a vast representamen, a great symbol of God's purpose, working out its conclusions in living realities" (5.119). He adds: "The Universe as an argument is necessarily a great work of art, a great poem—for every fine argument is a poem and a symphony—just as every true poem is a sound argument" (5.119). But there is not in Peirce's treatment of the universe the tendency to reduce nature to a symbol, to make it a dream or apparition. Thirdness or intelligibility is a truly constitutive feature of nature. But the secondness or otherness of nature is equally a defining trait. Emerson himself begins his discourse by defining Nature as what is *not me,* what is other than the self precisely in its unity with Soul (that is, my individual soul in its unity with the Over-Soul). But, in the next paragraphs, the otherness of Nature is rather quickly and completely absorbed into Spirit. In contrast, Peirce accords the natural world a more substantial ontological status. Its secondness, (in particular) its otherness from both its divine origin and human knowers, is in his judgment too pervasive, persistent, and forceful to warrant such metaphors as dream or apparition.

But it was James who pushed this emphasis on otherness to an extreme. The character of nature is too equivocal, divided, and even contradictory to enable nature to serve as a symbol for divinity. Such, at least, was the verdict of James. He observed:

> There were times when Leibnitzes with their heads buried in monstrous wigs could compose Theodicies. But those times are past; and we of the nineteenth century, with our evolutionary theories and mechanical philosophies, already know nature too impartially and too well to worship unreservedly any God of whose character she can be an adequate expression. Truly, all we know of good

and duty proceeds from nature; but none the less so all we know of evil. Visible nature is all plasticity and indifference,—a moral multiverse . . . and not a moral universe. To such a harlot we owe no moral allegiance; with her as a whole we can establish no moral communion.[9]

James thus insisted that "If there be a divine Spirit of the universe, nature, such as we know her, cannot possibly be its *ultimate word* to man." For him, Nature was, in fact, an unreliable word, an almost completely inadequate revelation. "Either there is no Spirit revealed in nature, or it is inadequately revealed there; and (as all the higher religions have assumed) what we call visible nature, or *this* world, must be but a veil and surface-show whose full meaning resides in a supplementary unseen or *other* world."[10] Unquestionably, James captured something central to traditional Judaism and Christianity when he confessed: "if I am to express my personal opinion unreservedly, I should say . . . that the initial step towards getting into healthy ultimate relations with the universe is the act of rebellion against the idea that such a God [as that solely knowable through Nature] exists."[11] The worship of Nature is, of course, a form of idolatry; moreover, worship of the God of Nature in the sense intended here may be little more than this. Principally for this reason, James refused to grant the natural world a sacramental status.

Peirce was aware of the possibility of such idolatry. Even so, on this matter Peirce stands closer to Emerson than to James, for he notes that "for the pragmaticistic logician, nature (including the deeds and works of man) is the sign of God to Humanity, and pure heuretic [or theoretical] science makes it [nature] the prayer book of an elevating worship" (MS 288, 181).[12] Like any other sign, especially one of staggering complexity and unfathomable significance, nature as a sign of divinity needs to be interpreted critically. It is one thing to claim nature provides no adequate revelation of the divine, quite another to break altogether with those religious traditions that accord the natural world a sacramental status.

But, as a scientist and scientifically oriented philosopher, Peirce was more concerned with idols of the theater such as mechanism and de-

9. William James, *The Will to Believe and Other Essays in Popular Philosophy* (New York: Longmans, Green, 1897; reprint, New York: Dover Publications, 1956), 43–44 in reprint edition.

10. Ibid., 44.

11. Ibid.

12. All references to Peirce's unpublished manuscripts will be given in accord with the identification of these in Richard S. Robin's *Annotated Catalog of the Papers of Charles S. Peirce* (Amherst: University of Massachusetts Press, 1967). MS of course refers to manuscript, whereas the number immediately following refers to the number used by Robin to identify a particular manuscript.

terminism than idolatry in its strictly religious sense. Insofar as materialism was identifiable with determinism and mechanism,[13] Peirce's opposition to it was as thoroughgoing as was Emerson's. Moreover, his intellectual kinship with his cultural elder is discernible in reference to other fundamental commitments. For Peirce would not hesitate to endorse Emerson's claim that "So much of man as he is ignorant of, so much of his own mind does he not yet possess. And, in fine, the ancient precept, 'Know thyself,' and the modern precept, 'Study nature,' become at last one maxim" (E 87). Nor would he hesitate to affirm Emerson's bias toward continuity and, to some extent at least, unity. In a letter to William James dated July 23, 1905, Peirce voiced his opposition to the Jamesian proposal of a finite God,[14] confessing, "the God of my theism is not finite. That won't do at all" (8.262). He went on to insist, "the human mind and the human heart have a filiation to God. That to me is the most comfortable [comforting?] doctrine. At least I find it most wonderfully so every day in contemplating all my misdeeds and shortcomings" (8.262). To James, as much a radical pluralist as a radical empiricist, Peirce then revealed that "Pluralism . . . does not satisfy either my head or my heart."[15] In his explicit opposition to the radical form of ontological pluralism being championed by James, Peirce in effect revealed his kinship to Emerson. Emerson after all insisted that, properly viewed, "the world lies no longer [before us as] a dull miscellany and lumber-room, but has form and order; there is no trifle, there is no puzzle, but one design unites and animates the farthest pinnacle and the lowest trench" (E 102). The totality of things was, for Peirce too, a cosmos: a far-reaching, perhaps even overarching, order is discoverable in this totality. But it is a cosmos *in the making,* for order is continually evolving out of chaos. The disruptive presence of chance is ineliminable; thus even the most secure patterns of order are precarious. The fluidity and dynamism of nature, so stressed by Emerson, are also emphasized by Peirce.

Despite these quite fundamental agreements, there are of course deep differences between Emerson and Peirce. Emerson is aware that when he speaks of nature in his characteristic manner, he has "a distinct but most poetical sense in the mind" (E 37).[16] He is in this, to use

13. Cf. Elizabeth Flower and Murray G. Murphey, *A History of Philosophy in America,* 2 vols. (New York: Capricorn Books, 1977).

14. See, e.g., William James, *A Pluralistic Universe* (New York: Longmans, Green, 1909; reprint, Cambridge, Mass.: Harvard University Press, 1975).

15. See, however, Sandra B. Rosenthal, *Charles Peirce's Pragmatic Pluralism* (Albany: SUNY Press, 1994).

16. But Emerson tends to blur the boundary between poetry and philosophy, though not erase it (see, e.g., E 67).

another one of his own expressions, a truly representative man: he represents the poet-priest for whom the woods and wilderness provide places of worship, sites of epiphany[17] and for whom a literature born of encounters with nature marks a path back to the very source of our being. The poetic sense of nature and especially the literary sensibility expressed therein are, however, distant from Peirce's treatment of this topic.[18]

The way toward an understanding of nature was, for the first generation of American pragmatists, *not* principally the way of poetry; it was *not* that of a poetic sensibility, yet in the case of Peirce it was unapologetic about its reliance upon a religious lexicon. Poetry was certainly not irrelevant to these thinkers; however, their approach to nature was more patient, painstaking, and detailed.[19] It aspired to be more straightforwardly scientific and also more conventionally philosophical, thus paying more explicit, careful attention to methodological questions and to formal argumentation.[20] When he approached completion of his *Principles of Psychology*, William James wrote to his brother Henry, indicating "I have to forge every sentence in the teeth of irreducible and stubborn facts."[21] So, Emerson's poetic sensibility stands in marked contrast to the scientific temperament of both Peirce and James, thinkers who conscientiously forged their assertions and arguments in the teeth of facts, attending especially to those that seemed to contradict their own positions. But this kinship between Peirce and James suggests a context for appreciating their differences.

JAMES'S INCLINATION TOWARD NOMINALISM

Both Peirce and James came to philosophy from a training in science.[22] This is relevant to an understanding of their work as philosophers. It is widely known that James taught courses in psychology before offering ones in philosophy, but it is not as well known that he

17. See the essay by Russell Goodman in this volume, 3–5.

18. This claim needs to be qualified, for Peirce depicts the universe as a vast poem and true poetry itself as possessing a truth higher than other modes of human discourse.

19. For example, John Dewey drew inspiration and insight from the Romantic poets.

20. See John Dewey, "Emerson—The Philosopher of Democracy," in *The Middle Works of John Dewey*, vol. 3, ed. Jo Ann Boydston (Carbondale: Southern Illinois University Press, 1976–83), 184–92, on the question of whether to count Emerson as a philosopher.

21. My source for this quotation is Whitehead, *Science and the Modern World*, 3 in the original edition.

22. Vincent Colapietro, "Peirce the Contrite Fallibilist, Convinced Pragmaticist, and Critical Commonsensist," *Semiotica* 111-1/2 (1996): 75–101 and Paul Jerome Croce, *Science and Religion in the Era of William James: Eclipse of Certainty, 1820–1880* (Chapel Hill: University of North Carolina Press, 1995).

began his illustrious teaching career by teaching courses in anatomy and physiology. His medical training prepared him to teach little else. The only book written solely by Peirce and published during his lifetime was *Photometric Researches,* a scientific monograph growing out of his work at the Harvard Observatory. He took his philosophical investigations to be of a piece with his more strictly scientific ones. In one place, he revealed that "I came to the study of philosophy not for its teaching about God, Freedom, and Immortality, but intensely curious about Cosmology and Psychology" (4.2). Moreover, the temperament Peirce originally brought to philosophy was one he maintained throughout his life. For he insisted that, *as philosophers,* the best we can ever do is to offer and test hypotheses. He described his own philosophy "as the attempt of a physicist to make such conjecture as to the constitution of the universe as the methods of science may permit, with the aid of all that has been done by previous philosophers" (1.7). Peirce spelled out the polemical implication of this self-description: "Demonstrative proof is not to be thought of. The demonstrations of the metaphysicians are all moonshine" (1.7).

Their training in science, however, did not result in an antipathy toward religion. Central to the mission of both thinkers was a critique of the ideologues of scientism who tried to use the authority of science to browbeat others out of their religious convictions and traditional beliefs. Here we need only recall James's defense of the individual's right to believe and Peirce's defense of the humble musings by which even a clodhopper[23] comes to perceive signs of divinity in the world of our experience.[24]

One marked difference between Peirce and James in this connection needs to be stressed. James mounted his defense of an individual's right to believe on the basis of the theoretically undecidable nature of theological and metaphysical disputes. In contrast, Peirce mounted *his* defense on the basis of theoretically defensible claims regarding the reality of God. Peirce and James were, thus, scientifically trained philoso-

23. "It is that course of meditation upon the three Universes which gives birth to the hypothesis and ultimately to the belief that they, or at any rate two of the three, have a Creator independent of them, that I have throughout this article called the N.A., because I think the theologians ought to have recognized it as a line of thought reasonably productive of belief. This is the 'humble' argument, the innermost of the nest. In the mind of a metaphysician it will have a metaphysical tinge; but that seems to me rather to detract from its force than to add anything to it. It is just as good an argument, if not better, in the form it takes in the mind of the clodhopper" (6.484).

24. Douglas R. Anderson, "Three Appeals in Peirce's Neglected Argument," *Transactions of the Charles S. Peirce Society* 26 (1990): 349–62, and chapter 11 of Christopher Hookway, *Truth, Rationality, and Pragmatism* (Oxford: Clarendon Press, 2000).

phers who were disposed to defend religious belief and also to take up anew (at least) some of the central questions of traditional metaphysics.

They differed, however, not only in their manner of defending religious belief but also in their attitude toward various parts of Western philosophy. While William James wrote disparagingly of scholastic philosophy and consistently maintained his distance from Aristotle, Peirce frequently identified his work, its general spirit as well as specific doctrines, with medieval scholasticism. In addition, Peirce often identified himself with the tradition of Aristotle. Peirce's reclamation of teleology and his declaration of realism[25] are two obvious examples of why he felt inclined to identify himself with Aristotle.

Arguably, the demise of scholastic thought was bound up with a transformation of medieval culture due to a host of cultural forces, not the least of which was the effects of a resurgent nominalism. This is, at least, Peirce's way of narrating the sequence of events by which modern thinkers such as Descartes and Locke came to eclipse medieval ones such as Thomas and Scotus.

The term *nominalism* is of course ambiguous; in particular, Peirce's use of this word can be quite elastic, for he tended to stretch it to cover an array of doctrines or even dispositions not obviously equivalent to or (for that matter) not simply connected with one another. More than one commentator has even suggested that the word came to be used by Peirce simply as a signal of disapproval or rejection, a label for anything with which he was disposed to disagree! But this is inaccurate and thus unfair, for Peirce had a more or less precise, albeit complex, conception of what this word should be taken to mean. The obvious historical referents of the term *nominalists* helped Peirce to establish the core of this conception, namely, the denial of universals or (to use Peirce's preferred term) generals as anything more than linguistic or conceptual instruments. Peirce tended to characterize nominalism as primarily an ontological position of a highly reductivist cast, for it reduced all modes of being to that of individuality, existence, or actuality. Accordingly, realism here turns out to be a defense of modes of being not reducible to

25. "In a long notice of Frazer's *Berkeley*, in the *North American Review* for October, 1871, I declared for realism. I have since very carefully and thoroughly revised my philosophical opinions more than half a dozen times, and have modified them more or less on most topics; but I have never been able to think differently on that question of nominalism and realism. In that paper I acknowledged that the tendency of science has been toward nominalism; but the late Dr. Francis Ellingwood Abbot in the very remarkable introduction to his book entitled 'Scientific Theism' [1885], showed on the contrary, quite conclusively, that science has always been at heart realistic, and always must be so; and upon comparing his writings with mine, it is easily seen that these features of nominalism which I pointed out in science are merely superficial and transient" (1.20).

that of existence. In particular, it becomes principally a defense of the reality of generals (not in the sense of General Grant or General Lee!). "Not only may generals be real, but they may also be *physically efficient*, not in every metaphysical sense, but in the common-sense acception [or acceptation] in which human purposes are physically efficient" (5.431).

> When society is broken into bands, now warring, now allied, now for a time subordinated one to another, man loses his conceptions of truth and of reason. If he sees one man assert what another denies, he will, if he is concerned, choose his side and set to work by all means in his power to silence his adversaries. The truth for him is that for which he fights. (1.59)

In a series of lectures, arranged by James, Peirce announced (no doubt, partly for the benefit of his benefactor James): "I stand before you an Aristotelian and a scientific man" (1.618).[26] For Peirce, only biases against Aristotle required him to stutter in this fashion, for being Aristotelian and being scientific should not be separated into apparently distinct affirmations: they were in Peirce's mind (though not in those of his listeners) of a piece. "Above all Aristotle was an Asclepiades, that is to say, he belonged to a line every man of whom since the heroic age had, as a child, received a finished training in the dissecting-room" (1.618). The result of such training was clear to everyone but those blinded by biases: "Aristotle was a thorough-paced scientific man such as we see nowadays, except for this, that he ranged over all knowledge" (1.618). What Peirce proclaimed in a different context also merits recollection here: "Aristotle was by many lengths the greatest intellect that human history has to show. . . . So gigantic is his power of thought that those critics may almost be excused who hold it impossible that all of the books that have come down to us as his should all have been produced by one man" (6.96).

Highlighting this point of difference provides an occasion for bringing into focus an important but neglected facet of Peirce's philosophy—the extent to which Peirce took himself to be following in the footsteps of Aristotle. While Peirce tended to think that scholastic thinkers attached too much weight to traditional authorities (see, however, 1.32), he portrayed Aristotle as the highest of all possible authorities (1.88), deserving nothing less than the painstaking attention of his medieval commentators. Nor did Peirce think of these scholastic expositors as slavish scribes unable to think for themselves. In his judgment, they certainly were not the obscurantists they were depicted to be by

26. Peirce immediately went on to stress the difference between theory and practice, etc.

the inaugural figures of modern science and literary humanism.[27] Peirce noted that

> originality of thought was not greatly admired, but . . . on the contrary the admirable mind was his who succeeded in interpreting consistently the dicta of [say] Aristotle, Porphyry, and Boethius. Vanity, therefore, the vanity of cleverness, was a vice from which the schoolmen were remarkably free. They were minute and thorough in their knowledge of such authorities as they had, and they were equally minute and thorough in their treatment of every question which came up. (1.31)

These traits reminded Peirce "less of the philosophers of our day than of the men of science" (1.32). Even with respect to the weight attached to authority, the medieval authors exhibited a truly scientific character, one standing in marked contrast to the highly individualistic temperament of modern metaphysicians.

Thus, while James disparaged scholastic philosophy as "common sense's college-trained younger sister,"[28] insinuating thereby pedantry and pretension, Peirce praised the medieval schoolmen for "their restless insatiable impulse to put their opinions to the test" (1.33). He saw in them scientific brethren animated by a truly scientific spirit (1.34), the Eros to discover what we do not know and to test strenuously what we suppose we know.

Underlying this sense of kinship, there is the Peircean vision of human knowing as essentially a communal activity in which the cultivation of certain virtues and attitudes is indispensable. The Cartesian attitude toward tradition has become itself traditional, so that we have a dominant though unacknowledged tradition of anti-traditionalism.[29] The repetition compulsion of adolescent rebellion thus becomes a defining feature of intellectual life. A more balanced and respectful attitude toward our own intellectual traditions requires greater maturity than that characteristic of the Cartesian temperament. (Our own anti-traditionalism tends to be directed toward *our own* traditions, for those shaped by it can often be observed in the posture of prostrating them-

27. "The humanists were weak thinkers. Some of them no doubt might have been trained to be strong thinkers; but they had no severe training in thought. All their energies went to writing a classical language and an artistic style of expression. They went to the ancients for their philosophy; and mostly took up the three easiest of the ancient sects of philosophy, Epicureanism, Stoicism, and Scepticism" (1.18). Cf. Whitehead, *Science and the Modern World,* ch. 1, esp. 10–18, of the original edition.

28. William James, *Pragmatism and the Meaning of Truth* (Cambridge, Mass.: Harvard University Press, 1975), 92.

29. Vincent Colapietro, "Tradition: First Steps toward a Pragmaticistic Clarification," in *Philosophy in Experience: American Philosophy in Transition,* ed. Richard E. Hart and Douglas R. Anderson (New York: Fordham University Press, 1997), 14–45.

selves before Eastern—or European—traditions.)[30] Such, at least, is the judgment of Peirce.

Descartes marks [he notes] the period when Philosophy put off childish things and began to be a conceited young man. By the time the young man has grown to be an old man, he will have learned that traditions are precious treasures, while iconoclastic inventions are always cheap and often nasty. He will learn that when one's opinion is besieged and one is pushed by questions from one reason to another behind it, there is nothing illogical in saying at last, "Well, this is what we have always thought; this has been assumed for thousands of years without inconvenience." The childishness only comes in when tradition, instead of being respected, is treated as something infallible before which the reason of man is to prostrate itself, and which it is shocking to deny. (4.71)

It is significant that James in the same breath disparaged common sense and scholastic philosophy. He supposed that both are defined by their disposition to fix, once and for all, our descriptive terms and even our basic evaluations.[31] In contrast, Peircean empiricism enthusiastically embraces common sense, for it realizes that common sense is, at bottom, nothing other than the intergenerational experience of countless generations.[32] One reason why he does so is that he realizes common sense is, in principle, open to modification and development. Peirce asserts, simply but emphatically, that "Common sense corrects itself, improves its conclusions" (6.573). Hence, the absolutism and dogmatism James ascribes to common sense and its younger sister are, in Peirce's judgment, utterly unfair.

Common sense *is*, to some extent, a junkyard for metaphysical doctrines and, more generally, discredited theories, so that critical vigilance is required. I know of no better statement of the dialectical balance needed here than the one offered by Paul Weiss: "Any view that wholly abandons common sense is at best a fiction or a fantasy. Any view that refuses to examine it is at best uncritical and dogmatic. Reflection and reason require one to stand somewhere between these two extremes."[33] This stance is in effect what Peirce defended under the title of "critical commonsensism."

In his respectful attitude toward common sense and scholastic philosophy, Peirce revealed himself to be a critical traditionalist. He did so also in reference to traditional metaphysics. Indeed, his very preoccu-

30. Of course the identification of what is one's own tradition is always in some measure part of a self-identification.

31. James, *Pragmatism and the Meaning of Truth*, 92.

32. See, e.g., 1.654 and Colapietro, "Tradition."

33. Paul Weiss, "Common Sense and Beyond," in *Determinism and Freedom*, ed. Sidney Hook (New York: Collier Books, 1958), 232.

pation with questions of being exhibited his respect for this tradition of reflection.

Pragmatism is often linked to positivism and, in particular, to the demand to purge philosophy of any trace of metaphysics. But this is a distortion of pragmatism, at least as envisioned by its originator.[34] "Find a scientific man who proposes to get along without any metaphysics . . . and you have found one whose doctrines are thoroughly vitiated by the crude and uncriticized metaphysics with which they are packed" (1.129). Philosophy is not to be set in opposition to science, but rather it is to be conceived as an integral part of a vast array of (potentially) related inquiries. It is a defining exigency of human reason, when humans refuse to arrest arbitrarily the press of their own questions. Peirce here appeals to the figure to whom Albert and Thomas, appealed: "We must philosophize, said the great naturalist Aristotle—if only to avoid philosophizing. Every man [and woman] of us has a metaphysics, and has to have one; and it will influence his life greatly. Far better, then, that that metaphysics should be criticized and not be allowed to run loose" (1.129).

A central part of philosophical reflection is the explicit critique of the implicit metaphysics to which any human mind is committed. Reliance upon common sense does not alleviate the necessity for this formal critique. "A man may say 'I will content myself with common sense.' I, for one, am with him there, in the main" (1.29). Peirce denies that "there can be any *direct* profit in going behind common sense—meaning by *common sense* those ideas and beliefs that man's situation forces upon him."

But "metaphysics has always been the ape of mathematics" (1.130) and, in its being so, metaphysicians have tended to make monkeys of themselves! This is nowhere more evident than in the countless efforts of metaphysicians to offer demonstrative proofs for their conclusions. "The best that can be done is," according to Peirce, "to supply a hy-

34. Pragmatism "will serve to show that almost every proposition of ontological metaphysics is either meaningless gibberish—one word being defined by other words, and they by still others, without any real conception ever being reached—or else is downright absurd; so that all such rubbish being swept away, what will remain of philosophy will be a series of problems capable of investigation by the observational methods of the true sciences—the truth about which can be reached without those interminable misunderstandings and disputes which have made the highest of the positive sciences a mere amusement for idle intellects, a sort of chess—idle pleasure its purpose, and reading out of a book its method. In this regard, pragmaticism is a species of prope-positivism. But what distinguishes it from other species is, first, its retention of a purified philosophy; secondly, its full acceptance of the main body of our instinctive beliefs; and thirdly, its strenuous insistence upon the truth of scholastic realism" (5.423).

pothesis, not devoid of all likelihood, in the general line of growth of scientific ideas, and capable of being verified or refuted by future observers" (1.7). He occasionally identified his own hypothesis as a guess at the riddle of the sphinx, thereby alluding to one of the central metaphors in the writings of his transcendental elder.

TOWARD A RECLAMATION OF TELEOLOGY

Peirce's guess at the riddle of the universe was animated by a concern to explain, rather than explain away, the reality of growth.[35] The reclamation of something akin to vital forms ("ideas" as *inherently* dynamic) was, in his cosmology, of a piece with his rejection of thoroughgoing reliance on dead mechanisms as the primordial actualities from which all natural beings allegedly derive.

Josef Pieper has suggested that scholasticism died not because there was any lack of worthwhile ideas but because there was a paucity of truly able thinkers.[36] Peirce would be disposed to dissent from this suggestion for a reason bearing upon our topic. Given the importance of this matter, allow me to quote Peirce at length:

> Do you think that, notwithstanding the horrible wickedness of every mortal wight, the idea of right and wrong is nevertheless the greatest power on this earth, to which every knee must sooner or later bow or be broken down; or do you think that this is another notion at which common sense should smile? Even if you are of the negative opinion, still you must acknowledge that the affirmative is intelligible. Here, then, are two instances of ideas which either have, or are believed to have, life, the power of bringing things to pass, here below. Perhaps you may object that right and wrong are only a power because

35. In response to the necessitarian's claim there are "no observed phenomena which the hypothesis of chance [or doctrine of tychism] could aid in explaining," Peirce points "first to the phenomenon of growth and developing complexity, which appears to be universal, and which, though it may possibly be an affair of mechanism perhaps, certainly presents the appearance of increasing diversification. Then, there is variety itself, beyond comparison the most obtrusive character of the universe; no mechanism can account for this. Then, there is the very fact the necessitarian most insists upon, the regularity of the universe which for him serves only to block the road of inquiry. Then, there are the regular relations between [or among] the laws of nature—similarities and comparative characters, which appeal to our intelligence as its cousins, and call upon us for a reason. Finally, there is consciousness, feeling, a patent fact enough, but a very inconvenient one to the mechanical philosopher" (6.64). An adequate cosmology must be a cosmogony, an account of how the cosmos possibility came into being. It must also account for growth (hence, increase in complexity and variety such as is observable in various parts of the natural world), variety, regularity, the lawful relationships among various natural laws, and finally consciousness.

36. Josef Pieper, *Scholasticism: Personalities and Problems in Medieval Philosophy*, trans. Richard and Clara Winston (New York: McGraw-Hill, 1964), 25.

there are, or will be, powerful men who are disposed to make them so; just as they might take it into their heads to make tulip-fancying, or freemasonry, or Volapük a power. But you must acknowledge that this is not the position of those on the affirmative side. On the contrary, they hold that it is the idea which will create its defenders, and render them powerful. They will say that if it be that freemasonry or its foe, the Papacy, ever pass away—as perhaps either may—it will be precisely because they are ideas devoid of inherent, incorruptible vitality, and not at all because they have been unsupplied with stalwart defenders. Thus, whether you accept the opinion or not, you must see that it is a perfectly intelligible opinion that ideas are not all mere creations of this or that mind, but on the contrary have a power of finding or creating their vehicles, and having found them, of conferring upon them the ability to transform the face of the earth. (1.218)

Some ideas appear to manifest "inherent, incorruptible vitality." The idea that ideas are utterly lifeless, wooden things arbitrarily generated and manipulated by a purely inward consciousness is a distinctively modern idea. The forms by which we understand things and processes (in a word, ideas) are continuous with the forms by which those things and processes are structured. In a long review of Fraser's edition of Berkeley's works in which Peirce traces the roots of Berkeley's nominalism to its medieval antecedents, Peirce also stresses that the realist refuses to "sunder existence out of the mind and being in the mind as two wholly improportionable modes. When a thing is in such relation to the individual mind that that mind cognizes it, it is [or can be said to be] in the mind; and its being so in the mind will not in the least diminish its external existence. For he [the realist] does not think of the mind as a receptacle, which if a thing is in, it ceases to be out of" (8.16).

At the very least, nature is the *proximate* cause of everything we encounter in our experience. For Emerson, however, spirit is the root from which nature is generated, the source from which nature flows. Nature is itself a language and, as such, a source of the metaphors needed to bring to explicit, vivid consciousness our ultimate origin and ontological status. But the supposition that nature is, at bottom, a dream conjured by divinity seems to deprive nature of her solidity and sufficiency. The explanatory principles learned from our more mundane engagements (precisely those discovered by such experimental practices as chemistry and carpentry) might go a much farther distance in explaining the workings of nature than the transcendentalist poet allows.

Indeed, these principles might go the whole distance. For it might be possible to explain nature in her entirety and also in all of her particulars simply by recourse to immanent, natural principles and processes. Put more simply, there might not be any need to go beyond nature in order to explain nature. This supposition is, at any rate, worthy of careful consideration.

A handful of important points need to be made at this juncture. First, our experience of nature cannot be limited to the deliberately artificial contexts of experimental investigation. Nature is more than what science reveals, though the disclosures of experimental science must be square with those from other experiential domains. In other words, the full testimony of human experience must be accorded a judicious hearing. Second, the weight of this experience tends to underwrite what Aristotle and Peirce jointly claim. In particular, two of these claims merit recollection here. So, third, a natural principle just is an immanent one. Fourth, mutability no less than immanence needs to be thrust into the center of this discussion. In *A Pluralistic Universe,* James asserted, "nature is but a name for excess."[37] Peirce would more likely claim that nature is but a name for alteration, for the sphere in which alteration is manifest and myriad. Fifth and finally, nature is aptly personified as our mother, for she is truly the matrix whence life in all its forms, and thus our own species, issues. The alterations to which we are attuned include the coming-to-be and ceasing-to-be so manifest in the biosphere. Natality and mortality are defining features of the immediate foreground of the natural world in which human beings have secured for themselves, thus far, a sustainable habitat.[38]

The Peircean reclamation of final causality is a central part of a more inclusive reclamation of both scholastic philosophy and, behind this appropriation of certain insights from the schoolmen, Aristotelian metaphysics. Near the center of this reclamation is a cluster of theses bearing directly upon nature, several of which indeed bear upon the nature of nature. The most important of these is that our word *nature* still to some extent carries the force of *natura* and also that of *physis* in something close to their original Latin and Greek meanings, respectively. Nature is the matrix and arena of alteration (or, as this word suggests, othering), of things becoming other than they are. Alteration here goes all the way down, for it concerns the very being of what has come into being and is yet in process of coming to be. That is, nature is a domain in which we witness coming-to-be and ceasing-to-be in their most radical sense, that of generation and destruction. But, despite his

37. James, *Pluralistic Universe,* 129.

38. Cf. George Santayana, "Dewey's Naturalistic Metaphysics," in *The Philosophy of John Dewey,* ed. Paul Arthur Schilpp (New York: Tudor Publishing Co., 1939).

various reservations about certain aspects of the Darwinian account of evolutionary change, Peirce was convinced that the forms of alteration are themselves alterable, that species are mutable and thus not eternal, that order evolves out of chaos, and that absolute chance plays a significant role in cosmic and other forms of evolution.

A metaphysics of nature thus includes an account of alterability in which the most radical alterations are imagined (or conjectured) to be part of the self-constitution of nature, including of course the ongoing evolution of a cosmos out of chaos. So, the question of nature is, for Peirce no less than for Aristotle, that of alteration in its myriad, perceptible forms. How are we to account for the changes we observe and indeed undergo?

But the problem is, of course, more complex than this. For our scientific orthodoxy has dulled or distorted—and, in some cases, even blinded—our perception of the alterations observable in nature. The mechanistic metaphysics with which modern science (more accurately, modernist self-understandings of modern science) is so entangled aspires to a monolithic explanation of all natural phenomena. In turn, this ideal precludes the recognition of finality in nature; it radically undermines our confidence in what appears to be manifest and undeniable—goal-directed, *natural* processes. From the perspective of mechanism, our attribution to nature is, at best, a convenient but misleading way of speaking about what can be translated without remainder into mechanistic terms; at worst, it is an instance of obscurantism. It is instructive to recall here that, for Peirce, there is, in philosophy and science, no greater sin than obscurantism or (in his own words) the sin of "blocking the road of inquiry." Yet Peirce thought that thoroughgoing mechanism, not natural teleology, constitutes an obscurantist tendency. Such mechanism impoverishes our observational and interrogative capacities, effectively denying us the disclosures of our own experience and the questions naturally prompted by these disclosures. This form of alienation—the condition of being so estranged from the disclosures of our own experience as to deny them their manifest evidential force—is intellectually, and arguably also spiritually, devastating, though the symptoms of this devastation tend to become, given the nature of the malady, harder and harder to discern as such. In any event, commonplace observations of goal-directed processes are marked down to superstition, projection, and other indefensible human propensities.

In direct opposition to monolithic mechanism, Peirce argued for a more nuanced position. Some natural processes are explicable simply in terms of mechanical principles or laws, whereas other ones are intelligible only in reference to a goal or function being realized or initiated in these processes. An example of the former is the dissipation of heat, while an example of the latter is the growth of an organism or the emergence of a species. Determinism allows no room for what seems so manifest—growth, thus the emergence of novelty. Hence, *tychism* (coined from the Greek word for chance) seems the more promising hypothesis. Though necessary, tychism is hardly sufficient: the disposition to acquire ever new dispositions, the tendency to replicate prior tendencies but in such a way as to modify these to surmount frustrations, is also a hypothesis worthy of consideration. The "law of mind" designates just this disposition or tendency. What is manifest in the case of mindful agents is, to the metaphysically unprejudiced mind, discernible in countless other instances of natural processes—the tendency to achieve a goal in flexible and alterable ways, wherein the improvisational success of alternative routes becomes a more or less stable tendency (though not a rigidly mechanical habit).

Teleology is the mark of mind, taking *mind* in a very broad sense (a sense coextensive, at least, with the biosphere). The physical is identified by its more or less rigid adherence to mechanical law, while the psychical (or "mental") is identified by its abiding susceptibility to qualitative transformation and, thus, its inherent tendency to grow in novel ways (cf. 6.24). The law of mind is, at bottom, the law of growth: "underlying all other laws is the only tendency which can grow by its own virtue, the tendency of all things to take habits" (6.101). This "law" or tendency is at once primordial and pervasive, so much so that for Peirce it provides an empirical warrant for "objective idealism." Materialism (or mechanism) supposes that the ultimate explanatory principles are physical laws such as the laws of thermodynamics (the laws governing mind thus being reducible to those definitive of mechanism), whereas such idealism supposes the ultimate explanatory principles are, in a sense, psychical laws. Peirce went so far as to assert: "The one intelligible theory of the universe is that of objective idealism, that matter is effete mind, inveterate habits becoming physical laws" (6.25). Hence, Peirce writes:

> The microscopist looks to see whether the motions of a little creature show any purpose. If so, there is mind there. Passing from the little to the large, natural selection is the theory of how forms come to be adaptive, that is, to be governed by a quasi purpose. It suggests a machinery of efficiency to bring about an end—a machinery inadequate perhaps—yet which must contribute some help toward the result. (1.269)[39]

39. Cf. William James, *The Principles of Psychology* (Cambridge, Mass.: Harvard University Press, 1981), 20–21.

At the macroscopic as well as microscopic levels, then, we observe patterns of persistence and transformation in which variability of means is a striking feature of these observable patterns. In some cases, "we find that as soon as the form is prevented from manifestation in one shape it immediately reappears in another shape" (7.469).

Aristotle's teleology upon a standard reading (I would contend a truly orthodox interpretation) affirms antecedently and immutably fixed forms and thus goals by which natural processes in all their mutability and dynamism are governed. In contrast, Peirce's *finiosity* posits historically emergent and mutable forms and goals as constitutive of some natural processes (e.g., the growth of an acorn into a tree). The felt need to introduce a new term (*finious* and indeed also its cognates) reflects Peirce's misgivings about *teleology* saying or implying too much—in particular, about the likelihood *teleology* implies there are antecedently fixed goals of a fully determinate character: "If teleological is too strong a word to apply to them [natural processes of a irreversible character], we might invent the word *finious,* to express their tendency toward a final state" (7.471). The dynamism and power of finious processes are crucial for explaining nature as an evolving cosmos out of a primordial chaos. Nature so envisioned is a symbol of the creative source of the natural world, a source not ultimately identifiable with this world itself. God's cosmic immanence is one with God's creative activity, but the Creator is also other than creation. A very traditional conception of divinity, one stressing both the immanence and the transcendence of the divine, is thus inscribed at the heart of Peirce's creative appropriation of Emersonian, Aristotelian, and other conceptions of nature.

CONCLUSION

At the outset of an important essay ("The Law of Mind"), Peirce remarked, in an autobiographical aside also worth quoting at length:

> I have begun by showing that tychism must give birth to an evolutionary cosmology, in which all the regularities of nature and of mind are regarded as products of growth, and to a Schelling-fashioned idealism which holds matter to be mere specialized and partially deadened mind. I may mention, for the benefit of those who are curious in studying mental biographies, that I was born and reared in the neighborhood of Concord—I mean in Cambridge—at the time when Emerson, Hedge, and their friends were disseminating the ideas that they had caught from Schelling, and Schelling from Plotinus, from Boehm, or from God knows what minds stricken with the monstrous mysticism of the East. But the atmosphere of Cambridge held many an antiseptic against

Concord transcendentalism; and I am not conscious of having contracted any of that virus. Nevertheless, it is probable that some cultured bacilli, some benignant form of the disease was implanted in my soul, unawares, and that now, after long incubation, it comes to the surface, modified by mathematical conceptions and by training in physical investigations. (6.102)

Emerson insisted that "Nature is made to conspire with spirit to emancipate us" (E 64). Peirce's evolutionary cosmology was an attempt to work out the details of this subtle conspiracy. He acknowledged that such an endeavor could hardly escape being anthropomorphic; but he strove in a manner unlike that of Emerson to avoid being anthropocentric and, more emphatically, egocentric. "Among vitally important truths there is one which I verily believe—and which men of infinitely deeper insight than mine have believed—to be solely supremely important. It is that vitally important facts are of all truths the veriest trifles. For the only vitally important matter is *my* concern, business, and duty—or yours" (1.673). He went so far as to claim that "Our deepest sentiment pronounces the verdict of our own insignificance" (1.673).

Our preoccupation with vitally important topics should give way to a concern for cosmically vital ideas. Human beings are "to find their highest occupation" in their cherishing concern for such ideas (1.673). Such concern is anything but a form of idolatry—anything but "a universal-worship . . . a bit of perverse sentimentalism, a philosophic 'idol of the cave.'"[40] Of course, the supposition in which such concern is rooted cannot but appear to be a form of insanity. At least materialistically minded people will judge such a supposition to be "stark madness, or mysticism, or something equally devoid of reason and good sense" (MS 290, 58).

But are ideas truly in every instance such wooden, dead things as materialists and mechanists suppose? Is their only possible locus the private consciousness of individual beings? Are the forms of intelligibility not themselves intelligible and vital in a manner and measure nearly miraculous? If these questions are symptoms of a transcendental virus, so much the worse for materialist health!

40. Ibid., 453.

7 Nature and Fact in Tocqueville's *Democracy in America*

HARVEY C. MANSFIELD

Today political science speaks of facts but studiously avoids speaking of nature or natural or what happens naturally. Classical political science, however, rests on nature and never speaks of facts. "Fact" is a modern term that seems to do the work, or some of the work, "nature" did for the ancients. Yet Tocqueville uses both terms. He is not unique in this; the practice of consulting "fact" was invented long before the term "nature" was abandoned under separate attacks from Nietzsche's historicism and scientific positivism. But Tocqueville's use of the two terms, now considered mutually exclusive, shows his awareness of their opposed meanings as well as a wish to bring them together. He was a modern liberal who took inspiration, in complicated ways, from liberalism's two main enemies, Christianity and classical political science.

Tocqueville might not seem the author in whom to seek heady thought on deep subjects such as nature and fact. He was a political man. He spent part of his life in politics and would have spent more if he had been successful and if the *coup d'état* of Louis Napoleon upon the Second French Republic in 1851 had not closed off his ambition. Tocqueville's writing too is very political and is often denied the name of philosophy. Although he speaks of philosophers, he does not analyze their thought but confines himself to describing their influence, which he generally denies. Descartes, for instance, is America's philosopher, for America is "the one country in the world where the precepts of Descartes are least studied and best followed."[1] Socrates is not praised for his questioning or philosophy but for his settled belief in the immortality of the soul. That doctrine, sustained by "the instinct and taste of the human race," is particularly important, he says, in times of

1. Alexis de Tocqueville, *Democracy in America,* trans. Harvey C. Mansfield and Delba Winthrop (Chicago: University of Chicago Press, 2000), II 1.1, 403; hereafter, parenthetical page references are to this edition.

democracy, which suffers from too much materialism in both theory and practice (II 2.15, 520).[2] The example of Pascal is invoked to illustrate the character of aristocracy. If Pascal "had envisaged some great profit, or even if he had been moved by the desire for glory alone, I cannot believe," says Tocqueville, "that he would ever have been able to assemble, as he did, all the powers of his intellect in order better to discover the most hidden secrets of the Creator" (II 1.10, 435). The faculty of contemplation is attuned to the high-minded idea of man in aristocracies, more than to the eagerness for present material enjoyments to be seen in democracies. Although Tocqueville distinguishes theory pursued for its own sake from its practical application, his fear is not for the safety of theory as such but that by neglecting theory democratic societies will fall into stagnation (II 1.10, 438).

In sum, Tocqueville seems most interested in the political, or social, difference between democracy and aristocracy. The latter is understood not in its literal sense of the rule of the best, though as we just saw, he awards aristocracy some high qualities. For him aristocracy is the landed nobility of feudalism, not the philosopher-kings of Plato's *Republic* (I 1.3, 46–47). It is factual aristocracy, now no longer the fact. It has been replaced by a new fact, the "equality of conditions" that Tocqueville calls "this primary fact" and "the generative fact" *(le fait générateur)* in the introduction to *Democracy in America.* This fact has come about in the democratic revolution, the seven-hundred-year-old trend that he calls a "providential fact" (I Intro., 6).[3] What surrounds and underlies a political regime, or as he prefers to say, a *social state,* is apparently not unchanging nature but providential fact.

The generative fact is one "from which each particular fact seemed to issue," and it was a "central point" at which Tocqueville's observations came to rest. He does not explain what he means by calling a fact "providential," but from his description in the introduction to *Democracy in America* of a long trend of events, all going in the direction of democracy, we can infer that he means that this was a trend of contingencies too consistent not to have been planned, yet not within the planning capacity of human beings, not even a full generation of

2. Lamberti says that Tocqueville repudiated metaphysics, but one may add that he looked at metaphysics politically, and in doing so repudiated still more the modern theorists who repudiated metaphysics. Jean-Claude Lamberti, *Tocqueville and the Two Democracies,* trans. Arthur Goldhammer (Cambridge, Mass.: Harvard University Press, 1989), 29.

3. This is the only time, among about 22 references to Providence in *Democracy in America* (apart from Providence, Rhode Island), that Tocqueville speaks of "providential fact." Note this phrase: "the social state that Providence imposes on men in our day" (I 2.9, 298). On the generative fact, see Pierre Manent, *Cours Familier de Philosophie Politique* (Paris: Fayard, 2001), 62–63.

them—hence providential. A providential fact would be in some sense sacred, not to be tampered with by men, and irreversible. Tocqueville wanted the reactionaries of his day to consider the democratic revolution irreversible, and the word "providential" may also have been chosen to appeal to them.[4] (Curiously, we today would probably call this a *secular* trend.) The first item he cites in the democratic trend, perhaps not incidentally, is the opening of the ranks of the medieval clergy to the poor and to commoners.

Yet there also seems something mysterious about the providential fact of democracy. Tocqueville is not reporting to us a rational philosophy of history, either of linear progress, such as implied in Edmund Burke's phrase, "the known march of providence," or of zigzag dialectical progress as in Hegel. Democracy would seem to be reversible by God, though this is not for humans to attempt, and aristocracy could return as another providential fact. In any case, democracy is not surely more rational than aristocracy in Tocqueville's view. Democracy is in a sense more natural than aristocracy because it requires less constraint, and Tocqueville says that democracy is more just. But democracy lacks qualities of soul that may be found in aristocracy: desire for greatness, the patience and determination needed for long-term achievement, the intense abstraction from worldly things required for contemplation. These qualities are not absorbed or retained when democracy has replaced aristocracy, but rather diminished or excluded. Providence does not bring the perfect or rational regime on earth.

To see better what Tocqueville means by providential fact we may turn to Machiavelli, who may be said to have introduced fact—in his case non-providential fact—to political philosophy. It may seem outrageous to connect Tocqueville, a moral man, to Machiavelli, a man of dubious morality, but let us not be indignant.[5] Machiavelli said in *The Prince* that it was more fitting to "go directly to the effectual truth of the thing than to the imagination of it."[6] This phrase, *verità effettuale,* could

4. "Thus there is no question of reconstructing an aristocratic society, but of making freedom issue from the bosom of the democratic society in which God makes us live" (II 4.7, 666). On the phrase "providential fact," see Seymour Drescher, *Dilemmas of Democracy: Tocqueville and Modernization* (Pittsburgh: Pittsburgh University Press, 1968), 27–29; Marvin Zetterbaum, *Tocqueville and the Problem of Democracy* (Stanford, Calif.: Stanford University Press, 1967), 4–21. See also Michael Hereth, *Alexis de Tocqueville: Threats to Freedom in Democracy,* trans. George Bogardus (Durham, N.C.: Duke University Press, 1986), 6; Larry Siedentop, *Tocqueville* (Oxford: Oxford University Press, 1994), 45.

5. For Tocqueville's thoughts on Machiavelli see II 3.26, 632–33; Letter of August 5, 1836 to Louis de Kergorlay, in Alexis de Tocqueville, *Oeuvres Complètes,* vol. 13 (Paris: Gallimard, 1951), 389–90; Letter of August 25, 1836 to Pierre-Paul Royer-Collard, *Oeuvres Complètes,* vol. 11, 19–20; "Notes sur Machiavel," *Oeuvres Complètes,* vol. 16, 541–50.

6. Machiavelli, Niccolò, *The Prince,* trans. Harvey Mansfield (Chicago: University of Chicago Press, 1998), 61.

be translated as the effectual, or the factual, truth. Machiavelli used it just this once in all his writings, and so far as I know, or have been told, it does not occur elsewhere in the Renaissance. A fact is an effect, not a cause; when a fact is a truth, it is a truth that cannot be disputed because it is visible, unmistakable, impossible to be ignored. Machiavelli used the word *effect* to mean both being an effect, a result, and making an effect, or display. A fact of this kind is a plain fact, plain as a pikestaff. Since the fact cannot be disputed, you have to reason from it, and not from an imagined cause that might be disputed. Reasoning becomes rationalization of impressive or sensational deeds; it is not permitted to human reason to disregard such deeds or facts on the ground that they are *unnatural* or merely *worldly*. Plato's *Republic* was an imaginary republic of the kind Machiavelli decries; St. Augustine's *City of God* was an imaginary principality. Neither can serve as a safe and certain guide for men because, being imaginary, they are disputable. Nor, one may add, does the science of logic resolve disputes. Machiavelli left the realm of philosophy to seek certitude in the popular understanding, one could say euphemistically. The kind of fact that brings assent is the sudden cruelty of an executioner's stroke, one that leaves the people "satisfied and stupefied."[7] *That* is a fact.

In its later history "fact" becomes the prosaical "matter of fact" (to use Hume's phrase), thus part of the systematization that is the main current of modernity. But whether in epistemology, science, or economics, Machiavellian "fact" reflects the purpose disclosed in its origin—to end dispute and bring assent. A fact is usually thought to be something objective, but in fact it is something subjective, though in a peculiar way. Its significance lies in how it strikes us. A fact is what resists that which we might wish, yet also signifies what we must accept; a fact is accepted or acceptable resistance to our will. It's a brute fact. A fact, therefore, erases Aristotle's distinction between a thing as it is for us and as it is in itself. The "in-itself" of a fact is that it is for us. As the American Declaration of Independence says, "let facts be submitted to a candid world." Fact addresses an audience.

To see better what is contained in Tocqueville's "providential fact," let us turn briefly to Aristotle. Aristotle does not discuss fact. Facts come and go, but truth is in what abides; in Aristotle's thinking, facts belong to the realm of chance or accident. What abides is nature, which is discussed in the second book of the *Physics*. There Aristotle uses alternative expressions for what happens "by nature" or "according to nature," a usage in which he does not draw a distinction between the

7. Ibid., 30.

two but apparently lets one be inferred. The distinction, if it is one, arises from what is said.[8] It appears that what happens "by nature" is spontaneous, and what happens "according to nature" is what one can see and say to be motion toward an end, the final cause. In Aristotle's *Politics* the difference between the two expressions becomes more pronounced as we learn that the city is by nature and yet does not have spontaneously a single form or end according to nature. The city is by nature, but it necessarily has several forms or regimes.[9] The best city, the city according to nature, requires human reflection and choice as to what is naturally best. Nature is not always its own agent, except perhaps in the very complicated way by which nature through the intervention of human beings corrects its own imperfections.

Thus in Aristotle there appears to be a working distinction, for some reason unstated, between nature as spontaneous and nature as reflected upon. In Tocqueville, however, nature seems to refer mainly to what is spontaneous, even though it may describe, for example, the way democrats spontaneously think. Tocqueville follows the modern, or eighteenth-century, usage epitomized in Adam Smith's phrase "the system of natural liberty," describing the operation of a market free from governmental interference. The spontaneity of that market does not mean, however, that a free market acts with its own intent, so to speak out of its own nature. The market is moved by all its factors of supply and demand, which are in turn directed by appetite or self-preservation or self-interest; the system of natural liberty is one of mechanical causation. Paradoxically, the thing that runs by itself does so only if it is understood as being run in reaction to impulses to which it is subject.[10] Hence the modern spontaneity of nature differs from Aristotle's understanding. In the *Nicomachean Ethics,* the voluntary actions of human beings are presented as a kind of spontaneity,[11] but in the modern view, spontaneous behavior is not voluntary or chosen.

It is no surprise to see liberalism prefer the nature that generates freely to the nature that might guide, and therefore control or curb, freedom. But there is a cost to setting oneself free from a guiding nature: one risks falling into the hands of a determining nature. One

8. Aristotle, *Physics,* 192b35–40.

9. Aristotle, *Politics,* 1279a25–31.

10. For Adam Smith's understanding of nature, see Joseph Cropsey, *Polity and Economy; An Interpretation of the Principles of Adam Smith* (The Hague: Martinus Nijhoff, 1957), 1–27; also Charles L. Griswold, *Adam Smith and the Virtues of Enlightenment* (Cambridge: Cambridge University Press, 1999), in which the account of the system of natural liberty, 254–56, needs to be connected to the account of nature, 311–17. For the phrase "system of natural liberty," see Adam Smith, *Wealth of Nations,* IV 9.51.

11. Aristotle, *Nicomachean Ethics* 1111b7–11, 1112a13–18. I take *to hekousion* for spontaneous and *to proaireton* for voluntary (or chosen).

needs a guide of some kind, after all. It may be a fine thing to set one's own goal in life, but which one? If only for the sake of self-satisfaction, one needs a guide. For this one needs to know: what is my self, and what will satisfy it? If one rejects a guiding nature because such a guide is too uncertain—who knows for sure what "self" is and whether it is "according to nature"?—then, for the sake of certainty, one is compelled to resort to a view of nature that leaves one no choice. In rebelling against all constraint one surrenders blindly to any constraint.

Tocqueville is a different sort of liberal, aware of this difficulty. He does not want to let democracy follow its instincts without guidance or self-control as in a policy of *laissez-faire.* At the same time he does not adopt nature as a guide; he does not speak approvingly of what is "according to nature." What is natural for him is the spontaneous, instinctive, and unreflective. Sometimes "natural" in this sense is good, or partly good, such as the intractability of soul that equality gives naturally to men; sometimes "natural" is bad, as in the natural inclination of democracy toward centralization of power.[12] Classical political science would not say that anything bad is according to nature, because for it, evil is a perversion or a privative of what is natural. But Tocqueville has his reasons for not adopting this view of nature. In his time the term "nature" was used by modern theorists in two ways he considered harmful. "According to nature" might mean accepting the notion of "state of nature" (originating in the seventeenth century) as a fair description, even as a suitable end, of mankind. It might then seem that the individualism Tocqueville feared in a democracy could not or should not be prevented. Or various scientific theories might teach democratic peoples that "they necessarily obey I do not know which insurmountable and unintelligent force born of previous events, the race, the soil, or the climate" (II 4.8). The first notion of nature leaves men weak; the second leaves them impotent. In sum, Tocqueville feared that the notion of "according to nature" would be applied in favor of the modern philosophy that had rejected nature as a guide. That very rejection had become a guide.

Yet Tocqueville does not simply drop the idea of using nature as a

12. These are in the titles of successive chapters, II 4.1, 2. A further sampling of Tocqueville's usage: the "natural vice" of democracy (I 1.8, 128); "natural weakness" (I 1.8, 139); "natural instincts" of democracy that are bad (I 2.5, 189); "natural style" of democracy that is partly good, and the "natural dignity" of the human species (I 2.5, 194); "natural defects" of democracy (I 2.5, 217); "natural inequality being very great" (II 1.9, 431); "a malady so natural" (II 2.4, 486); Americans are "natural, frank and open" (II 3.2, 540); democratic peoples "naturally desire" peace, democratic armies "naturally desire" war (II 3.22, 617); in democracy, centralization will be the "natural government" (II 4.3, 645)—centralization also being called a "necessary fact" (II 4.4, 647); democratic peoples "naturally" need forms and "naturally" respect them less (II 4.7, 669).

guide; he finds a substitute. He replaces nature in this sense with providential fact, the providential fact that makes democracy of some sort irresistible now and for the foreseeable future. But democracy of some sort leaves us with the choice that the scientific theories foreclose, between democratic tyranny and democratic liberty. How does human choice consist with the providential fact? Tocqueville claims in his book that he has never "knowingly succumbed to the need to adapt facts to ideas instead of submitting ideas to the facts" (I Intro., 14). In the distrust of theory characteristic of his liberalism, facts are to be the judge of ideas. Yet Tocqueville departs from Machiavelli, who uses the effectual or factual truth to present men not with a choice but with an apparent necessity, a fact that brooks no disagreement. Contrary to Machiavelli, Tocqueville says that "there is nothing so difficult to appreciate as a fact" (I 2.5, 205). He apparently denies that one can make a trade of disputable nature for indubitable fact.

Thus the fact Tocqueville presents seems to serve the function of nature in Aristotle's phrase "according to nature." It constrains human choice but also requires human choice in cooperation with it; human beings are neither raised to gods nor reduced to puppets. To see Tocqueville's peculiar respect for fact, we should look at the beginning of *Democracy in America,* after the introduction. The first chapter is on the geography of America, and the second is on America's "point of departure," the Puritans. Why does he not begin with the point of departure? It is because he wants to show the limits of God's providence (and nature's fertility). In lyrical prose the geography of America is interpreted teleologically and providentially, featuring above all the Mississippi Valley, "the most magnificent dwelling that God has ever prepared for the habitation of man" (I 1.1, 21). And yet it is a vast wilderness; the valley and the rest of America were inhabited only by Indians, who occupied it but did not possess it. Those who possessed it were civilized Europeans, the Puritans who came to America for the sake of an idea, a religious democracy breathing "an air of antiquity and a sort of biblical perfume" (I 1.2, 33). These men made themselves a "first cause," a political cause, or in cooperation with God's bounty, they made themselves the "first causes," political and natural (Tocqueville uses both singular and plural of "cause"; I 1.2, 28–29). Here we see the providential fact of democracy, on the advance for seven hundred years, now brought out "in broad daylight" (*au grand jour,* a favorite Tocquevillian phrase), deliberately adopted by men, who to signify that they came to America for a serious idea, and not for money or adventure, called themselves "pilgrims." Their religion was a political theory, and they came not so much under Providence as actively willing it.

Tocqueville then backs away from the deliberateness of the Puritans, and from their passion for regulation, and introduces a new concept, clearly a feature of the new political science for the new world promised in the introduction, termed the *social state* (I 1.3, 45). He defines it as ordinarily the product of a fact, sometimes of a law, which "one can consider" as the first cause of the laws, customs, and ideas that regulate the conduct of nations. It is a product of the fact (not chosen) and law (chosen) that may be considered a first cause; so a democratic social state is partly by choice, partly not. Tocqueville frequently refers to the social state as causing in a loose sense, sometimes "naturally suggesting" (II, Notice, 399); for example, it is the democratic social state of Americans that, as we have seen, causes them simultaneously to be both followers and non-readers of Descartes. As first cause, the first cause can be the generative fact issuing particular facts that Tocqueville spoke of. If the social state is a fact, Tocqueville also awards it the status of having a nature. The frequency of the term "nature" in *Democracy in America* comes from its being used not only to denote what is unchanging in humans and around them but also in the sense of "second nature."[13] Democracy and aristocracy as social states have natural penchants, for good and ill, that need to be identified and dealt with.

Clearly the concept of social state in Tocqueville's political science replaces the notion of regime in Aristotle's. Aristotle holds more firmly to the sovereignty of the political, the form of government that, he says, "chiefly" determines what the city will be. He would say that democracy causes a democratic society, and not the reverse as Tocqueville appears to do. Yet in defining the social state as both product and cause, Tocqueville seems rather to cover over the question of the primacy of politics than to answer it. He may not quite deserve the praise he gets for being sociological. If the social state replaces the regime, one can also say that it serves the same function as cause, and that it is partly political. The first two chapters of Tocqueville's book, on geography and on the point of departure, do resemble Aristotle's procedure in the *Politics,* where he too tries to understand the city as caused by nature in Books 1 and 2, and then turns to human and political cause, derived from an inquiry into citizenship, in Book 3.[14]

What Tocqueville wants to avoid is the choice of regimes offered in Aristotle's political science. For although man is by nature a political

13. Pierre Manent connects the two meanings of nature: "The danger of democracy is its nature, which is nature." Pierre Manent, *Tocqueville and the Nature of Democracy,* trans. John Waggoner (Lanham, Md.: Rowman and Littlefield, 1996), 74.

14. See my account in Harvey C. Mansfield, *Taming the Prince: the Ambivalence of Modern Executive Power* (Baltimore, Md.: Johns Hopkins University Press, 1989), 31–44.

animal for Aristotle, there is no single regime that arises by nature, reflecting man's political nature. The several regimes reflect partisan interpretations of different aspects of human nature, particularly the democratic propensity to emphasize what is common to human beings and the corresponding oligarchic desire to claim honors reserved for the few.[15] Aristotle asserts that there is one regime that is the best everywhere according to nature,[16] but it is very unlikely to come into being—as is a mixed regime combining the two partisan deviations that typify politics as we humans experience it. The two regimes—those of the few and of the many—are both rooted in human nature, hence arguable, and yet in their exaggeration they both display the perverseness of human partisanship. Aristotle regards them as constantly, if not equally, possible at any time, but also equally vulnerable over the long run because of their bias. He does not speak of aristocratic or democratic epochs, still less of a providential fact; the long run for him is a cycle of regimes, none of them lasting.

Tocqueville provides no best regime and declares the mixed regime to be a chimera (I 2.7, 240). He presents aristocracy and democracy as successive epochs, not as constant possibilities. While accepting the unity of human nature, he is always contrasting aristocracy and democracy, and says quite prominently at the end of the book that "they are, as it were, two distinct humanities" (II 4.8, 675). In the chapter on parties, Tocqueville speaks of two great parties "as old as the world" to be found "in all free societies," one of them seeking to narrow the use of popular power, the other to extend it (I 2.2, 167). These parties, he says, have aristocratic or democratic passions as their foundation, somewhat like Aristotle's oligarchic and democratic regimes that are rooted in human nature. But Tocqueville does not follow Aristotle in conceiving the oligarchic and democratic aspects of human nature as presenting claims or arguments capable of being judged and mediated by political philosophy. Tocqueville's contrasts of aristocracy and democracy do not point toward common ground in the mixed regimes, but rather conclude, as he says, almost with two distinct humanities. One could also say, however, that the two great parties are seen from the democratic point of view, centering on the people, not the nobility.

To summarize so far: Tocqueville introduces democracy as a providential fact, irresistible and irreversible, emphatically not as a regime to choose or avoid. Yet to prevent it from being overwhelmed by this fact, he very soon shows that Americans have adopted it and made it their

15. Aristotle, *Politics* 1280a6–15.
16. Aristotle, *Nicomachean Ethics* 1134b5.

deliberate intent, taking over from God and nature, though with due respect, so as to make themselves their own first cause. Thus Americans become the generative fact as they practice the democracy that has been given to them. The social state serves the same function as Aristotle's regime of bringing nature under the honorable rule of human beings, "the sovereignty of the people," but it does so at a lower level of choice, one might say. The providential fact, which was made *for* men in the Old World before it was made *by* men in the New World, covers over the best regime that inspires and haunts Aristotle's political science.

That being said, we must immediately add that the central event of Christianity is not absent from *Democracy in America.* Tocqueville says: "it was necessary that Jesus Christ come to earth to make it understood that all members of the human species are naturally alike and equal" (II 1.3, 413).[17] In this interesting statement we see that nature does not have the power on its own to make itself recognized; a supernatural event was needed to make natural human qualities generally understood. The Coming of Christ was prepared by Providence (II 1.5, 420) but is not part of Providence, a term Tocqueville reserves for what can be inferred by human reason without resort to faith. Faith, he says, was necessary to get men to believe in the equality that is naturally true. But once the belief is established in democracy, men begin to think themselves independent of one another, and of authority, and "humanity always seems to run by itself" (II 1.3, 413). Democrats then *believe* that Providence has made them independent—which means, independent of Providence and God. "The dogma of the sovereignty of the people" is not religious dogma but seems to replace it. It is "the great maxim on which civil and political society in the United States rests," namely that "Providence has given to each individual, whoever he may be, the degree of reason necessary for him to be able to direct himself in things which interest him exclusively" (I 2.10, 381).

In this view of Providence—one that Tocqueville does not share—democracy receives its beginning from Christianity, and then, ungratefully and almost unwittingly, turns its back on Christianity. Democracy actually claims to receive from Providence its independence from Providence. This is not true Providence but rather "an inflexible providence" or a "blind fatality" (II 1.20, 478). Tocqueville, one could say, does his best to restore democratic belief in Providence. Without a be-

17. See Peter Augustine Lawler, *The Restless Mind: Alexis de Tocqueville on the Origin and Perpetuation of Human Liberty* (Lanham, Md.: Rowman and Littlefield, 1993), 144–45; Lamberti, *Tocqueville and the Two Democracies,* 160–62.

lief in Providence, democrats tend to believe in pantheistic doctrines that treat free human beings as directed by great, impersonal, material forces they can do nothing about. "Pantheism" sees God everywhere and levels all differences between God and man, the consequences being to deprive God of intelligence and to make man a subject and victim (II 1.7). Providence, however, presupposes the difference between God and man and thus protects the human freedom that God, within limits, permits. Tocqueville ends each volume of *Democracy in America* with a striking appeal to Providence. At the end of the first volume, he contrasts two advancing peoples, the Russian and the American, representing despotism and freedom: "Each of them seems called by a secret design of Providence to hold the destinies of half the world in its hands one day" (I 2.10, 396). He closes the second volume more promisingly, denouncing "false and cowardly doctrines" that require men to obey unintelligent force, and proclaiming that Providence has created man, and peoples, "powerful and free" (II 4.8, 676).

Clearly there can be no providential fact without Providence. Tocqueville uses the providential fact to show the limits to choice and Providence to assure us that nonetheless we have the power to choose.

Nor is natural right absent from *Democracy in America.* We note that although natural similarity and equality were made understood by Christ, natural right was not. Tocqueville says that democracy has more naturalness in the sense of spontaneous ease than aristocracy (particularly in the family; II 3.2, 540; II 3.12, 573; II 3.13, 577), and that in its practice of equality it has greater justice than aristocracy (II 4.8, 675). He reserves the phrase "natural right" mostly for occasions of authority within regimes, the right of a father in aristocracy or of a judge in democracy (II 3.8, 559; II 3.16, 586; I 1.6, 96, 98). On one occasion he contrasts "natural right" arising from common humanity to the "political right" of feudal society (II 3.1, 536). He says of man universally that "the taste for the infinite and the love for what is immortal . . . have their immutable foundation in his nature" (II 2.12, 510). But he does not apply natural right generally to regimes as wholes. For Tocqueville, "according to nature" is not swallowed up by the spontaneous "by nature," but it lives closer to spontaneity and to the deliberative practice of democracy arising from its spontaneous nature than in Aristotle. Tocqueville is a liberal, but his main enemy is not Aristotle; it is liberal or modern theorists who are critical of Aristotle. Unlike those theorists, Tocqueville departs from Aristotle in a manner Aristotle might appreciate. Let us see what Tocqueville makes of "natural" in the general sense of "according to nature."

A notable passage in the long chapter on the three races in America pictures the contrast in view for a traveler being carried down the Ohio River, as was Tocqueville himself on his visit to America. On its opposite banks are fertile soil and equable climate, and each of them is the border of a large state. On the left the traveler sees nature fertile and men idle in the slave state of Kentucky; on the right, in the free state of Ohio, he sees industry, rich harvests, elegant dwellings, and happy workers. Here and elsewhere Tocqueville remarks the effects of slavery on the masters as much as, or more than, on the slaves. Slavery shows "the order of nature reversed," and while the consequences for slaves are horrible, their masters are made to suffer a natural—that is, spontaneous—punishment for what they are doing (I 2.10, 331–2, 348). It is a punishment somewhat disguised from them, yet perhaps they sense it even as they repress it. How can Southern masters not see the greater prosperity of the North?[18]

Tocqueville in his situation does not address the naturalness of slavery as does Aristotle. Speaking of aristocracy, he says that the serf "regarded his inferiority as an effect of the immutable order of nature," obviously a delusion (I Intro., 8). What Tocqueville calls aristocracy has to do with landed proprietorship, and not with any natural superiority of which Aristotle speaks. Hierarchy within human nature may exist according to Tocqueville, but it does not sustain a regime of the few. Tocqueville's natural right is more democratic than Aristotle's. He does say that "the idea of rights is nothing other than the idea of virtue introduced into the political world" (I 2.6, 227). Virtue belongs to great individuals and is too far above politics to become political. But it becomes accessible to a society or a people when transformed into rights. Rights are humanly defined, and they need to be inculcated in men—better by getting them to practice rights, Tocqueville says, than by trying to teach them rights in theories. The transformation of virtue into rights seems to have occurred historically as Americans learned their rights from the honorable resistance of English noblemen to the king. But although rights are aristocratic in origin, they are democratic in present practice (II 4.4, 646). Tocqueville would rather derive rights from virtue than from the liberal theorists' state of nature—that is true. But he does not suggest that virtue (which he does not call natural) puts nature on the side of aristocracy.

Freedom is sustained by the doctrine of self-interest well under-

18. See Tocqueville's vivid example of the white man who had had children by a slave mother, and who, about to die, suffered from horrible images of his sons being sold and passing from paternal authority to the whip of a stranger: "I then understood that nature knew how to avenge herself for wounds the laws had given her" (I 2.10, 347).

stood. Tocqueville calls this an American doctrine and leaves it unclear how far he himself subscribes to it (I 2.10, 359). Its basis, in turn, is that interest is the "only immobile point in the human heart" (I 2.6, 228). But unless interest is well understood, it can bring a citizen to submit to despotism. The mild despotism that Tocqueville believes to be the special danger to humanity in the democratic age works through interest rather than fear—the interest, perhaps perverted, that induces impotent individuals to seek help from the centralized state (II 4.6). To counter that danger, interest must be well understood. In *Democracy in America* there are two instructors of self-interest: the Americans, who have a doctrine derived in some part from philosophers (II 2.9, 504) but mostly from their own practices, and Tocqueville himself, who wants to "instruct democracy" in his new political science (I Intro., 9). Tocqueville blends the two instructions so that it is difficult to tell what he is proposing on his own from the facts he is recounting.

In order to appreciate this combined instruction we may look at the picture given of American government in the first volume of *Democracy in America.* Tocqueville's account begins with the New England township and goes to the federal Constitution. The township is said to be spontaneous in origin; it is "so much in nature that everywhere men are gathered, a township forms by itself" (I 1.5, 57). Tocqueville uses the township, not the state of nature and the social contract, to explain why a free people would obey government. They do so not because they are inferior to their governors but because it appears useful, and they grow attached to the township because it engages their ambitions, draws them into its forms, and gives them a love of order. Obedience begins from evident self-interest and develops into an elemental patriotism through the observances of free government. What a distance from John Locke's curt phrase that from the state of nature men are "quickly driven into society"![19] Yet if at the beginning of Tocqueville's account the township is spontaneous, at the end the Constitution is described at length as a "work of art," a complicated structure contrived from political theory and achieved only after careful deliberation.[20] What Tocqueville says about the federal Constitution is indebted to *The Federalist,* but his presentation of American government differs markedly because it adds the element of local spontaneity that animates the

19. John Locke, *Two Treatises of Government* II 127.

20. "The sovereignty of the Union is the work of art. The sovereignty of the states is natural; it exists by itself without effort, like the authority of the father of a family" (I 1.8, 157–158). Here "natural" is explained as what "exists by itself without effort," like a father's authority. Natural right, for Tocqueville, is unforced and carries with it a willing acceptance of authority.

whole. His presentation opposes liberal social contract theory in form and character: it is an analysis of the facts of American politics rather than abstract theory, and it finds an admirable active interest in self-government rather than cowardly or defensive fear to be the basic motive. Here again Tocqueville brings his conclusion closer to Aristotle by departing from Aristotle to consult fact rather than nature. With America he shows us man's political nature more accurately than the liberal philosophers on whom Americans have depended.

Tocqueville relies on fact to correct theory in his famous but not very carefully read discussion of associations. Associations, he says, are the means by which Americans combat individualism, a malady, born of theory, that he was the first to identify. Individualism is distinct from run-of-the-mill egoism because it is a mistaken judgment, not a blind instinct. Each democratic individual, taught by liberal theorists or "democratic historians" that he is subject to large, impersonal forces beyond his control, decides to isolate himself from the mass and live as an entire whole (*tout entier;* II 1.20, 2.2). Americans combat this enervating weakness with the associations they practice so well, and this fact is supported by human nature in the spontaneous sense: "After the freedom to act alone, the most natural to man is that of combining . . . and acting in common." The right of association is "almost as inalienable in its nature as individual freedoms" (I 2.4, 84).[21] Tocqueville is untroubled by the theoretical difficulty of an almost inalienable right, by the ridicule to which he might be subjected by the ghost of Thomas Hobbes. He makes a major correction in Aristotle's direction of the state of nature postulate, against its all-or-nothing rigor at the expense of truth and liberty. Hobbes had simplified human nature in order to find a single motive that would universally take precedence and always operate. Tocqueville sees the desire to combine *next to* the desire to act alone. His view is not so simple and so leaves room for human choice. He finds both a practical art and a science in the fact of association, the art of how and why to associate, the science on the theoretical presuppositions. The latter are not argued in *Democracy in America.* They suddenly appear now and again and quickly leave the scene. Tocqueville announces the need for a new science of politics, but he does not supply it except in hints left unelaborated and in new concepts the reader must connect to one another on his own.

Self-interest well understood is not altogether in tune with human

21. See Harvey C. Mansfield and Delba Winthrop, "Liberalism and Big Government: Tocqueville's Analysis," in *Tyranny and Liberty* (London: Institute of United States Studies, 1999), 1–31.

nature. Tocqueville points out "the disinterested and unreflective sparks that are natural to man"—a spontaneous motion contrary to self-interest—as he remarks that in maintaining their doctrine of self-interest, Americans "would rather do honor to their philosophy than to themselves" (II 2.8, 502). "The taste for the infinite and the love of what is immortal" that he asserts to be founded in human nature cannot be destroyed, but they can be perverted, and he shows how Americans do pervert them. At this point the divergence between Tocqueville and his Americans comes to view. Americans see the moral and political use of religion in this world, but Tocqueville reminds them that its principal use is eternal felicity in the other world (II 2.9, 505). The desire for eternal happiness, he says, is in their nature, yet so, too, is the taste for material well-being. We learn in the following chapter that this taste is "natural to men who are excited and limited by the obscurity of their origin or the mediocrity of their fortune"—the middle class (II 2.10, 507). How do we reconcile the natural taste for the infinite and immortal with the natural taste for material well-being?

Tocqueville's Americans are materialistic but not grossly venal. They want what is necessary for material well-being, and they want to hold on to it. Their materialism does not corrupt them but softens them. They are not seekers of power and money without limit as Hobbes and Locke affirm men to be. They are not great sinners, and Tocqueville reproaches them for being absorbed in *permitted,* not forbidden, enjoyments (II 2.11, 509). But at times, he adds, their natural love of the infinite asserts itself, and their souls break the material bonds that restrain them and escape toward Heaven. Nor are Americans cheerful with their decent materialism; they are on the contrary grave, sad, and restive. They know they cannot get all the goods they want; they are defeated by the impossibility of complete happiness in the world (I 2.13). Though Tocqueville does not say it, they are punished for their materialism, just as the Southern masters were punished for holding slaves. In both cases the facts testify against Americans that they do not live according to nature. No doubt Tocqueville agrees with Aristotle that a whole people cannot live according to nature. Certainly democracy is more natural, more spontaneous, than aristocracy. But it does not reach the heights of aristocracy, nor does it aim so high.

Yet democracy can achieve greatness. The French Revolution in its early phase of the Constituent Assembly was a noble effort according to Tocqueville; so were the deeds of the Puritans and the American Founding, and more successful too. The entire project of democratic progress, the democratic revolution that still advances, in Tocqueville's day and in ours, is surely something great. Although the advances may have come through great individuals who were not always democrats, still the result has been to put into relief "the natural greatness of man" (I Intro., 5). The idea of that project is the indefinite perfectibility of man (II 1.8). Indefinite perfectibility is promoted by equality. Equality destroys the traditional authority that enshrines the fixed inequalities of an aristocracy, leaving usages, customs, and laws open to change and the reason of each individual sovereign in the making of change. With the downfall of aristocracy the idea of rational control arises to replace it. Despite the potential hostility between rational control and popular sovereignty, the two have advanced together to create modernity, joined in such a fashion that it is hard to say whether rational control is a means to democracy or democracy a means to rational control. The two movements converge in the Enlightenment, in which reason is brought to the people—or is it that popular will is imposed on reason? The progress of rational control is featured more in Tocqueville's later work *The Old Regime* than in *Democracy in America.* Perhaps the project of applying reason to society is the deliberate side of the undeliberated providential fact bringing ever more democracy. To read Descartes you might not see that the founder of modern rationalism was also a prophet of democracy, but Tocqueville has shown us why he was to become America's unofficial, unread philosopher.

The difficulty in the idea of progressive rational control is that it has no end. It is perfectibility without a notion of perfection. It is indefinite; it does not know when to stop. Democratic man "tends ceaselessly toward the immense greatness that he glimpses confusedly at the end of the long course that humanity must still traverse" (II 1.8, 427). What is the rational life? Who is the perfect democrat? These questions have no answers but in a vague democratic vision of the future. We today in America have only since 1964 seen the progress of democracy that first equalized blacks and whites, then women and men, and now gays and straights, each stage presented as if it were the last, yet succeeded by another. Who among us now, presently unknown to us, are due for promotion and inclusion in the next wave of greater democracy? Tocqueville tries to set limits to visionary perfectibility by reminding us that both human beings and the social state of democracy have natures that limit and define our restive democratic ambition.

I conclude with three further observations on nature and fact in Tocqueville's great work. If the project of rational control of human life begun long ago in the old regime were to succeed, there would be no liberty for those subject to it. Every move would be planned for them by bureaucrats. That rational control does not work in individual instances is no check to its ambition because any particular attempt, however clumsy, is always full of hope, and the project as a whole is never reconsidered. In case of failure one just turns to a fresh experiment in the same thing. In the *Old Regime* Tocqueville devoted what seems inordinate attention to the administration of the king's ministers. But they are the agents of rational control, of human perfectibility. What stands against them in the first line of defense is human intractability, the irrational insistence on not being governed even or especially when it is for one's own good. This intractability is natural, and it is spontaneous. It disposes Americans "to consider all authority with the eye of a malcontent" (II 4.1, 639). Tocqueville approves of this primitive instinct as the basis of political liberty. However irrational democratic elections may be—and he compares a presidential election to the passage of a storm—they give security against the junior Cartesians who want to run things rationally. Various and frequent elections counter the democratic tendency toward centralization of power in the "Immense Being," the state. Centralization, he says, is the "natural government" in democratic times, both spontaneous and normal; independence and local liberties are the product of art (II 4.3, 645). At bottom, democracy is intractability, but it aims at rational tranquility. Tocqueville in his political science wants to use the former to counter the latter. Intractability appears in democratic practice, rational control in democratic theories. Tocqueville wants to separate democratic practice from democratic theory, and to substitute his own theory, derived from practice and based on natural spontaneity.

Is there no natural order, no natural end to serve as a guide, an "according to nature"? Tocqueville admittedly idealizes some of the facts he presents, those he wants to be exemplary. His pictures of the Puritans, of the New England township, and especially of American women, are too beautiful to be true. Aristotle says in his *Rhetoric* that you can offer advice by praising someone; what you praise him for is what he, or others listening to the praise, ought to do.[22] In this way the desirable is presented as fact, as good choices made by Americans rather than universal rules derived from natural rights.

In the last chapter of the book, entitled "General View of the Subject," Tocqueville speaks of God. He summarizes the goods and evils of democracy, concluding that equality is less elevated but more just than aristocracy, and that its justice makes for its greatness and its beauty. Then he ascends and strives to enter, he says, into the point of view of God. What does God see? God sees the whole, including all human beings with their similarities and differences (II 1.3, 411). What God sees

22. Aristotle, *Rhetoric* 1367b35–1368a10.

is nature; we see it only partially. We choose to see all human beings as alike *(semblables)*, which is democracy, or as separate and unequal beings in aristocracy. Democracy and aristocracy, the two distinct humanities, are partial truths and incomplete wholes. They are united in the invisible nature of things that only God sees perfectly, that Tocqueville sees imperfectly, and that we would do well to leave alone, lest it lead us into the folly of failing to consider democracy in its own terms, as fact.

8 Holmes on Natural Law

ROBERT P. GEORGE

My dear Laski: . . .

Your remark about the "oughts" and system of values in political science leaves me rather cold. If, as I think, the values are simply generalizations emotionally expressed, the generalizations are matters for the same science as other observations of fact. If, as I sometimes suspect, you believe in some transcendental sanction, I don't. Of course, different people, and especially different races, differ in their values—but those differences are matters of fact, and I have no respect for them except my general respect for what exists. Man is an idealizing animal—and expresses his ideals (values) in the conventions of his time. I have very little respect for the conventions in themselves, but respect and generally try to observe those of my own environment as the transitory expression of an eternal fact.[1]

So the eighty-eight-year-old Oliver Wendell Holmes wrote to Harold Laski on September 15, 1929, just weeks before the stock market crashed, plunging the world into depression.

What are we to make of Holmes's statements? "Values," he says, are merely "generalizations emotionally expressed." As such, they are "matters for the same science as other observations of fact." They have no "transcendental sanction." Of course, different people, and, especially, different peoples, "differ in their values." These differences are mere "matters of fact" and deserve no particular respect beyond the respect owed to "what exists." "Man is an idealizing animal." He expresses his ideals in "conventions." The "conventions" themselves aren't worthy of any particular regard, but it makes sense for people generally to observe the conventions of their environment as "an expression," albeit a "transitory" one, of "an eternal fact."

What is Holmes affirming and what is he denying?

In affirming that "values" are "generalizations emotionally ex-

1. Oliver Wendell Holmes and Harold J. Laski, *Holmes-Laski Letters: The Correspondence of Mr. Justice Holmes and Harold J. Laski 1916–1935*, vol. 2 (Cambridge, Mass.: Harvard University Press, 1953), 1183.

pressed," I take him to be denying that there are objective truths about what it is ultimately *reasonable* to want and to consider worthy of acting to realize, attain, preserve, promote, and participate in. "Values" are, rather, subjective, according to Holmes, inasmuch as they are given by emotion, which varies from person to person and from culture to culture, and are not susceptible to rational evaluation. People act in light of their values, but values provide merely emotional, and not rational, motivation.

Thus it is that values are, according to Holmes, matters for "the same science as other observations of fact," that is to say, *positive* science—the science of "what is." Holmes disbelieves in the possibility of *normative* science or rationality—the use of intellectual faculties to determine objective truths about what one ought to want, what is worth wanting, and what isn't. Hitler's hatred of Jews, or ancient Rome's quest for glory in the conquest and domination of other peoples, are, or were, expressions of subjective values. Under Holmes's view, they are intrinsically neither more nor less rational than the opposing values of others—say Mother Teresa and the Quakers. Of course, reason—positive science—can inquire whether Hitler *really* hated Jews, and, if he did, what caused his hatred; it can inquire whether the Romans *really* sought glory in conquest and domination, and, if so, why. But reason is powerless to judge the rightness of wrongness of Hitler's values or Rome's, whatever they were, nor can it identify the values of Mother Teresa as rationally superior to Hitler's, or the values of the Quakers as more reasonable than those of the Romans.

From the point of view of rational inquiry, according to Holmes, people's values are just facts about the world—like the fact that sharks kill and eat seals, or that a typhoon recently struck Taiwan, or that AIDS is ravaging sub-Saharan Africa. We may, according to our own "value system," deplore Hitler's values; indeed, we may, in light of our own subjective values, be willing to fight and die to frustrate Hitler's ends. But our ultimate values are, from the point of view of rational inquiry, neither more nor less rational than Hitler's. Our values, too, are mere facts about the world. All that rational inquiry can do is to record them as facts, and, perhaps, explore possible psychological and sociological causes of their existence. "Ethics" or "moral philosophy," considered in Platonic and Aristotelian fashion as disciplines of rational inquiry into putative truths about what is worth having and doing—what is right and what is wrong—are mere pseudo-sciences. They futilely seek what Holmes refers to, with evident derision, as "some transcendental sanction"—some standard by which to judge rationally the meaningfulness and significance of facts about which the universe is ultimately indifferent.

It seems to me that Holmes's reference to "some transcendental sanction" ought not to be taken merely as an expression of religious skepticism, though it certainly includes that. I don't think he was worried about Harold Laski getting religion. The skepticism it pleased Holmes to assert was comprehensive. It denied the possibility of reason's functioning (in the practical or prescriptive domain) as anything more than Hume's "slave of the passions," that is to say, a faculty for identifying how to get what we want, but not one capable of identifying what is intelligibly *wantable,* what is rationally *worth wanting.*

Is this because man has no nature that can serve as the ultimate criterion for distinguishing reasonably between what is fitting and unfitting, noble and base, right and wrong? Well, plainly Holmes doesn't think that anything, including human nature, provides such a criterion. But just as plainly he believes in human nature. Indeed, he says something about his understanding of human nature in the fragment I quoted from the letter to Laski. "Man," he asserts, "is an idealizing animal." In other words, it is characteristic of human beings—it is our nature—to *have* values considered precisely as "generalizations emotionally expressed." Human beings in all times and all places have values. It is a fact about us. Hitler had values; so did Mother Teresa. Similarly, human cultures constitute, promote, and express a sharing of values. The Romans had values; so did the Quakers.

But, of course, the fact that man is an idealizing animal—a being that characteristically has values—is merely a fact about man. It doesn't imply or entail anything about putatively objective ethical duties. It is a truth that is attained by positive observation of human beings and cultures and inquired into more deeply in the disciplines of psychology and sociology. And these inquiries reveal that while "having values" is a constant fact of human existence, values themselves vary from person to person, and especially from culture to culture. Reason has no power to adjudicate these differences. They too, Holmes insists, are "just facts." The respect they deserve is merely the respect owed to "what exists," as he put it, whether it is a shark, a typhoon, a virus, a hatred, a belief in the glory of conquest—that is, the demand that facts be recognized as and for what they are.

Holmes's final point in the fragment concerns social conventions. There is, of course, a sense in which conventions, as such, are more than merely subjective. They are shared. But, again, as such, neither are they objective in any meaningful sense. They are, one might say, intersubjective. Moreover, conventions do not *have to be* what they are, by virtue of anything, including norms of rationality. For example, in our culture, it is a convention for men to wear tuxedos to certain sorts of social events. This convention provides a way of expressing certain values that, while widely shared, are, Holmes would insist, necessarily subjective. Where there is a sharing of values, however, conventions arise precisely to express these shared values. It is not as if shared values are capable of being expressed in some way apart from conventions. Still, conventions cannot be any more objective than the shared subjective values they express. Indeed, they are, despite being shared, *arbitrary*. There are countless alternatives to the tuxedo that would serve just as well to express the shared values that wearing tuxedos to certain functions expresses. But someone who genuinely shared those values would not express what he wanted to express if he attended such a function dressed in, say, a toga—even a particularly elegant toga. Of course, it is not as if togas are intrinsically incapable of expressing the values expressed for us by tuxedo-wearing. It is merely that, as a matter of contingent historical and sociological fact, in our culture togas don't express these shared values. Tuxedos, not togas, are the convention. A fellow who shows up at a formal wedding wearing a toga is expressing something, to be sure, but he is not expressing the shared values that the other men present are expressing by wearing their tuxedos.

Holmes's statement about having very little respect for conventions "in themselves" is meant, I believe, to say that he recognizes the ultimately arbitrary nature of social conventions. At the same time, his point about "trying to observe" the conventions of his own culture ("environment") as "the transitory expression of an eternal fact" is meant to show his appreciation of the indispensable social function of conventions for "idealizing animals" for whom a certain sharing of values makes society possible. To repeat: Conventions are needed to express shared values, yet particular conventions are contingent and, in that sense, arbitrary. Still, once conventions are established, the sensible person realizes that it is irrational to defy them unless one's intention is in fact to signal one's personal dissent from the shared values expressed by conforming to the conventions.

It seems to me that what Holmes says about the historical and sociological contingency and, in a sense, arbitrariness of social conventions is true. There are, no doubt, natural psychological limits to what forms of dress, speech, and behavior can express what, but ordinarily social conventions could be otherwise than as they are, while still fulfilling their social function perfectly well.

Further, I think that Holmes is right about the role and importance of social conventions. Across the range of dimensions in which human life is lived, and certainly across human cultures, conventions play an indispensable role. They make possible things (e.g., the formality of a wedding) that would not be possible without them. Very, very often, it makes sense to follow a convention because the convention, as a matter of fact, enables one's personal goals, or the goals of a group, to be achieved, despite the fact that a different convention would have worked just as well had *it* been (as a matter of contingent historical and sociological fact) the convention in place for the purpose.

It would, perhaps, not particularly please Holmes to know that an important dimension of these basic ideas about the role and importance of social conventions was elaborated skillfully by Thomas Aquinas in his discussion of the relationship of positive to natural law. Famously, Aquinas held that all just positive law is derived, in some sense, from natural law.[2] Of course, natural law, for Aquinas, was nothing like Holmes's caricature of a "brooding omnipresence in the sky,"[3] but more on that point in a moment. The point here is that, as Aquinas understands the matter, the task of the legislator is to give effect to relevant principles of right order and natural justice in the shape of positive laws for the common good of society. However, the legislator accomplishes this task, according to Aquinas, in two distinct ways, representing two forms of "derivation."

Natural law, on Aquinas's understanding of the matter, is the body of principles, including moral norms, providing practical reasons, that is to say, reasons for action and restraint. Some positive laws, such as those prohibiting murder, rape, theft, and other grave injustices, are derived from the natural law by a process akin to the deduction of demonstrable conclusions from general premises in mathematics and the sciences.[4] Other positive laws, however, cannot be derived from the natural law in so direct and straightforward a fashion. Where law is required to solve a coordination problem, it is often the case that a variety of possible solutions, each having its own advantages and disadvantages, are rationally available as options. One solution must, however, be authoritatively chosen if the problem is to be solved.

Consider the regulation of highway traffic. From the basic principle of natural law that identifies human health and safety as goods to be preserved, together with the empirical fact that unregulated driving, even among motorists of goodwill, places these human goods in jeopardy, it follows that a scheme of coordination (and, thus, of legal regulation) is necessary for the common good. Yet, typically, different rea-

2. *Summa theologiae,* I-II, q. 96, a. 4.

3. Oliver Wendell Holmes, *The Essential Holmes: Selections from the Letters, Speeches, Judicial Opinions, and Other Writings of Oliver Wendell Holmes, Jr.,* ed. Richard A. Posner (Chicago: University of Chicago Press, 1992), 230.

4. *Summa theologiae,* I-II, q. 96, a. 4.

sonable but incompatible schemes are possible. For the sake of the common good, then, the relevant authority must stipulate *one* from among the different possible schemes. In selecting the scheme, the lawmaking authority operates not by any process analogous to the deduction of demonstrable conclusions from premises, but rather by a process of choosing between reasonable, yet incompatible, options—a process that Aquinas refers to as *determinatio*.[5]

Laws that come into being as *determinationes,* according to Aquinas, have their binding force not from reason alone, but also from having been laid down by valid lawmaking authority.[6] But for the law's enactment, no one would be under any general moral duty to behave as it requires. Indeed, despite the fact that the lawmaking authority could, compatibly with natural law, have selected a different rule or scheme of regulation, "its directiveness derives not only from the fact of its creation by some recognized source of law (legislation, judicial decision, custom, etc.) but also from its rational connection with some principle or precept of morality."[7]

Now, mention of custom in this regard links us back to Holmes's points about convention. For even where custom lacks the status or force of law—where, that is to say, it is *merely* a social convention—it can provide a reason, indeed, a conclusive reason, for compliance—even where the custom or convention could be different from what it is and still fulfill its valuable social function. Of course, Holmes's underlying moral skepticism and non-cognitivism cause him to treat compliance with law, custom, convention, or any other norm as merely a matter of hypothetical imperatives. Anyone holding, as Aquinas does (and I do), a contrary metaethical position will see the matter differently. Often, that is to say—not always, but often—one will have conclusive moral reasons to contribute to the realization of ends and achievement of goals that a custom or convention serves. And where compliance with the custom or convention provides the unique way of making that contribution (as it often will), then one's strict moral obligation is to comply with the custom or convention. Because the imperative is categorical, rather than hypothetical, one can truly say that one's moral obligation is to comply—again, despite the fact that the custom or convention could have been otherwise than it is without substantial loss—and even, perhaps, with gain.

5. See John Finnis, *Aquinas: Moral, Political, and Legal Theory* (Oxford: Clarendon Press, 1998), pp. 266–74. See also Robert P. George, "Kelsen and Aquinas on 'the Natural Law Doctrine,'" *Notre Dame Law Review* 75 (2000): 1625–46, from which material in the text is largely drawn.

6. Summa theologiae, I-II, q. 104, a. 1.

7. Finnis, *Aquinas,* 267.

Holmes's insistence on the purely hypothetical nature of imperatives is fully on display in the only essay of which I am aware in which he squarely confronts the doctrines of natural law. It appeared in the *Harvard Law Review* in 1918 under the title "Natural Law." There he argued as follows:

> It is true that beliefs and wishes have a transcendental basis in the sense that their foundation is arbitrary. You cannot help entertaining and feeling them, and there is an end of it. As an arbitrary fact people wish to live, and we can say with varying degrees of certainty that they can do so only on certain conditions. To do it they must eat and drink. That necessity is absolute. It is a necessity of less degree but practically general that they should live in society. If they live in society, so far as we can see, there are further conditions. Reason working on experience does tell us, no doubt, that if our wish to live continues, we can do it only on those terms. But that seems to me the whole of the matter. I see no *a priori* duty to live with others and in that way, but simply a statement of what I must do if I wish to remain alive. If I do live with others they tell me that I must do and abstain from doing various things or they will put the screws on to me. I believe that they will, and being of the same mind as to their conduct I not only accept the rules but come in time to accept them with sympathy and emotional affirmation and begin to talk about duties and rights.[8]

Holmes makes it clear that there is all the difference in the world between, on the one hand, the psychological phenomenon of coming to accept and approve social rules initially complied with merely as conditions of achieving one's ends (including, preeminently, the end of staying alive), and, on the other hand, what he describes as "the supposed *a priori* discernment of a duty or the assertion of a preexisting right."[9] He summarizes the matter in one of his famous aphorisms: "A dog will fight for his bone."[10]

Well, yes: the psychological phenomenon of approving and accepting rules is not the same thing as having, nor is it very good evidence for believing that there are, good reasons that are not reducible to mere emotions for valuing the ends the rules are designed to procure or protect. By the same token, of course, the rejection of the rules by some, or the willingness of people to comply merely under threats or as a means of achieving their goals, or the diversity of beliefs and practices within a society or across cultures, does not establish the non-existence (or non-obtaining) of such reasons. Values may be objective even if nobody considers them to be so, and even if lots of people, or indeed

8. Oliver Wendell Holmes, "Natural Law," in *The Collected Works of Justice Holmes: Complete Public Writings and Selected Judicial Opinions of Oliver Wendell Holmes*, ed. Sheldon M. Novick, vol. 3 (Chicago: University of Chicago Press, 1995), 446–47.

9. Ibid., 447.

10. Ibid.

everyone, does not accept or hold them. Differences of wants, or of beliefs about what people should want, do not negate the possibility that people can have reasons to want things even if they happen not to want them, or the possibility that people can have reasons not to want things that they happen to want.

Here, I think, is the crux of Holmesian skepticism. The question is whether our basic wants are mere sub-rational, emotional, *givens*. At the end of the day, is it that we necessarily want whatever we happen to want, and reason has no power to criticize our wants? Holmes states his view clearly in the "Natural Law" article: "I see . . . no basis for a philosophy that tells us what we should want to want."[11] (This is central among the views that qualify Holmes, in Richard Posner's apparently approving judgment, as "the American Nietzsche.")[12]

But is there a basis for a philosophy—and Holmes's claims, however skeptical, are plainly philosophical—that tells us that that there is no possibility of rationally adjudicating among wants—in other words, a philosophy that tells us that there are no fundamental (in the sense of non-instrumental or more-than-*merely*-instrumental) reasons for wanting things? What could that basis be? What would be the status of the philosophy on which it is built?

The problem that Holmesian (like Humean, and, for that matter, Nietzschean) philosophy faces is retorsion, with its threat of self-refutation. Any philosophy worth entertaining must be capable of providing an intelligible (coherent, internally consistent, plausible) account of itself. Its claims must square with its own premises, other claims, and implications. This is true of skeptical philosophies as much as non-skeptical ones. And the problem is not simply logical, though logical inconsistency, if proven, is damning to any philosophical claim, for the canons of reasoning include elements that go beyond the demand for logical consistency. If, for example, a philosopher lays claim on our attention to consider a proposition he is asserting, we are entitled to count it against his assertion that the claim itself, even if internally consistent, is being asserted not as true, but as, say, merely his opinion, where he has detached the idea of "opinion" from the concept of truth, such that his opinion is put forward as something other than an opinion about the truth of what he is asserting. Similarly, we needn't, and shouldn't, credit a claim being asserted as something other than a proposition we ought to hold because the reasons for holding it are, all things considered, sound, or, at least, sounder than the reasons, if any, for not holding it.

11. Ibid.

12. Richard A. Posner, "Introduction," in Holmes, *The Essential Holmes*, xxviii.

Now back to Holmes. He runs a couple of arguments against belief in natural law that are easily disposed of. First, he claims that believers in natural law draw an unwarranted inference from the merely familiar to the natural, in the sense of the morally good and right. "The jurists who believe in natural law," he protests, "seem to me to be in the naïve state of mind that accepts what has been familiar and accepted by all men everywhere."[13] But this is plainly a false charge. It certainly does not apply to Aquinas or his most influential forebears and successors in the tradition of natural law theorizing. Indeed, as Leo Strauss observed in *Natural Right and History,* it is the diversity of human practices and moral opinions that motivates the philosophical quest to discover principles of natural law or natural right that provide criteria for their moral-critical evaluation.

Holmes's second charge is that natural law theorists confuse their own certitude with certainty. "We have been," he says, "cock-sure of many things that were not so."[14] Well, yes, of course we have been. But this fact, if anything, should strengthen our resolve to be self-critical and practice intellectual humility. It should make us more aware—dare I say more certain, more cocksure?—of our own fallibility. And this applies to everyone, not just natural law theorists. (Indeed, it strikes me as defamatory to assert that it applies with any special force to natural law theorists. Consider that St. Thomas sets forth, "sympathetically and plausibly," as John Finnis says in his fine book on Aquinas, "more than 10,000 objections to the positions he proposes and defends" in the *Summa theologiae* alone.)[15] Skepticism has no better record than any other philosophy on this count. Ditto for pragmatism, Darwinism, utilitarianism, and other philosophies that impressed Holmes in various ways. Holmes himself was a man of many certainties of belief—certainties, often rooted deeply in his philosophical skepticism, that appear highly dubious today. In the very discussion of certitude, in the course of making his point against the natural law theorists, he asserts without qualification or the slightest shade of doubt that "what we love most and revere generally is determined by early associations."[16] Really? Now, there is a claim that, if interpreted in such a way as to raise it above the level of the banal, is highly questionable, to say the least.

Now, back to the problem of retorsion and self-refutation. Holmes asserts his skeptical claims as true, or, at least, rationally warranted. His criticisms of natural law theory and other cognitivist accounts of ethical obligation are assertions that their claims are wrong, or, at least, ration-

13. Holmes, "Natural Law," 446.

14. Ibid.

15. Finnis, *Aquinas,* p. 10.

16. Holmes, "Natural Law," 446.

ally unwarranted. He thinks that people who hold false, incorrect, or at least unwarranted opinions on these matters ought to change them. They ought to replace them with the contrary opinions that Holmes himself asserts as true, correct, or at least uniquely warranted from the rational viewpoint. For example, the claim about the general determination of what we most love and revere is put in place to set the stage for a distinction that is meant to have the practical impact of causing people to change their views in order to conform them to what Holmes thinks ought to be believed. "While one's experience . . . makes certain preferences dogmatic for oneself," he says, "recognition of how they came to be leaves one able to see that others, poor souls, may be equally dogmatic about something else. And this again means skepticism."[17] But if this is true, if this really warrants skepticism, indeed, if it makes any real sense to assert it and urge the adoption of moral skepticism, then it means that a fundamental belief—indeed a belief of great practical significance—can be changed by reasoning, and it ought to be changed, fundamental desires and emotions to the contrary notwithstanding. A practical implication of the assertion is that people ought to embrace the skeptical position, desires and emotions to the contrary, again, notwithstanding, because it is true, correct, warranted, and the contrary positions are false, erroneous, unwarranted. And this, in turn, appeals implicitly but inescapably to the practical reasonableness of acting and believing on the basis of what is sound, correct, true—in other words, it treats truth (or, at least, warranted belief) as providing a valid practical reason, an *objective value,* something with a claim on us that transcends our wishes and emotions, and thus, in precisely the sense Holmes himself derided (if I understand him correctly), a transcendental sanction.

Holmes position is not saved from a retorsive or self-referential argument along these lines by his claim that one's recognition of the validity of skepticism will leave in place (or at least needn't displace) "one's belief or love."[18] First, this is problematic in itself. Recognition that a "belief or love" one believed to be rationally and morally warranted or even required is, in truth, a mere subjective emotion with no objective rational or moral warrant is unlikely to leave that belief or love unaffected even in respect to the emotional intensity with which one holds it. Second, and much more importantly, whether or not one's belief or love stays in place, Holmes's argument asserts a skeptical position that does not sit easily with his own assertions that skepticism is true, or at

17. Ibid.
18. Ibid.

least uniquely warranted from the rational viewpoint, and should *therefore* be embraced even by those who wish it were otherwise.

Holmes says that "deep seated preferences cannot be argued about—you cannot argue a man into liking a glass of beer—and therefore when differences are sufficiently far reaching, we try to kill the other man rather than let him have his way. But that is perfectly consistent with admitting that, so far as it appears, his grounds are just as good as ours."[19] But the issue I am raising is not about a glass of beer. There really isn't a reason to like a glass of beer if one happens not to like it. One likes it or one doesn't, and there, as Holmes would say, is the end of it. The issue is whether people ought to believe and act on the basis of what is true, correct, sound, warranted; Holmes's assertion of his view presupposes that they should, and thus presupposes that people can and should grasp the point—the basic, more-than-merely-instrumental, point and value—of truth, knowledge, reasonableness, rationality. But if they can, then it is a mistake to suppose that all values are subjective, and it is time to launch, or continue, the quest to distinguish mere matters of taste (a glass of beer) from those aspects of human well-being and fulfillment (such as practical and theoretical knowledge of truth) that have objective worth, and thus standing as "natural law."

19. Ibid.

9 Dewey's Metaphysics of Existence

JOSEPH MARGOLIS

I

One reasonable suggestion about how to read John Dewey's epistemology—which, on Dewey's conviction, requires attending to his metaphysics as well—holds that Dewey agrees with Hegel about replacing the fiction of Kant's Transcendental Ego with actual human beings; and that, as a result, Dewey binds his own calling in exorcising every vestige of "Cartesianism" and every vestige of Kantian transcendentalism; *and* that, succeeding there, he turns against the idealist extravagances of his own early efforts until they yield the leanest naturalistic realism that can escape the paradoxes of the pre-Kantian and Kantian (and even Hegelian) tradition.

You may see in this a warning that the effective arguments of past metaphysics were deemed successful only on the assumption of an unalterable space of argument removed from practical life, hence from the conditions of knowledge, which Kant and Hegel effectively dismantled on grounds of insuperable paradox. Dewey's originality, like Hegel's before him, may then be seen to depend on converting every previous metaphysical privilege in his own favor. But victories gained that way are themselves uncertain. For it is surely the most vexed question of modern philosophy how to judge the validity of competing metaphysical and epistemological visions whose own evolving claims seem to carry in their wake the decisive, the privileged, conditions on which their victory is assured.

Opportunists may seize one or another "evident" first principle in order to gain a victory of sorts or, anticipating a possible stalemate, to repudiate every proposal for bridging the divide between competing intuitions in order to condemn as utterly pointless the continued pursuit of metaphysics and epistemology. The first line of argument risks falling back to refurbished options that were thought to have been decisively defeated (like the Cartesian and Kantian options); the second leads to what is now called "postmodernism," which, paradoxically, seems unable to state the grounds for its own validity, since, if successful, it might appear to redeem the very discipline it rejects. Contemporary metaphysics seems caught between the horns of this dilemma.

I must, therefore, insist on a corollary clue in speaking about Dewey's conception of nature, if we mean to allow his proposal any inning at all. Ever since Kant—in particular, ever since philosophy agreed on the primacy of resolving the essential paradox of "Cartesian" realism—it has become increasingly clear that a certain "benign antinomy" constitutes a necessary condition for every would-be resolution: namely, that metaphysics and epistemology are indissolubly linked, so that neither can be meaningfully said to take precedence over the other and that, nevertheless, within that symbiosis, each may be accorded a different priority of its own that cannot rest on stronger metaphysical or epistemological resources than the original symbiosis permits. The tradition that runs from Kant, through Hegel, through a variety of philosophical beneficiaries including Dewey, has thereby effectively transformed the conceptual setting in which alone metaphysical arguments may be judged to be defensible. They hold, in effect, that the paradoxes of Cartesian realism cannot be surmounted without embracing one or another version of the symbiotic doctrine just mentioned (that is, the antinomy and what it entails) and that there is no point to any further metaphysics that ignores that precondition. But, the argument goes on, the paradoxes can be successfully resolved.

It is a startling fact, nevertheless, that Cartesianism lives!—handsomely in fact—in late analytic philosophy. You have only to remark the extraordinary confidence of the first three maxims of Michael Devitt's well-known (and even well-received) recent attempt to recover what may be fairly viewed as the leanest version of Cartesian realism. Here they are:

> Maxim 1. In considering realism, distinguish the constitutive and evidential issues.
>
> Maxim 2. Distinguish the metaphysical (ontological) issues of realism from any semantic issue.
>
> Maxim 3. Settle the realism issue before any epistemological or semantic issue.[1]

This is both explicit and admirably brief. The only difficulty with Devitt's proposal is that he offers no reason at all to believe we could ever

1. Michael Devitt, *Realism and Truth,* 2nd ed. (Princeton: Princeton University Press, 1991), 3–4.

follow his recommendation strictly. (It's as if Kant and Hegel had never practiced their trade.) Devitt is obviously an unrepentant Cartesian, and Dewey would have been his instant nemesis.

More than that, Dewey was himself challenged by theorists as diverse as Arthur Murphy, Bertrand Russell, George Santayana, Hans Reichenbach—on grounds that can only be called Cartesian—as having produced a terrible muddle by conflating science's knowledge of the independent world and the "merely" instrumentalist conditions by which, occasionally, it actually succeeds.[2] By "Cartesianism" (or "Cartesian realism"), I should say at once, I mean any attempt to advance a realism on grounds that construe belief or perception in such a way that actual beliefs or perceptions lack realist import as such and cannot, therefore, provide epistemic grounds for any realism regarding the physical or natural world. For example, a causal theory of belief or perception that could not rightly convey epistemic grounds for affirming the realist standing of the beliefs and perceptions it would explain (causally) would yield no more than a form of Cartesianism. Much of analytic philosophy influenced by W. V. Quine and Donald Davidson favors Cartesian realism by default—in effect, tends to produce realisms *manqués*. Thus, anything like Locke's representationalism, or Devitt's segregation of metaphysics and epistemology, or a merely causal theory of belief and perception set in a realist context cannot count for more than alternative forms of Cartesian realism.

Not surprisingly, the critics mentioned converge on something very similar to Devitt's undefended (but very fashionable) policy. Murphy's complaint will have to serve as proxy for all those arguments:

> [W]e know both what the world is like under the conditions of observation and enjoyment and also what, in a much more general and approximate way, the unexperienced environment is by which experience is conditioned. If we could not know this there would be no sense in calling this environment "nature" and regarding experience as our means of finding out about it. . . . But to suppose that the whole meaning of what science tells us about the physical environment is reducible to this instrumental function is to treat one context in which things come to us as ultimate for metaphysics, and this is an irreparable mistake.[3]

I trust it will be enough to say that Murphy's challenge is simply a "Cartesian" rebuff, updated for the times, utterly unresponsive to the novelty of Dewey's conception. Dewey's reply supposes that *any* such re-

2. All four are commentators in Paul Arthur Schilpp, *The Philosophy of John Dewey*, 2nd ed. (New York: Tudor, 1951).

3. Arthur E. Murphy, "Dewey's Epistemology and Metaphysics," in Schilpp, 223–24. I have reversed the order of two citations.

buff is past being readmitted: the space of argument, Dewey might say, has changed so much through a series of reasonable interventions that no realism can now pass muster that would leave the Cartesian paradoxes in place. Dewey maintains that "experience" is a real ingredient in the world; that it never constitutes or constructs the "independent world"; that the world, when "known," is known under the condition of the inseparability of the subjective and the objective; that knowledge of the world emerges from some real but non-cognitive experience (or "ingredient") of (and in) the world; and that whatever we view as the features of the "independent" world are, epistemically but not ontically, artifacts of our evidentiary sources.

Dewey's answer to Murphy and his other critics is admirably straightforward, even if we should wish to contest it. All inquiry, science included, arises out of what Dewey calls a "problematic situation," by which he means "a non-cognitive situation" that engenders a practical and unavoidable impasse for a human subject "out of what [as he explains] knowing develops."[4] On the suggestion sketched, the resolution of such a practical impasse yields a viable form of constructivism or constructive realism that need no longer be thought to be an idealism.

Relative to a "problematic situation," Dewey reminds Murphy, he distinguishes between "subject-matter, object, and contents," which (roughly) is to say he distinguishes between the initial "situation," what is real in it, and whatever comes to be known of the real world in instrumental terms fitted to the resolution of the initial impasse. In that sense, as he explicitly says, all three terms "designate these different statuses of experienced material."[5]

I cannot see how it can be denied that, at least at a first pass, Dewey has plainly met Murphy's Cartesian objection. He has done so by an economy that catches up the very nerve of pragmatism. I suggest that it is also an extremely spare (very distant) reading of Hegel's own general solution of the realist problem, without mention of Hegel's master theme of the historicity of thought or any of Hegel's conceptual devices.

Arguing from the other horn of our dilemma, Richard Rorty, the resident "postmodernist" critic of metaphysics and epistemology, seems hell-bent on reading Dewey as a prescient postmodernist who anticipates himself. Extraordinary piece of stage-setting. "It is [Rorty affirms]

4. John Dewey, "Experience, Knowledge, and Value: A Rejoinder," in Schilpp, 566. These themes are central to Dewey's *Logic* and *Experience and Nature.* See John Dewey, *Logic: The Theory of Inquiry* (New York: Henry Holt, 1938); and *Experience and Nature,* 2nd ed. (New York: Dover, 1958).

5. Dewey, "Experience, Knowledge and Value," 566.

easier to think of [Dewey's *Experience and Nature*] as an explanation of why nobody needs a metaphysics, rather than as itself a metaphysical system."[6] Whatever does Rorty mean? It cannot be "easier" for anyone who actually reads *Experience and Nature.*

To pick up the corrective theme of what I have cited from Dewey's Reply to his critics in the Schilpp volume, by turning back to the fuller account of *Experience and Nature,* we cannot fail to see that Dewey surely explains what *he* means by "metaphysics" read in the revisionary sense he intends—against the old hegemonies: "If philosophy be criticism, what is to be said of the relation of philosophy to metaphysics?"[7] There cannot be an end to metaphysics there. Dewey's theme of course is the unrelieved "contingency" of nature and how its discovery is "the beginning of wisdom."[8] That is what separates him from the classic metaphysicians. There is no postmodernism there, because there are no longer any absolutes to provoke it. Metaphysics itself clearly remains in play.

The only path from Dewey to Rorty that could possibly vindicate postmodernism as pragmatism's own sweet lesson would require, first, Dewey's repudiation of Cartesianism, Kantian transcendentalism, Aristotelian essentialism, and similar philosophical weeds that count against the deep contingency of nature; and then, and for that reason alone, his concluding that wherever the first step is taken, we may as well admit there is no way to recover philosophy's systematic disclosure of the "metaphysics of existence," that is, the metaphysics of the deep contingency of nature. Dewey certainly champions the first step, but he never supports the second. That is a complete fantasy on Rorty's part—and a non sequitur to boot. For you cannot find in all of Rorty's prose a single argument to support his judgment, unless it is the one that rests on the false lead just offered.

We may make the correction easily enough by recalling Dewey's words at the close of *Experience and Nature,* which plainly anticipate, in 1929, the metaphysics he insists on in 1939 against his critics. You may read what he says as also explaining what he means, in the *Logic* in 1938, by the troublesome expression, a "problematic situation," which is surely the most compact clue to his entire doctrine:

> In mind, thought, this situation, this predicament, [that is, this "problematic situation,"] becomes aware of itself. . . . The one cord that is never broken is

6. R. Rorty, "Dewey's Metaphysics," in *Consequences of Pragmatism (Essays: 1972–1980)* (Minneapolis: University of Minnesota Press, 1982), 72.

7. Dewey, *Experience and Nature,* 412.

8. Ibid., 413.

> that between the energies and acts which compose nature. Knowledge modifies the tie. But the idea that knowledge breaks the tie, that it inserts something opaque between the interactions of things, is hardly less than infantile. Knowledge as science modifies the particular interactions that come within its reach, because it *is* itself a modification of [such] interactions. . . . The generic insight into existence which alone can define metaphysics in any empirically intelligible sense is itself an added fact of interaction. . . . The universe is no infinite self-representative series, if only because the addition within it of a representation makes it a different universe.[9]

There is no more perspicuous or timely statement of Dewey's metaphysics than this. It's a compendium of everything already said and a perfectly reasonable specimen of Dewey's distinctly original conception of nature. It is also, I should say, noticeably more agile than the most up-to-date realisms now proposed by John McDowell and Hilary Putnam.

II

The skill and grand economy of Dewey's metaphysics may elude you. It obviously eluded the "Cartesian" critics of his own day, and it baffles Rorty still. Dewey, however, is quite straightforward. The invention of the "indeterminate situation" is pragmatism at its existential best. At one stroke, it completely outflanks Cartesianism (in Peirce's original sense), all the while it construes meaning and truth and knowledge of reality within the pragmatist priorities of practical intelligence. (Here, it favors James and goes against Peirce's notion of the "long run.") That explains why Dewey treats knowledge as "a modification of interactions [*non-cognitive* interactions]" between organism and world. By that single slim adjustment, Dewey disables every form of cognitive privilege and draws the realist standing of *savoir* dependently from the standing of *savoir-faire,* which is itself a pragmatist construction from the realist import of our animal interactions with the world.

You see the trick of Dewey's strategy: the realist standing of our science is ultimately justified constructively from *within* the realist interactions of a viable life, which, from time to time, trap us in one existential (sub-cognitive) impasse or another requiring improvisations of a dawning cognitive sort that we eventually judge to be continuous in some degree with the objective regularities of nature. Realism is therefore a late artifact of our scientific and philosophical reflections, *not* a first principle of any kind; hence, never more than provisional, perspectived, "in-

9. Ibid., 414–15.

strumentalist" (if you wish), fluxive, constructed, lacking any assurance of fixity or invariance or necessity or essential *telos* or privilege or unique validity. All of this comes from a single maneuver demonstrably superior to any of the more recent analytic attempts to displace it or entrench Cartesianism—hence a fair alternative to every earlier realism spanning, say, Aristotle and Hegel. That is the pragmatist's most important challenge.

The fact is, Cartesian realism and analogues of Cartesian dualism are very much with us still at the start of the twenty-first century. The entire twentieth century and a good deal of the late nineteenth century, particularly in English-language philosophy, were almost completely occupied with one or another form of Cartesian realism. It was of course Peirce's original pragmatist target, itself drawn from Kant and Hegel, and now from James's sensible (even necessary) misreading of Peirce's doctrine in the latter's *Pragmatism* (which transforms Peirce's theory of meaning into a theory of truth), that leads directly to Dewey's all but official version of what we now take pragmatism to be.

You have only to add that Dewey's notion of an "indeterminate situation" signifies that his realism is a metaphysics of *existence*—which is precisely what ensures the amplitude and plasticity of his entire doctrine. There are, for Dewey, no *a priori* fixities to be drawn from the *natures* of things; "features," kinds, essences cannot be more than what we surmise answer to the piecemeal animal potencies implicated in responding to existential impasses.

There you have the deft reason Dewey discards Aristotle's habit of assigning potency and actuality to fixed "natures" (or essences) or essences to fixed potencies: an existentialized metaphysics precludes the need for, and the plausibility of, any such doctrine. The existential theme supports no more than one version or another (or of course plural versions) of the theory of the flux. Teleology is now no more than an idealization from the inventive trajectories of animal intelligence—it cannot set any changeless normative constraints on human life and conduct; it accommodates instead the completely open-ended purposiveness and continually improvised values that mark the contingent episodes of human life. Neither Aristotle nor Kant need be entirely discounted, but there is no longer any necessity or near-necessity in anything they say about nature or reason. In fact, the defeat of modal necessities in metaphysics and epistemology—once privilege is set aside—follows at once from the normal coherence of *any* plausible account ranging over human improvisation and history. That is an extraordinary gain at absolutely no cost.

To see the force of all this is to see how radical and spare Dewey's metaphysics actually is. No wonder Rorty misses its lesson. It's true that Dewey is unconditionally opposed to ancient, medieval, and early modern and Kantian metaphysics and epistemology. But if you accept the essential nerve of the pragmatist conception of meaning and truth, and if you add to that your acceptance of Dewey's notion of the "indeterminate [or problematic] situation," you will find it well-nigh impossible to avoid adopting something akin to his metaphysics of existence. The important point is that Dewey's *is* a coherent doctrine that arises in a debating space that had, already by Hegel's time, completely transformed the canonical milieu in which figures such as Aristotle and Descartes and Kant could have counted on providing the exemplars for all admissible metaphysics.

To defeat Dewey now—or any of the more interesting progeny of the Hegelian turn—you must demonstrate at least that the doctrine of the flux is itself false (the *faute de mieux* thesis that there are no necessities *de re* or *de cogitatione,* that no such necessities can be demonstrated); so that flux cannot thereafter be invoked to defeat the *a priori* division between eligible and ineligible metaphysics or epistemologies.

The postmodernist will still insist on his pointless triumph: for, if the modal argument fails, he says—and it surely fails—then all philosophy must be at an end. But Dewey's example confirms the reasonableness and coherence of carrying the issue further in the pragmatist's direction. Beyond that, we cannot but fall back to the usual dialectical scuffles among competitors. It had, you realize, taken the better part of a century to thin down the extravagances and opaque machinery of the Hegelian system to arrive at Dewey's impressive economy; and it has taken the better part of another century to align Dewey's conception (in a dialectically manageable way) against the strongest challenges of late twentieth-century analytic philosophy.

It is now, therefore, nearly two centuries since Hegel's *Phenomenology* appeared. *"Geist"* has been abandoned; all traces of teleologism have been put at risk; Hegelian vestiges of Kantian transcendentalism are no longer in vogue; the idea of the historicity of thought, which had flourished until recently, is now neglected by pragmatists as well as the champions of nearly every English-language movement (and, increasingly, by their European counterparts). The startling fact is that the latest pragmatists (Hilary Putnam and Richard Rorty) as well as the most influential recent analytic philosophers (notably, Donald Davidson) are still committed to protecting one or another version of the Cartesian paradigm, all the while they act to exorcise Cartesian faults in one another. At the very beginning of the twenty-first century, we are, it seems, still engaged in resolving the puzzles that confronted Kant and Hegel in the span of little more than the last quarter of the eighteenth century!

The strength of Dewey's solution, which is much clearer now than it was before the present dominance of American analytic philosophy, depends on Dewey's ingeniously simple union of the essential themes of Peirce's and James's theories of meaning and truth, of Hegel's radical treatment of empirical contingency and flux (shorn of all reference to historicity), and Dewey's own biologized conception of the "indeterminate situation." There you have the bare bones of Dewey's metaphysics of existence. Its peculiar resilience is better demonstrated, however, by following the mixed fortunes of the lesser pragmatists of our own day. To make the case is to justify the strong revival of interest in pragmatism's options.

Without a doubt, Putnam, more than Rorty, must be credited with the attempt to bring James's and Dewey's conception of realism into line with the strongest pressures of late twentieth-century analytic philosophy. Putnam's own variant, which Putnam calls "internal realism," obviously counted on resolving the usual paradoxes of Cartesian realism by featuring a symbiosis of the subjective and the objective in epistemic terms without denying the ontic independence of the physical world. (That is the point of the "benign antinomy" I mentioned earlier.) The maneuver had already been developed by Dewey, most fully in *Experience and Nature,* but it was of course the essential thread of Hegel's *Phenomenology* as well. Putnam's argument is best rendered in his *Reason, Truth and History* (1981) and more or less summarized in *The Many Faces of Realism* (1987). You have only to compare the prefaces of both books to see that Putnam remained committed to opposing "the dichotomy between 'objective' and 'subjective' views of truth and reason."[10] His constant target remained Cartesian realism, which he labeled "metaphysical realism," a doctrine committed to there being "One True Theory" in accord with which the mind "copies" the world.

You have, here, already, a fatal equivocation affecting Putnam's realism. Putnam never explained the disjunctive difference (in epistemological terms) between there being many partial descriptions compatible with some single, ideally neutral and comprehensive description of the world in accord with the "One True Theory" and a plurality of partial or fragmented descriptions generated by our diverse and changing existential interests—always partly blind epistemically (in Dewey's sense of animal life)—that, nevertheless, are antecedently known (if known

10. Hilary Putnam, *The Many Faces of Reason* (La Salle: Open Court, 1987), 1. The same phrasing appears in Putnam, *Reason, Truth and History,* ix.

at all) to be compatible with whatever a realism of the independent world would require. *If* Putnam had indeed held faithfully to the symbiosis doctrine, he could not have defended his own pluralist answer. There's an obvious lacuna in his argument. But if he has no answer, then it is impossible that he should escape the charge of relativism that Rorty, for one, brings against him.[11]

Two observations are worth remarking here. For one, Putnam goes to great lengths to demonstrate that there is no single, uniquely valid description of the world; that, relative to our interests, we may even individuate the things of the world in plural ways that nevertheless do not generate any paradox or incompatibility regarding truth. This is the burden of Putnam's pluralism, as if that doctrine were enough to capture the pluralism of James and Dewey. It is not.

Putnam puts his thesis very neatly: "realism [by which he means, interchangeably, 'internal realism' or 'pragmatic realism'] is *not* incompatible with conceptual relativity."[12] Fair enough: we may always, he explains, invoke something akin to the play between Carnap's standard view of individuation and some Polish logician's mereological alternative, so as to arrive at *plural* ontologies that are compatible with one another (in the relevant sense) and consistent with a strong view of the independent world. But how could we ever, *on* the symbiotizing thesis alone, *show that* such divergent descriptions *were* no more than alternative ways of describing *the same part of the same world?* There seems to be no answer; there you have the point of relativism's "menace." For, it is against this precise worry (my second observation) that Putnam invents out of whole cloth his notorious *Grenzbegriff* of truth and rationality—that is, to offset the threat of relativism. But now, on the symbiotizing thesis, the *Grenzbegriff* cannot possibly serve any pertinent epistemological or methodological function.

Putnam has now abandoned (with qualifications) his internal realism (or what he now counts as internal realism).[13] But the reason has nothing to do with the difficulties mentioned. It seems that, having been seduced much earlier (as he admits) by James's attraction to a form of representationalism (on the strength of which James built an

11. See, for instance, Richard Rorty, "Hilary Putnam and the Relativist Menace," *Philosophical Papers,* vol. 3 (Cambridge: Cambridge University Press, 1998).

12. Putnam, *Many Faces of Realism,* 17.

13. See, particularly, Hilary Putnam, "Sense, Nonsense, and the Senses: An Inquiry into the Powers of the Human Mind" (The Dewey Lectures 1994), *Journal of Philosophy* 91 (1994): 461 n. 36, 463 n. 41. The entire text has been included, unaltered, in Hilary Putnam, *The Threefold Cord: Mind, Body, and World* (New York: Columbia University Press, 1999). Putnam has added some essays to this last volume, but they do not appear to alter the position advanced in the Dewey Lectures.

idealist picture of reality, which Putnam now rejects),[14] Putnam has belatedly discovered that his own version of representationalism was always hostage to the same Cartesian paradoxes he labored to expose.

It is not entirely clear whether, in rejecting (quite correctly) "Cartesian" representationalism, Putnam also means to abandon what he now understands to be "internal realism."[15] It hardly matters, except to get clear about Putnam's own solution. For, for one thing, the doctrine of the symbiosis of the subjective and the objective *is* independent of representationalism and, on the evidence, affords the only viable way to overcome the paradoxes; and, for a second, given the argument of the flux, in particular given the rejection of cognitive privilege, "internalism" (in effect, symbiosis) plainly puts Putnam at risk of yielding to one or another form of relativism (assuming, as I do, that relativism can be formulated coherently and consistently).

I should say therefore that Putnam unqualifiedly failed in his realist undertaking. You must remember that the whole purpose of the Paul Carus Lectures *(The Many Faces of Realism)*—much the same is true of the older *Reason, Truth and History*—was, in Putnam's own words, "to further specify the alternative that I see to metaphysical realist [that is, Cartesian] views of reality and truth, on the one hand, and to cultural relativist ones, on the other [by which he means to include at least Rorty's postmodernism]."[16]

I emphasize the outcome, because Putnam's was surely the most sustained (very nearly the only) effort in late twentieth-century American philosophy to recover the pragmatist strategy on realism—Dewey's strategy, I should say—in a way that matched the best rigor of analytic philosophy. By that Putnam meant (as I interpret matters) to show that the penchant for "metaphysical realism" he discerned in the unity of science movement and such affiliated undertakings as Donald Davidson's was indeed something of a return to Cartesian realism. Putnam, of course, believed (still believes) that relativism is as incoherent as

14. See Putnam, "Sense, Nonsense, and the Senses," 448 and n. 8.

15. The key passage appears in Putnam, "Sense, Nonsense, and the Senses," 463 n. 41. I judge that Putnam has not given up the rejection of "a sharp line between properties we 'discover' in the world and properties we 'project' onto the world"; but I cannot be sure that that now entails the symbiosis of the subjective and the objective. If the entailment holds, then Putnam remains "Hegelian" (or at least a somewhat Hegelian reader of Kant); but if it does not, then, I'm afraid, Putnam will have fallen back to Cartesian realism or to a somewhat Kantianized version of the Cartesian position (*sans* representationlism, of course). Putnam's recent book, *The Threefold Cord,* which adds to the Dewey Lectures the text of the Josiah Royce Lectures (1997), does not take up the unanswered question. We shall have to wait to see how Putnam plays his new hand.

16. Putnam, *Many Faces of Realism,* 1.

Cartesianism. But that hardly shows that Dewey's realist strategy fails, even if it should favor or yield to relativism.

Dewey's strategy *is* "internalist" (in the sense at stake) and (I should argue) hospitable to relativism, though that is almost never spelled out. Apart from the interpretation I am now suggesting, I am aware of very little more than the briefest mention of the essential connection (in Dewey's doctrine) between relativism and realism. Arthur Murphy, who adopts a Cartesian stance against Dewey (as we have seen) remarks in the briefest way that the dependence of realism, in Dewey's account, on the peculiarities of the "indeterminate situation" does indeed introduce an ineliminable touch of relativism.[17] He means this as a polite objection, but the charge *is* valid and (I think) entirely acceptable. It may be read as the barest trace of the original Hegelian doctrine (which both Murphy and John Herman Randall conventionally label "objective relativism," that is, the effect of the inescapable but also contemporaneously impenetrable horizon of our historical existence).[18] It is the same point I have brought against Putnam's pluralism.

Dewey escapes all the conceptual traps, *if* (as I believe) relativism and even incommensurabilism are coherent. Ralph Sleeper has ventured the single line, bearing on Dewey's metaphysics of existence, that Dewey's ontology "is pluralistic and relativistic, of course, since Dewey accepts no eternal objects or permanent kinds."[19] Sleeper means his claim to rely on the import of the original "indeterminate situation," which, as I say, confounds Putnam's own version of realism. Dewey's master stroke rests with the double fact (1) that our animal interactions with the real world (which are themselves parts of reality) are more fundamental than, and not reducible to, our *cognitive* connections with the world, and (2) that our cognitive connections are themselves entitled to a realist reading for that very reason—are not merely "representational" in any Cartesian or mentalist sense.[20] If you hold all this together, you see the stunning simplicity of Dewey's metaphysics of existence.

17. Murphy, 219–21.

18. See John Herman Randall Jr., "Dewey's Interpretation of the History of Philosophy," in Schilpp.

19. R. W. Sleeper, *The Necessity of Pragmatism: John Dewey's Conception of Philosophy* (New Haven: Yale University Press, 1986), 161.

20. I should like to draw attention to a very skillful rendering of this lesson in John R. Shook, *Dewey's Empirical Theory of Knowledge and Reality* (Nashville: Vanderbilt University Press, 2000), 7. Shook does not pursue the relativistic issue further. Its absence does, however, confirm that Dewey himself did not pursue the matter.

III

I should say that, ultimately, Dewey's theory favors two strategies: one, to prefer existence over essence, which (let me assure you) is not to prioritize "existence" over "nature"; the other, to relativize all metaphysical and epistemological questions (which, though distinct, are not separable) to the pre-cognitive and fluxive "indeterminacies" of the existential impasses from which cognition first arises and gains its own realist standing. I regard this formula as the key to any acceptable summary of Dewey's grand labor. I believe it must yield in the direction of relativism and even incommensurabilism; and I find that that is entirely acceptable. It catches up in a coherent and balanced way all of Dewey's speculations about metaphysics, epistemology, logic, and practical norms and values.

But I must still collect the true fire of the argument.

Dewey, as I say, prefers a metaphysics of existence over essences. He draws his account of nature, therefore, from the fluxive condition of reality, which poses the decisive philosophical bet that no one will be able to demonstrate the modal necessity of *de re* or *de cogitatione* invariances. The sheer coherence and wide range of application of Dewey's metaphysics constitute a proof that the ancient, admittedly coherent canon—the entire Parmenidean clan, if I may name an honorable history thus—has been led astray: because the clan's own argument rests on the assumption that the denial of reality's invariant structure must yield to paradox or contradiction "somewhere" (as Aristotle pointedly says). But if you cannot show the incoherence of Dewey's alternative, defended as a close analysis of the human condition, you must consider yielding in favor of Dewey's economies. The argument is thoroughly *"naturalistic"* of course, in the sense the classic pragmatists preferred; that is, it eschews all conceptual resources that, by its own lights, would count as "supernatural" (or even fictional), and it prefers to be guided by (though not to submit to) the authority of the epistemological and methodological practices of the sciences.[21]

Dewey's metaphysics is not, however, of the *"naturalizing"* kind—that is, not the naturalism so strenuously espoused by Davidson and Rorty or, more equivocally, by Quine, that insists, beyond the mild policy just mentioned, that all explanation is ultimately causal; disallows all separate epistemic and legitimative discourse; and favors physicalism and extensionalism over all other options, whether in reductive, elimina-

21. See, further, John Ryder, ed., *American Philosophic Naturalism in the Twentieth Century* (Amherst: Prometheus Books, 1994), including Ryder's introduction.

tive, or non-reductive terms.[22] The extreme doctrine—"naturalizing," in Davidson's idiom—depends, as far as I can see, on the doubtful dictum of "the causal closure of the physical world."[23]

I say "doubtful," because, of course, if flux holds, then the would-be exceptionless laws of nature must be contingent idealizations of the observed or conjectured regularities of the experienced world. (There is good reason to think that necessary laws are idealizations anyway.) In short, the status of nomological universals is not a different issue from that of validating something like Dewey's metaphysics of existence or, more specifically, the irreducibility or ineliminability of the symbiotizing claim. The Deweyan maxim, then, finally comes to this: "Natural but not naturalizable."[24]

If you grant all this, then, if you recall the sense in which Putnam's realism fails to escape the charge of relativism—in effect, the sense in which we prioritize the existential indeterminacies of Dewey's "problematic situation" over any merely formal or *ad hoc* measures meant to bring philosophy safely back to Cartesian or transcendental or invariantist assurances (without toil, as by invoking Putnam's *Grenzbegriff!*)—you begin to see the deeper thrust of Dewey's boldness. Dewey obliges us at every turn to explain precisely why we are entitled to suppose that the solution to our epistemological questions should lead back, reliably, to one or another form of the canon that spans, say, Aristotle and Kant.

As early as 1891, reflecting on the instruction of children regarding the difference between percepts and concepts, Dewey had already realized that, taken in strictly pragmatist terms, a concept [think of a triangle constructed in imagination] is

> "ideal" not sensual . . . it is a mode or *way of mental action,* it cannot be felt or seen or heard. *It can be grasped only in and through the activity which constitutes it.* . . . The concept, in short, is knowledge of what the real object is—the object taken with reference to its principle of construction, while the percept, so called, is knowledge of the object in a more or less accidental or limited way.[25]

22. See Donald Davidson, "A Coherence Theory of Truth and Knowledge," and Richard Rorty, "Pragmatism, Davidson and Truth," both in Ernest Lepore, ed., *Truth and Interpretation: Perspectives on the Philosophy of Donald Davidson* (Oxford: Basil Blackwell, 1986). Something of the labile nature of both Rorty's and Davidson's style of argument may be gleaned from W. V. Quine, "Let Me Accentuate the Positive," and Donald Davidson's "Afterthoughts, 1987," appended to the reprint of "A Coherence Theory . . ." in Alan R. Malachowski, ed., *Reading Rorty* (Oxford: Blackwell, 1990).

23. See Jaegwon Kim, *Philosophy of Mind* (Boulder: Westview Press, 1996), ch. 6, particularly 147–48.

24. See, further, Joseph Margolis, "Reconstruction in Pragmatism," *Journal of Speculative Philosophy* 13 (1999): 221–39.

25. John Dewey, "How Do Concepts Arise from Percepts?" in *The Early Works,*

Concepts, then, are modes of active intervention; percepts are not. There can be little doubt that this is, in essence, the import of Dewey's biologized account of resolving an existential or "indeterminate" impasse. It shows the near-necessity of preferring flux over invariance and practical know-how over theoretical knowledge.

The idea of an indeterminate situation is a remarkably spare conceptual device that ensures the symbiosis of the subjective and the objective at an existential level well below any cognitive presumption, though compatibly with realism and the acceptance of the flux. It obliges us to explain the emergent powers of cognition and theoretical reason epistemically in terms that acknowledge the biological continuity of resolving practical impasses (despite our lacking any sufficient science) and cognate animal competences. It affords a privitive strategy: namely, it advises us to count—in the pragmatist sense of meaning and truth—all invariances, necessities, essences, universals, natural kinds, fixed concepts, meanings as no more than instrumental constructions or improvisations or gropings (or gradually developing know-how), until we have (equally pragmatized) evidence to the contrary. It turns the tables on all the pieties of standard epistemology. That is undoubtedly what misled Rorty so disastrously: Dewey does not reject epistemology; he merely refuses to countenance its usual circular and self-serving assurances. Rorty is a Cartesian *manqué,* because he believes that a viable metaphysics must rely on privilege and invariance despite the fact that that's impossible!

Dewey's pragmatism is committed to a kind of holism therefore. But it saves itself from vacuity: by nesting *savoir* and *savoir-faire* uncompromisingly in non-cognitive but real encumbrances, and by adhering very strictly to the leanest possible reading of meaning and truth that could be drawn from Peirce's and James's original guesses.

I emphasize Dewey's holism, because it suggests a telling comparison with Quine's well-known but more baffling holism, which is required (as Quine sees matters) if we are to ensure the spare physicalism and extensionalism of the best of analytic philosophy. Quine introduces *ad hoc* a doctrine favoring original "holophrastic sentences"—never properly analyzed, possibly impenetrable to analysis—that nevertheless claims the obvious advantage of possessing realist import, functioning empirically in a quasi-foundational way, and altogether free of "ontic commitment" (in Quine's familiar sense).[26]

1882–1898, vol. 3, ed. Jo Ann Boydston (Carbondale: Southern Illinois University Press, 1969), 144–45.

26. See W. V. Quine, *Pursuit of Truth,* rev. ed. (Cambridge, Mass.: Harvard University Press, 1992), ch. 1.

Although Quine is often said (with some justice) to be a pragmatist, Quine's holophrastic doctrine—which, mind you, cleverly permits him to advance a more moderate "naturalizing" stance than Davidson's (*a fortiori,* than Rorty's)—secures his physicalist and extensionalist invariances without ever having to meet anything like Dewey's pragmatist scruple.[27] I should say that Dewey and Quine were, in effect, vying to define a suitable form of realism free of any charge of idealism.

You see the superiority of Dewey's strategy if you bear in mind that Dewey's originating holism (the "indeterminate situation") is initially cast entirely in non-cognitive terms; whereas Quine's counterpart (originating) holism is outfitted from the start with the strongest possible cognitive advantages, without yet violating the familiar constraints Quine imposes by way of his notion of the "indeterminancy of translation" and the effort of exposing the analytic/synthetic "dogma." But if you concede all that, you cannot fail to see that Davidson's recovery of realism (without risking any epistemology), Putnam's appeal to his *Grenzbegriff,* and Rorty's "ethnocentric solidarity" are all failed vestiges of Cartesian realism that ignore the pragmatist scruple.

The right way to read Dewey, then, is to hold, without compromise, to the pragmatist account of meaning and truth. In a fair sense, the whole of the texts of *Logic* and *Experience and Nature* is occupied with explaining what Dewey intends by his "indeterminate situation." But you cannot read his formula without featuring flux over fixity, know-how over knowledge, adequacy of directed action here and now over correspondentist and neutral truth, and endless instrumentalities over changeless final ends.

Let me offer, in closing, then, two small textual clues to fix the lesson of the entire argument. First, in *Experience and Nature,* Dewey identifies Aristotle as the metonymic bearer of the doctrine he utterly opposes and dismisses without ceremony; in effect, he says, Aristotle "bequeathed to the modern world through Latin Christianity . . . the consequences of taking the universal which is instrumental, as if it were final."[28] I cannot imagine a more succinct indictment of one and an affirmation of the other of the two completely opposed systems of thought I have been tracking: Dewey's and what is now called Cartesianism. But the deeper explanation of Dewey's doctrine (the second clue) is focused most memorably in the following well-known formula:

27. See W. V. Quine, "Epistemology Naturalized," in *Ontological Relativity and Other Essays* (New York: Columbia University Press, 1969).

28. Dewey, *Experience and Nature,* 116.

Inquiry is the controlled or directed transfomation of a indeterminate situation into one that is so determinate in its constituent distinctions and relations as to convert the elements of the original situation into a unified whole.[29]

The decisive lesson is this: in the symbiotized, pre-cognitive, but real situation in which effective cognition first arises, all the "objects" that are marked off as real are provisionally constituted and reconstituted *as* the human agent works deliberately to capture whatever begins to dawn as an acceptable resolution of his impasse. It is the "situation" and *its* "objects" that are transformed, *not* any supposedly independent objects by way of the power of mere thought; Dewey is no idealist. The evolving "situation" is both part of reality and the medium through which the stablest features of what we take the independent world to be are gradually mapped and continually revised.[30] Dewey's thesis is that there is no end to the process, no privileged or total picture of reality, no final or essential *telos* in anything, and no need for same. *Nature,* on Dewey's argument, is whatever answers to that. That's all!

"[K]nowledge of nature, but not nature itself, [he says] 'emanates' from immediate experience": he is paraphrasing and parodying George Santayana's severe criticism of his own doctrine. He also allows the rest of Santayana's well-known objection: "everything remote emanates from something immediate," Santayana offers—meaning by that that "everything immediate emanates from something biological." But for the questionable "aura" of the single term "emanate," Dewey counters, he agrees completely that "the view stated in the last sentence is also mine."[31]

Santayana's criticism of Dewey's naturalism is one of the best-remembered indictments of Dewey's entire *oeuvre,* but it also inadvertently explains the decisive advantage of Dewey's conception of nature. Here is what Santayana says:

This question, which is the crux of the whole system, may be answered, I think, in a single phrase: *The dominance of the foreground.* In nature there is no foreground or background, no here, no now, no moral cathedra, no center so really central as to reduce all other things to mere margins and mere perspectives. A foreground is by definition relative to some chosen point of view, to the station assumed in the midst of nature by some creature tethered by fortune to a particular time and place. If such a foreground becomes dominant in a philosophy naturalism is abandoned.[32]

29. Dewey, *Logic,* 104.
30. See Dewey, *Experience and Nature,* ch. 2, particularly 67–69.
31. Dewey, "Experience, Knowledge and Value," 533–34.
32. Santayana, "Dewey's Naturalistic Metaphysics," 251. The passage cited, which Dewey straightforwardly co-opts, appears in Santayana's text, 258 n. 1.

Dewey's answer I judge to be utterly compelling. First of all, he shows that Santayana is forced to concede *some* "foreground" of his own in order to justify speaking of nature at all: in effect, Santayana concedes the need for *some* "interplay" between ourselves and nature, which term Dewey takes (incorrectly, I would say) to be "synonomous" with his own term "interaction."[33] Second, the implied concession opens the door to subverting every form of the ancient canon or the more recent Cartesianism that pragmatists were bound to oppose from the attenuated vantage of their own Hegelian origins. And, third, Dewey explains the benignly equivocal sense (against Santayana again) in which *he* starts "with experience as the manifestation of interactions of organism and environment" (that is, the post-Kantian pre-cognitive symbiosis termed, *per* James, "experience" as well). So that what comes to be distinguished as real or merely imagined is marked off by "different modes of interaction" (or "experience," within the larger space of what is also called "experience").[34]

Once you realize that Dewey's "indeterminate situation" is a very lean version of the Hegelian critique of both Kant and Descartes, biologized in the pragmatist way, you see the entire fluxive account of nature that Dewey intends. The only conception that's missing in Dewey, as far as I can see, is an up-to-date paraphrase of Hegel's notion of historicity. But I am certain that that too can be restored, now that the pragmatist advantage has been made clear. Dewey was perhaps too sanguine about the equivalence of Santayana's term "interplay" and his own "interaction": for the first is meant to be relational *at* the cognitive level (which is a Cartesian notion), whereas the relationship marked by the second is entirely benign epistemically, since it is cast initially in biological and non-cognitive terms.

What Dewey offers in the way of a disciplined realism is, therefore, more than the equal of John McDowell's fashionable rejection of a relational "interface" between belief and world (which rejection Putnam now endorses in place of his earlier internal realism).[35] The fact is, Dewey provides a detailed (pragmatist) account of what should replace the "interface" (in effect, the Cartesian gambit), whereas McDowell's resolution is never more than abstract and formal and without any epistemic details at all.

Dewey forces the implied contrast on our attention in a number of

33. Dewey, "Experience, Knowledge and Value," 330.

34. Ibid., 331.

35. See John McDowell, *Mind and World* (Cambridge, Mass.: Harvard University Press, 1996); also Putnam, "Sense, Nonsense, and the Senses."

compelling papers that explain why "natures," "kinds," and similar distinctions are rightly cast in terms of the similarity of *pragmatist interventions* rather than in terms of the sameness or similarity of *perceived qualities:*

> No amount of direct inspection and comparison of [the] qualities [of two *browns,* he says] will yield the needed conception or definition [of *brown*]. What is common and constant is not the quality as quality but the logical function assigned it as an evidentiary sign of something else. Instead of being directly given for comparison and abstraction, the commonness in question is the *product* of operations that depend upon a universal or conception being already at command [that is, common operations deliberately fitted to collected instances].[36]

This is as clear a formulation of the pragmatist conception of nature as any I know. I think it can be said to justify, by its originality and power, all of Peirce's and James's more primitive intuitions about meaning and truth. Dewey's principal discovery is this: that if knowledge is originally biologized, it must favor practical know-how over facultative expertise; and if that is so, then all invariances are the artifacts of flux.

36. John Dewey, "What Are Universals?" in *The Later Works,* vol. 11, *1935–1937,* ed. Jo Ann Boydston (Carbondale: Southern Illinois University Press, 1987), 111; see also "Characteristics and Characters: Kinds and Classes," in the same volume.

10 Perspectives on Nature in American Thought

NICHOLAS RESCHER

THE CONCEPTUAL BACKGROUND: NATURE AND ITS CONTRARIES

Understanding our human situation in the world individually as persons and collectively as a species is—either way—a complex project that has many different aspects. Natural philosophy—the project of comprehending how things go in the world about us—is clearly one of them. Traditionally it has been largely focused on the business of *explanation.* But there is also another aspect, that of *orientation,* of relating ourselves to our setting in the world's scheme of things with a view to matters of appreciation and evaluation—the requisites for guidance in matters of thought and action. The development of our conception of nature is an important part of this project.

The *Oxford English Dictionary* defines the relevant sense of *nature* as "The material world, or its collective objects and phenomena, esp. those with which man is most directly in contact; freq. the features and products of the earth itself, as contrasted with those of human civilization."[1] The term "nature" thus has two principal applications, according to whether the natural universe at large or merely our more localized natural environment is taken to be at issue. The former goes back to the Greek idea of *physis* with its cosmic ramifications. The latter, by contrast, has a view to our proximate environs. For present purposes it is the second of these that is at issue—the localized stage-setting of human life here on earth. Nature in this sense encompasses the sort of thing that gets depicted in landscape painting, which is, in fact, a topic that will be the focus of these present deliberations.

One very useful way to clarify a concept is through contrasting it

1. *The Oxford English Dictionary,* 2nd edition (Oxford: Clarendon Press, 1989), s.v. "nature."

with its contraries. Now in this contrastive regard, the concept of nature goes back to the dawn of philosophy in pre-Socratic Greece, where its definitive role was to provide one pole for the contrast between what is so by nature *(physis)* and what is so by human convention *(nomos)*. So what ultimately emerges here is a view of nature based on the dichotomy between works of nature and works of man. This leads to the classical view of the matter based on the perspective of

I. *Artifice-Contrastive Nature:* physical reality as contrasted with human artifice.

From this perspective, as John Herman Randall put it: "Between man, his 'mind' and experience on the one hand, and Nature on the other, there yawned a chasm. . . . Thus human experience was removed from Nature and made [merely] 'subjective.'"[2]

However, once man comes to be seen as himself constituting an integral component of nature, there also arises the prospect of what might be characterized as an enlarged view of nature that *combines* physical reality and human artifice and accordingly regards this endangered nature from a man-made evaluative perspective.[3] What we have in this case is the integrated perspective of a naturalism based on "the refusal to take 'nature' or 'the natural' as a term of distinction [between our own works and the rest of reality]."[4] The upshot is a stance of

II. *"Spiritually" Oriented Nature:* nature from a man-made evaluative perspective.

Within this perspective, there are divisions, based on whether nature is seen in a positive or negative light or neutrally. There is first of all

IIA. *Axiological Naturalism:* physical reality + human artifice (seen in an evaluatively positive perspective).

The concept of nature now undergoes a virtually revolutionary transformation based on the shift from a contrast of extra-human reality with human *productions* to a contrast with the "spiritual" domain of human *aspirations and evaluations.*

A brief comment on the use of "spiritual" here is unavoidable: In

2. John Herman Randall, "The Nature of Naturalism," in *Naturalism and the Human Spirit,* ed. Y. H. Krikorian (New York: Columbia University Press, 1944), 354–82 (see 371).

3. Against this setting there is also the contrast with the super- or preter-natural, which is of no particular concern to us here.

4. Randall, "The Nature of Naturalism," 357.

particular, it needs to be stressed that it is not intended to have a specifically religious bearing, nor yet is it used with ghostly connotations. Rather it looks to those value-laden factors which constitute the judgmental and orientational perspectives of the human intellect. It thus comprises what relates to the human spirit rather than being specifically confined to the divine, and more generally to matters of thoughtful reflection rather than mere observation and to issues of value rather than issues of mundane fact. In sum, the term is now used to enlarge the domain of mundane reality, so as to encompass also the mechanisms of judgment, broadly construed in its relation to matters of meaning and value.

All of this being understood, it should be noted that with the rise of idealism with its revulsion against the eighteenth-century mechanization of the world, nature came to be endowed with a humanly "spiritual" dimension, so to speak. It took on an evaluative, axiological, normative dimension. We can speak in this connection of an Emersonian revolution in the conceptualization of nature. For this expanded view of nature is due in its essentials to Ralph Waldo Emerson, who wrote in his 1836 book *Nature* as follows:

> All that is separate from us [as experiencing, thinking, and evaluating individuals], all of which philosophy [ordinarily] designates as the NOT ME, that is both nature and art, all other men and [even] my own body, must be numbered under this name, NATURE.[5]

As Emerson saw it, value infuses nature because—as he saw it—"nature always bears the colors of the spirit."[6] It is the destiny of man to spiritualize nature, for man "is not designed to be an idle eye before which [physical] nature passes in review, but by his action is enabled to learn the irresistible properties of *moral* nature."[7]

What we have here is a turn to normativity that pivots on the salient perspective of traditional philosophical idealism. Nature, so regarded, is infused by spirit and viewed as a theater of operation where human purposes and values both arise through and find their application in nature's processes and furnishings. The interests of an emergent intelligence in matters of purpose and value are not excluded from—let alone antagonistic to—the realm of nature.

However, for those who are not idealistically inclined—who are skeptical in relation to this spiritual dimension, at it were—this spirit-

5. Emerson, *Collected Works*, vol. 1, 8.
6. Ibid., 9.
7. Arthur C. Giffert, ed., *Young Emerson Speaks* (Boston: McGiffert, 1938), 208.

contrastive conception of nature can also provide a basis for a neutral position in the evaluative sphere. Thus the natural now stands opposed to an extra-natural realm that is regarded as not just supra- but as outright super-natural and on that basis rejected as essentially empty. This yields another perspective of spiritually oriented nature:

IIB. *Modernistic/Scientistic Naturalism:* physical reality + human artifice (seen in an evaluatively neutral perspective).

This concept of nature sees the works of physical nature and of human technical artifice in a value-free perspective, to the exclusion of those spiritual-evaluative factors. Insofar as value is allowed to play any role at all—that is, insofar as we go beyond value nihilism—the only values whose role is acknowledged are those at issue in an avowedly value-neutral science.

Such a scientistic naturalism inclines in effect toward becoming value negating in a way that rejects the entire "spiritual" dimension of evaluative concern as illicitly transcendental or supernatural. It tends to be accompanied by an imperialist tendency to view nature in terms revealed by science at large, with nature viewed in an all-embracing cosmic scheme in which spirit is exiled to the realm of fiction and make-believe.

And, of course, beyond such a neutralism there is also the third negativistic option of spiritually oriented nature:

IIC. *Nihilistic Naturalism:* physical reality + human artifice (seen in an evaluatively negative perspective).

Reality and humanity along with it are now regarded as inherently worthless, contaminated alike by the world's harshness and man's brutality. Though this perspective initially took root in the nihilism of European fin-de-siècle iconoclasts and their camp followers in American *avant garde* circles, such a position came into rapidly increasing prominence in the wake of the cynicism and disillusionment engendered by the First World War and its aftermath.

All the same, however, a far more generous construction of nature is also possible once the spiritual aspect is seen as itself part of the natural domain at large. This would result in the perspective of

III. *Comprehensively Holistic Nature:* physical reality + human artifice + "spiritual" factors.

What we have in this case is an integrated view of human artifice and non-human nature conjoined into a coordinated whole under the aegis of a "spiritual"—that is, value-governed—standpoint. The result is an enlarged view of nature, where extra-human nature, human agency, and the manifold of spiritual factors coexist in a collaborative synthesis to underwrite a worldview that takes a comprehensive, open, and more humanely user-friendly view of the overall domain of the "natural." Nature now serves not as a contrast of sectors within reality, but as a contrast between what is real with what is unreal and merely fictional.

The overall situation as regards the categories in terms of which nature has been viewed is set out in Display 1. Clearly, what is at issue is a complex historical dialectic in which the concepts of nature interact with those of power and value.

This brief survey leads to three distinctive conceptions of nature subject to an increasingly ample construction of what is involved in nature and what counts as being natural, moving from an initial nature/artifice contrast to a final view where not only the material productions of man, but even the larger aspirations encoded in his intellectual productions and spiritual values, are seen as qualifying for a place within the realm of the natural.

Display 1. Summary of Perspectives on Nature

Key: N = nature; P = physical nature; A = human artifice; S = spiritual/evaluative factors

I. *Pre-Emersonian (Artifice-Contrastive Nature)*
—power oriented ($N = P$; P being contrasted with A)
- A. nature > artifice, that is, $N > A$
- B. nature < artifice, that is, $N < A$
  - 1. viewed favorably
  - 2. viewed unfavorably
- C. nature ~ artifice, that is, $N \cong A$

II. *Post-Emersonian ("Spiritually" Oriented Nature)*
—value oriented ($N = P + A$ with $P + A$ being viewed S-perspectivally)
- A. (evaluatively positive)
- B. (evaluatively neutral)
  - 1. scientistically value-neutral
  - 2. totally value-nihilistic
- C. (evaluatively negative)

III. *Holistic (Comprehensively Holistic Nature)*
—a synoptic tripartite amalgam of nature, artifice, and value ($N = P + A + S$)

This categorization of perspectives on nature can serve an instructive descriptive function in relation to the development of American culture. In particular, it can help us understand and categorize various approaches encountered in the history of American art, the history of American thought, and the history of their interrelationship. From the angle of present concern, however, the issue is not one of styles or genres but one of themes—or more specifically subthemes within the general topic of ways of looking at nature. Viewed in this light, what is involved is not a matter so much of temporal *phases* but of repeatable *themes,* so that the aspect of periodization—of phases or stages—enters in only indirectly, in line with the historically varying historical prominence or even predominance of certain themes.

ART HISTORICAL PERSPECTIVES

Let us see how this idea works itself out, profiting by the opportunity to illustrate those tendencies of thought through their manifestations in the history of American landscape art—broadly construed to encompass town-scapes and sea-scapes as well.

Much of the work that needs to be done here can be accomplished in terms of that initial conception of artifice-contrastive dualism. However, four quite different approaches emerge in relation to the *works of man/works of nature* dichotomy, depending on how one regards the power priorities here. Is it the works of man or those of nature that are seen as occupying the driver's seat?—so to speak.

> 1. To begin with: in the setting of the artifice-contrastive dualism of a *works of man/works of nature* dichotomy, one can view nature as the dominant partner and man as a comparatively puny being existing within a preponderantly powerful natural realm that unfolds all about him. The basic relationship is: *nature > artifice.*

This represents an older Western tradition that saw nature as fearful—wild and dangerous. Only with the rise of Romanticism in the late 1700s was nature viewed in the more favorable light. But this perspective came into the New World slowly. Americans long envisioned a sharp contrast between on the one hand puny man and his works, and on the other their setting within vast, virtually overpowering environing nature that dwarfs man and his puny works. As Lord Bryce put it in his classic work on *The American Commonwealth* (1888), Americans in large part "lead a solitary life in the midst of a vast nature."[8] It is helpful to

8. James Bryce, *The American Commonwealth* (London: Macmillian, 1888), *III* civ. 497.

FIGURE 1. *A View of the Mountain Pass Called the Notch of the White Mountains (Crawford Notch)* by Thomas Cole. Courtesy National Gallery of Art, Washington, DC

consider some art-historical illustrations, which are readily found in the work of the Hudson River School of landscapists, whose work is exemplified by the splendid canvas of Thomas Cole presented in Figure 1.

What we have here is a sharply dualistic view of the American natural scene—one that is brilliantly illustrated in the majestic landscapes depicted in the great canvasses of Albert Bierstadt—set-pieces that depict diminutive man in the majestic nature of America as an "untamed continent." We are offered such scenes as the following: a few explorers huddled together for warmth around a fire in a vast valley; a log cabin perched on the slope to a vast mountain; a lost wanderer being beset by wolves and confronting a nature "red in tooth and claw." In these pictures—and many others of the same tendency—man stands in awe and perhaps even fear before the vast powers of nature. He confronts the challenges that face a weak but determined and ambitious creature maintaining a precarious existence within a vast and potentially hostile natural environment.

This view of things found an earlier philosophical expression in the Jeffersonian spirit that launched Lewis and Clark and the "Corps of Discovery" forth in their exploration of the Pacific Northwest. And it has later resonances in Theodore Roosevelt's robust and constructive Americanism that emphasized the development of personal character in a contest with the primordial powers of nature.

However, under the aegis of technology, man ultimately gained the upper hand in this struggle. Accordingly—

> 2. A variant, inverted version of the artifice-contrastive dualism is also possible—one in which a role reversal takes place, with man dominant over nature. The basic relationship here is: *artifice* > *nature*.

But two very different perspectives are now available regarding this artifice-contrastive nature, depending on whether we are to view the dominance of artifice in the positive light of technological triumphalism or the negative light of technological endangerment. Again it is instructive to consider an art-historical illustration, for example such positive vistas as Everett Warner's Pittsburgh winter scene of Figure 2 or the seascapes of Winslow Homer. Here human artifice has clearly achieved a secure mastery over nature (epitomized in the former case by dominant position of St. Paul's Cathedral).

Here artifice dominates a nature that, like it or not, stands tamed and domesticated by the impetus of human physical and intellectual powers. The ideology at issue came to active expression in the last third of the nineteenth century in the active proliferation of city parks that produced a nature tamed and manicured for the enrichment of urban life across the cities of the United States. On the artistic side, we encounter here a version of the aesthetic impressionism that endows its view of nature with the overt coloration of human response.

A philosophical manifestation of this *artifice* > *nature* perspective comes to view on its positive side in the proto-pragmatism of the enormously popular Herbert Spencer, who was a great favorite among the industrial tycoons of his day. However, the ideology of civic-mindedness and good citizenship that reflected such tendencies of thought was more alive in the wider community than among philosophers in specific, and was in these times heard more from lecture platforms than in philosophical classrooms.

In due course, man's conquest of nature became increasingly triumphant. Railway tracks and telegraph wires spanned the continent; the Panama Canal linked the oceans. Could this process perhaps be carried too far? Increasingly, the power of man over nature can also be viewed in negative terms. The dominance of human artifice (including science and technology) comes to be viewed as constituting a threat to nature. Nature is now seen as not just tamed and domesticated by human artifice but as overwhelmed and endangered by it. Man and his

FIGURE 2. *Panther Hollow* by Everett Warner. Courtesy Westmoreland Museum of American Art, Greensburg, PA

works are taken to dominate and even negate the natural environment. Technological triumphalism is absurd because in the contest between human artifice and nature, artifice comes out on top in a way that is ultimately not really beneficial to human interests. One can, in short, regard the matter in the light of the ideological orientation nowadays commonly characterized as "green."

Again, art-historical illustrations are easy to come by. There is, for example, a plethora of painting of foundries amidst a stygian gloom, but the point is also clear in such less gloomy pictures as Figure 3, with its distressing vista of man's impact upon the beautiful Hudson.

Such a negative perspective is represented on the philosophical side by Thoreau, homeopathy, Christian Science, and a variety of other technology-aversive and science-distrusting tendencies. Here technology is viewed as an instrument for the subjugation of humans, science is

FIGURE 3. *Storm King on the Hudson* by Samuel Colman. Courtesy Smithsonian American Art Museum of Art, Washington, DC

seen as an unfriendly critic that views man as no more than a somewhat more developed ape, and industrial modernism is seen as a corrosive force that pollutes and degrades an inherently pristine nature.

In that natural dialectic of things, the view elicits sympathy for poor theoretical nature. Earlier on, when nature had been seen as dangerous, the salient task was to subdue, tame, and domesticate it. But once this task has been achieved, the relentless mark of individual progress changed matters radically. Now it becomes a matter of safeguarding, maintaining, and preserving. Nature is now not a threat but a treasure.

There thus emerges the "Endangered Nature" school of thought that views human artifice as the corrupter of nature's attractions. A new sensibility arises—one that sentimentalizes nature and endows it with a moral weight that engenders a responsibility on our part for its protection and preservation: a line of thought that engenders eco-philosophy and an ethic of conservation. The neo-animistic orientation of some sectors of environmentalism affords a vivid latter-day illustration. Thus the emergence of nonstandard ethics concerned not only for the welfare of humans but also for the putative rights of animals and even of plants and trees and natural terrains is another aspect of this tendency of thought.

3. However, there is also yet another way of construing artifice-contrastive dualism: For man and nature can also be regarded as coordinated co-equals. A state of peaceful coexistence is reached where the two parties, artifice and nature, coexist in fruitful symbiosis. The basic relationship now takes the form: *artifice ~ nature*. Man comes to terms of peaceful coexistence with nature, and nature for her part takes on a "user-friendly" aspect.

This approach confronts us with a view of man-nature coordination, where both factors exist in connected interlinkage. In architecture, this is captured in the "Prairie Style" of Frank Lloyd Wright and the ideology he characterized as "usonian." In landscape painting, we encounter numerous instances such as Figure 4, George Inness's panorama of the Lackawanna Valley where the works of industrial production and the fields of agriculture form a seamless whole with nature's surrounding hills and forests. Man and nature have now achieved a position of a harmonious equilibrium. They have come to terms of peaceful coexistence with one another.

As regards philosophy, what we have here is a view of man-nature cooperation that envisions a unification of nature and artifice in a reciprocally fruitful and constructive symbiosis. Such a position was clearly manifest in the cosmic philosophy of John Fiske and in some of the motivating tendencies of early pragmatism. For as children of the industrial revolution, early American proto-pragmatists did not want to hear about impotence and limits, let alone conflict. They took an essentially Darwinian approach that saw man and his works as an integral part of nature. Their motto was not "Man against nature" but "Man in nature." What those proto-pragmatists wanted was a naturalism that assigned to Homo sapiens his proper and appropriate part as an effective cog within the vast mechanism of the world's natural processes. Instead of an antagonistic opposition between the works of man and the works of nature, they sought to reject bifurcation and dualism in favor of the seamless whole of a man-encompassing nature. Their watchword was an inclusive *naturalism* of the sort that envisioned a comprehensively complex man-plus-nature coordination.

With the emergence of developmental geology and evolutionary biology, nature became the theater of operations of tendencies of a fundamentally progressive and innovative character. Thinkers like Herbert Spencer saw nature as a power that ongoingly brought higher forms of being to realization. Nature, in sum, was a progressive agency. Evolution—cosmic, geological, and biological—forged an important new link between nature and modernity through its linkage with the themes

FIGURE 4. *The Lackawanna Valley* by George Inness. Courtesy National Gallery of Art, Washington, DC

between success and progress. This became one of the central themes of American pragmatism.

To this point we have developed our descriptive perspective in terms of a contrast between the works of man and the works of nature, by asking the power-oriented question: Who is to be seen as being the top dog, nature or man? But let us now shift our angle of vision from the question of *power* to that of *value* and take into view the spirit-contrastive nature characterized above. We turn, accordingly, to the realm of spiritual features in the above-indicated sense of a focus on matters of meaning and worth.

There are several possibilities here, depending on which sort of evaluative perspective one has upon nature.

4. Clearly one prospect here is a value-pervaded view of nature, with value seen as a guiding principle and some mind-imposed evaluative perspective taken to provide a determinant factor in the organization of nature itself.

On the artistic side we find examples of this standpoint in the art of symbolic idealization as well as in some of the neo-Romanticism of the late nineteenth century, typified by the splendidly imaginative vista of Figure 5 and the innumerable birds and mammals of John James Audubon. In all such works, the presentation of nature becomes strikingly and explicitly subject to some explicitly mind-imposed orienting principle of positive tendency. Reality is subordinated to an idealized image. The human face of a specifically evaluative orientation comes to the fore here.

The philosophical expression of this sort of approach is represented by idealism. In particular, Emerson's nature-idealism captures this tendency of thought. With Emerson we do not just observe nature. Rather someone who authentically experiences nature is actively engaged in applying an evaluative perspective of his own, and indeed the very purpose of nature is to manifest the Universal Spirit that lies at the root of its apprehension: "The facts in natural history, taken by themselves, have no value, but are barren, like a single sex. But marry it to human history and it is full of life."[9] Spirit (in this Emersonian sense) unites and organizes nature and renders it apprehensible. The widespread influence of Alexander von Humboldt can also be seen as being at work here.

But there is also another, very different way of implementing the spirit-contrastive view of nature. The preceding value perspective is positive. But there are two other alternatives here: namely neutrality and negativity. Value neutrality leads to a view—let us call it *scientistic* or *modernistic*—that the natural realm (now broadly construed to encompass the works of man and nature alike) is evaluatively neutral or self-sufficient.

5. What we have here is a value naturalism that subordinates the realm of value to what can be encompassed in science. Such a position is at once spirit-contrastive and supernaturalism-rejective. In the end it amounts to scientism, for it looks to science itself as the ultimate basis of value. The fundamental relationship is one of imposing a value perspective on the analogy of physical reality and human artifice *(nature + artifice) → value.* This results in a value-minimalism: There is no need for a supra-natural basis of value: scientistic plus intellectualist values will do. Science and technology can replace the traditional value scheme. The result is a strictly "rationalized" view of nature that sees the scientific view of nature as comprehensive and self-contained and

9. Emerson, *Collected Works,* vol. 1, 19.

FIGURE 5. *Cattleya Orchid and Three Brazilian Hummingbirds* by Martin John Heade. Courtesy National Gallery of Art, Washington, DC

rejects what Dewey called *extra-naturalism* as something one better than super-naturalism and superstition.

With the artwork that exhibits this tendency of thought one often cannot tell whether one is looking at a work of artistic imagination or an illustration from a textbook of science or technology. Radical examples of this are present in architecture (for example in work inspired by the Bauhaus, such as that of Mies van der Rohe) or in works of photographic iconoclasm (such as those of Man Ray). What we have here is a minimalism that divorces art from any effective involvement with the science-transcending values that function in everyday life. "Decorative" is now a term of derogation.

Such a position finds strong resonance in the middle period of American pragmatism, especially in the thought of John Dewey—and also in such somewhat more eccentric thinkers as George Santayana. It rejects the older dichotomies between nature and spirit and between science and values, and instead seeks to relocate values within a scientific perspective. On this basis, it is marked by a minimalism on the side of those "spiritual" values. The austere values of economics are now dominant: symmetry, uniformity, systematicity. The range of traditional humanistic values (comfort, domesticity, charm, etc.) is deliberately put aside.

Carried to its logical extreme, this "modernistic" tendency of thought led to an explicit rejection of any "meaning" or "significance" beyond the abstract theoretical features of material reality. Such an evaluatively bland perspective opened the way to yet another ideological position, namely the modernist view of a value-free science that confronts us with a cosmos coldly indifferent to the wishes, needs, and aspirations of an obscure and puny creature clinging to a precarious existence on a fourth-rate planet. We arrive here at a modernist "scientism" that sees the scientific understanding of nature as a value-free replacement for a more idealistic view of things. The tendency at issue here was a commonplace in the philosophy of the inter-war years of the first half of the twentieth century. It was pervasively recurrent in a wide spectrum of philosophical approaches ranging from logical positivism to such ideologies as scientific socialism and various versions of dialectical materialism.

This tendency of thought ultimately also became a commonplace of American philosophical naturalism. Thus in his summarizing discussion on "The Nature of Naturalism" (in the classic Krikorian anthology on this topic) John Herman Randall wrote:

> Naturalism finds itself in thoroughgoing opposition to all forms of thought, which assert the existence of a supernatural or transcendental Realism of Being and make knowledge of that realm of fundamental importance to human living. There is no "realm" to which the [scientific] methods for dealing with Nature cannot be extended. This insistence on the universal and unrestricted application of "scientific method" is a theme pervading every one of the essays.[10]

However, there yet remains the third possibility of value negativism. By going down this road we arrive at an evaluatively negativistic or nihilistic position that sees the world as essentially meaningless. We are led to envision a vast but yet coldly indifferent natural universe encompassing a puny, shallow, and contemptible humanity. The resultant position is roughly as follows:

10. Randall, "The Nature of Naturalism," 358.

6. It is not just that value should be exiled from our view of nature but that value is to be dismissed period. Value in the larger sense of the term represents an illusion: reality excludes/negates value. The aficionados of traditional values are seen as hypocrites, as self-deluded, or both. What is in order is a negativism—or perhaps even nihilism—toward traditional values. The basic relationship is: *(nature + artifice) → no value.*

In art we see this theme reflected in works that view man and the stage-setting of his existence in a bleak light and also manifest an in-your-face negativism toward nature itself. The bleak landscape of Figure 6 presents one of the less drastic illustrations of such a gloomy perspective.

On the philosophical side, this sort of value negativity prepared the ground for a whole spectrum of ideological tendencies that envisioned a world in which spiritual values have no role outside the pages of the history of delusion. Its inclination is to see the human condition in a cold and essentially indifferent light. This tendency of thought manifested itself in some sectors of psychoanalysis as well as in logical positivism.

As this approach to art evolved, the name of the game became the pursuit of shock-value. The artist is called upon to manifest his seriousness by mocking traditional human values. As theorists of this tendency saw it, the guiding motto is *épater les bourgeois.* And its only true appreciators are an elite whose sophistication leads them beyond the demand of the unenlightened masses for beauty, meaning, and the other classical values of aesthetic appreciation.

Fortunately, however, a counter-revolution arose in due course through the natural dialectic of tendency and counter-tendency. This now engendered the resurgence of concern for spiritual and humane values. Once more such normative concerns became a significant tendency in American thought.

7. Reality is a meaningful whole under the aegis of spiritual values. Nature is a realm that is user-friendly to man as a home that has a place of human values: *nature + artifice + value.*

We have here what is a virtually Hegelian synthesis of earlier tendencies. Idealism involved a spiritualization of nature. Evolutionism envisioned a naturalization of man and his works. In a way the two reinforced one another, coming to agreement as it were, in conspiring to break down any clear-cut man/nature divide.

This phenomenon has some clearly observable manifestations on the artistic side. It issues in a new aesthetic sensitivity—one in which the

FIGURE 6. *Exiles* by Patrick Hennessy. Courtesy Hugh Lane Municipal Gallery of Modern Art, Dublin

works of man and nature are seen as such that neither is subordinated to the other but the two are coordinated—not by way of a utilitarian exploitation but by way of a complementarity of appreciation. This is manifested in the emergence of what might be called a "viewer-friendly" aesthetic that integrates the work of man and nature in a symbolic way that betokens a friendly and often even humorous approach. Vivid illustrations are afforded by the works of contemporary regional genre painters (see Figure 7) as well as by the proliferating fantasies of landscape-transforming sculptures and illustrations. (See Figures 8–9.)

The hallmarks of this thematic perspective are visible in works of art that are:

- not afraid to portray nature as appealing or even beautiful
- prepared to use artifice to enhance the appreciation of nature (and the reverse)
- prepared to use humor in a constructive or at least harmlessly playful way
- willing to function in the service of an enhanced quality of life, and not ashamed of playing a decorative role.

Within this orbit of thought, values are once more seen as playing an organically integrated part within the world's natural scheme of things—with "value" regarded not as a wholly artificial mere human contrivance, but as a positive factor or force encoded in the very fabric of nature. Such an enlarged humanistic perspective underwrites a point of view with a wide-ranging cultural impact, from which philosophy itself is emphatically not excluded. The recent flourishing of theoretical ethics and the rise of applied ethics are a part of this phenomenon. And so is the emergence of a greater respect for religion (as marked by the renaissance of philosophy of religion). But more of this anon.

What needs to be emphasized at this point is that American thought—like American art and American life in general—is marked by a complexity, variety, and fertility grounded in a creative energy of vast proportions. And on all sides alike this creative development manifests an ongoing negotiation both with nature itself and with the concept of nature in an endeavor to create a congenial home where people of pluralistically diversified interests and thought-orientations can coexist in fruitful and mutually profitable interaction. But let us look a bit more closely at the philosophical ramifications.

FIGURE 7. *Rooftop Image, January 2000* by Margaret Petterson. Courtesy The Margaret Petterson Gallery, Charleston, SC

PHILOSOPHICAL RAMIFICATIONS

American thought in the twentieth century witnessed an ongoing development and enlargement of a factor that is absolutely central in the development of recent American philosophizing—the role of *experience.* Such philosophizing has throughout the recent period been substantially empiricistic in the sense that human experience has been front and center in its deliberations. But there is an ongoing enhancement of experience, one that moves from the *cognitive* experience of the critical realists to encompass additionally first the *affective* experience of the pragmatists (and especially Dewey) and ultimately also the "spiritual" or religious experience that have come to figure more

FIGURE 8. *Spoonbridge and Cherry* by Claes Oldenburg. Courtesy Walker Art Center, Minneapolis, MN

FIGURE 9. *Trace* by Nancy Stephenson Graves. © Nancy Graves Foundation/ Licensed by VAGA, New York, NY

prominently in the contemporary scene. In this final part of the discussion I should like to dwell on this aspect of the matter more closely.[11]

11. I want to emphasize this aspect of the matter especially because John Herman Randall's otherwise excellent survey of naturalism (already cited above) resolutely calls a halt at the midpoint of this evolution. "Naturalism must combine the wisdom of Plato with the sanity of Aristotle. Is there any other enterprise in our vexed world today (1944) where this combination has been successful since in the practice of scientific inquiry? Assuredly the naturalists are right: our world is perishing for want of faith. The faith we need, the faith that alone permits salvation, is the faith of [scientific] intelligence" (382). This stirring paean to science was penned just before the atomic bombs exploded over Hiroshima and Nagasaki.

One particularly significant development in relation to American views regarding nature relates to an ongoing rapprochement between science and religion. To be sure, what is at issue here is not just a return to the past—to the old-style Anglican "natural religion" that looks to various aspects of nature as providing "evidences" or "traces" of the operation of a creator. Instead, what is emerging is a doctrinal stance that settles for a consonance or harmony between naturalism and theism and involves a holism that unites scientific knowledge and human concerns at large. The perspective at issue seeks to match the intelligence which inquires into the workings of nature with the conceptually sophisticated *modus operandi* manifested in nature's laws themselves. What it thus envisions is not a God of the gaps, but a view of divine efficacy and worldly process that provides for a seamless fusion between intelligent design of the object of inquiry and intelligent procedure on the part of its investigators.

I do not at this juncture have the time—nor on this occasion the mandate—to develop this theme at length. Suffice it for the moment merely to cite such obvious illustrations as big bang cosmogony, the dematerialization of matter in quantum physics, the role of anthropic theory in cosmic evolution, and the rise of intelligent design theory in evolutionary biology. While it would doubtless be stretching matters to see such developments as furnishing probative *evidence* for the existence of God, it is nevertheless clear that each is smoothly harmonious with and entirely congenial to a religious outlook. And the tendency of such innovations is to reject theology-excluding scientism that exiles God from nature and negates theism, affording instead the science of a nature that is not hostile toward aesthetic, ethical, and even religious concerns.

On this basis, what seems to be in process of realization—and what would certainly deserve the sympathy and support of committed theists—is a unitized worldview that envisions an intelligent design of nature itself in a way that invites a humanistically positive vision of reality within which meaningfulness, "spiritual" values, and even theistic perspectives play a formative role in the construction of a holistic, unified, and synoptic worldview.

And science apart, there are—happily—also various other signs that American thought is in the process of embracing the challenge of a great sea-change toward a holism that sees nature as a complex whole in which physical reality, artifice, and evaluative judgment all function in a coordinated way to afford us the opportunity of creating a congenial setting for human habitation. In sum, what we have here is the emergence of a view of nature that has made its peace with the manifold of human values.

In this regard, one bright hope for holism in American philosophy lies in the renovation of pragmatism. Not, to be sure, the currently all-too-prominent anti-cognitivist pragmatism of the James-Rorty tradition, nor yet the scientistic pragmatism of the Dewey tradition, but a more open-minded pragmatism operative of the sort at work in the thought of such realistic pragmatists as Peirce and even C. I. Lewis. It is, in my view, something of a tragedy that current American neo-pragmatism has been striving to turn into the wishy-washy normlessness maintained by Richard Rorty and his acolytes, a doctrine designed to provide a simple and sensible way of validating norms—namely, through their capacity to facilitate efficacy in realizing the aims of a purposive enterprise that is itself legitimate in meeting authentic human needs.

Such a traditionalistic and realistic pragmatism is—rather fortunately—marked not by a negativism toward norms and standards but by wide-ranging sympathies that make for an openness toward a variety of intellectual cultures. There is nothing crassly materialistic or cognitively nihilistic about such a pragmatism. Rather, it begins with the Peircean precept: "Never to bar the road of inquiry to the pursuit of further truth" but duly extends it with the precept "Never to bar the road of evaluation to the appreciation of life-affirming values." After all, it is—or should be—clear that there is no conflict between pragmatism and values. For pragmatism, in its root conception, centers on the idea of praxis in the realization of valid aims and goals. Its standard is applicative success in the service of valid ends. And it is exactly here that values play an essential role. At the center of such an axiologically oriented pragmatism there lies a generous, open view of the human condition driven by an impetus toward the enhancement of positive aspiration and values.

Such a value-oriented pragmatism has another aspect as well. Perhaps the greatest mistake in developing a pragmatic position would be that of practicalistic narrowness and exclusivity—of taking one particular purposive realm to be totally sufficient and all-controlling. For every range of purpose carries its own correlative natural teleology in its wake, each of which engenders its own department of pragmatism—its own dimension of purposive efficacy. What we have here is a praxis-concerned pragmatism whose concern is not just for the *standard of living* but for the *quality of life,* a pragmatism geared to a complex manifold of human desiderata that has a broad construction of human values encompassing not only the materialistic and the spiritual, but also the workaday and the playful.

To be sure, this holistic tendency of thought is perhaps still more prominent in other sectors of the wider society than in professional philosophy. In the philosophy-of-science community, for example, there yet largely prevails the reductive perspective of an exaggerated dedication to scientism, as attested by dedication to artificial intelligence, computer models of mind, and the like. And so, while new reconciling tendencies are, as we have seen, astir in the realms of art and even science, philosophers are sometimes among the last to get the word. But just here is the point where, as I see it, pragmatism's revolt against dualism is being—and deserves to be—carried further and implemented more vigorously. For just as the American pragmatists of the past rejected the dualism of a man/nature divide so we, their successors, should follow with enthusiasm the Emersonian rejection of a nature/value dichotomy. What is needed—and what seems in fact to be in the process of emerging—is a holistic pragmatism geared to efficacy in the realization of appropriate objectives across the whole range of human concern, including those of the domain here characterized as "spiritual."

Such an enlightened pragmatism that looks to the whole spectrum of human experience is predicated on taking a more generous and accepting stance that does not regard nature just as a physically viable home for man as an embodied being, but also as a spiritually viable home for man as a mind-endowed being concerned for intellectual attunement to the world-context of his existence. Nature is thus viewed as providing a user-friendly setting for intelligent beings with regard not only to the process but also to the product of their intellectual operations. And the naturalism that is now at issue envisions a world-picture in which human values and interests constitute a significant force that is able to function in a harmonious and fruitful collaborative symbiosis with the other realities of the human condition.

Contributors

Russell B. Goodman serves as Professor and Chair of the Philosophy Department at the University of New Mexico. He is the author of *American Philosophy and the Romantic Tradition* (1990), *Pragmatism: A Contemporary Reader* (1995), and *Wittgenstein and William James* (2002).

John Clendenning is Professor Emeritus at California State University, Northridge, where he served as Professor of English. He is the author of *The Life and Thought of Josiah Royce* (revised and enlarged edition, 1999) and *The Letters of Josiah Royce* (1970).

Karl-Otto Apel was designated Professor Emeritus after serving as Full Professor for Philosophy at the University of Frankfurt am Main. His books include *The Response of Discourse Ethics to the Moral Challenge of the Human Situation As Such and Especially Today* (2001), *Understanding and Explanation* (1984), and *Charles S. Peirce: From Pragmatism to Pragmaticism* (1981).

Jean De Groot is Associate Dean and Associate Professor in the School of Philosophy at The Catholic University of America, located in Washington, D.C. She is the author of *Aristotle and Philoponus on Light* (1991) and articles on Aristotle's philosophy of nature.

Stefano Poggi returned as Fellow of the Alexander von Humboldt Stiftung at the University of Heidelberg and Konstanz after recently serving as Chair of the Philosophy Department at the University of Florence. He is editor (with Maurzio Bossi) of *Romanticism in Science: Science in Europe, 1790–1840* (1994).

Vincent Colapietro is Professor of Philosophy at The Pennsylvania State University (University Park Campus). He is the author of *Peirce's Approach to the Self: A Semiotic Perspective on Human Subjectivity* (1989) and the editor of *Peirce's Philosophical Perspectives* (1996).

Harvey C. Mansfield is the William R. Kenan, Jr. Professor of Government at Harvard University. His books include *A Student's Guide to Polit-*

ical Philosophy (2001), *Alexis de Tocqueville, Democracy in America,* a new translation with introduction (2000, with Delba Winthrop), and *America's Constitutional Soul* (1991).

Robert P. George is the McCormick Professor of Jurisprudence at Princeton University, where he also serves as Professor of Politics and Director of the James Madison Program in American Ideals and Institutions. He is the author of *In Defense of Natural Law* (1999) and the editor of *Natural Law and Public Reason* (2000, with C. Wolfe).

Joseph Margolis is Professor of Philosophy at Temple University in Philadelphia, Pennsylvania. His books include *Reinventing Pragmatism: American Philosophy at the End of the Twentieth Century* (2002), *Flux of History and the Flux of Science* (1993), *Science without Unity* (1987), and *Pragmatism without Foundations* (1986).

Nicholas Rescher is University Professor of Philosophy at the University of Pittsburgh, where he also served for many years as Director of the Center for Philosophy of Science. His books include *Nature and Understanding* (2000), *American Philosophy Today, and Other Philosophical Studies* (1994), *The Limits of Science* (1984), and *Scientific Progress* (1978).

Bibliography

Anderson, Douglas R. "American Loss in Cavell's Emerson." *Transactions of the Charles S. Peirce Society* 29, no. 1 (Winter 1993): 69–89.

———. *Strands of System: The Philosophy of Charles Peirce.* West Lafayette, Ind.: Purdue University Press, 1995.

———. "Three Appeals in Peirce's Neglected Argument." *Transactions of the Charles S. Peirce Society* 26 (1990): 349–62.

Apel, Karl-Otto. *Auseinandersetzungen in Erprobung des transzendental-pragmatischen Ansatzes.* Frankfurt: Suhrkamp, 1998.

———. "C. S. Peirce and Post-Tarskian Truth." In *The Relevance of Charles Peirce,* ed. E. Freeman, 189–223. La Salle, Ill.: Monist Library of Philosophy, 1983.

———. *Charles S. Peirce: From Pragmatism to Pragmaticism.* Trans. John M. Krois. Amherst: University of Massachusetts Press, 1981. Reprint, Atlantic Highlands, N.J.: Humanities Press, 1995.

———. *Collected Essays.* New Jersey: Humanities Press, 1996.

———. *Der Denkweg von Charles Peirce.* Frankfurt: Suhrkamp, 1975. Trans. John M. Krois, *Charles S. Peirce: From Pragmatism to Pragmaticism.* Amherst: University of Massachusetts Press, 1981; reprint, New Jersey: Humanities Press, 1995.

———. "Einführung." In Charles Peirce, *Schriften* I, ed. K-O. Apel. Frankfurt: Suhrkamp, 1976.

———. "Husserl, Tarski oder Peirce?" In *I forste, andre, og tredje person: festskrift til Audun Øfsti,* ed. Solveig Bøe, Bengt Molander, and Brit Strandhagen, 3–94. Trondheim: Norges teknisk-naturvitenskapelige universitet, 1999.

———. "Das Problem der phänomenologischen Evidenz im Lichte einer transzendentalen Semiotik." In *Die Krise der Phänomenologie und die Pragmatik des Wissenschaftsfortschritts,* ed. M. Benedikt and R. Burger, 78–99. Vienna: Öesterreichische Staatsdruckerei, 1986. Trans. "The Problem of Philosophical Foundations in Light of a Transcendental Pragmatics of Language," in *After Philosophy: End or Transformation?* ed. K. Baynes, J. Bohman, and T. McCarthy, 250–90. Cambridge, Mass.: MIT Press, 1987.

———. "Pragmatism as Sense-Critical Realism Based on a Regulative Idea of Truth: In Defence of a Peircean Theory of Reality and Truth." *Transactions of the Charles S. Peirce Society* 37 (2001): 443–74.

———. *Selected Essays.* Ed. Eduardo Mendietta. 2 vols. Atlantic Highlands, N.J.: Humanities Press, 1994, 1996.

———. "Transcendental Semiotics and Hypothetical Metaphysics of Evolution: A Peircean or quasi-Peircean Answer to a Recurrent Problem of Post-Kantian Philosophy." In *Peirce and Contemporary Thought,* ed. K. L. Ketner, 366–97. New York: Fordham University Press, 1995.

———. *Transformation der Philosophie.* Frankfurt: Suhrkamp, 1973, vol. 2, 157–77. Selected essays translated by Glyn Adey and David Frisby. *Towards a Transformation of Philosophy.* London: Routledge and Kegan Paul, 1980; reprint, Milwaukee: Marquette University Press, 1998.

———. "What Is Philosophy? The Philosophical Point of View after the End of Dogmatic Metaphysics." In *What Is Philosophy?* ed. S. Heidt and C. P. Ragland. New Haven: Yale University Press, 2001.

Ash, Mitchell. "Wilhelm Wundt and Oswald Külpe on the Institutional Status of Psychology." In *Wundt Studies,* ed. W. G. Bringmann and R. D. Tweney. Toronto: Hogrefe, 1980.

Ash, Mitchell, and W. Woodward, eds. *The Problematic Science: Psychology in Nineteenth Century Thought.* New York: Praeger, 1982.

Ashley, Benedict. "Does Natural Science Attain Nature or Only the Phenomena?" In *The Philosophy of Physics,* ed. Vincent E. Smith, 63–82. Jamaica, N.Y.: St. John's University Press, 1961.

Auxier, Randall E., ed. *Critical Responses to Josiah Royce.* 2 vols. Bristol, UK: Thoemmes Press, 2000.

Ayer, A. J. "What Is a Law of Nature?" *Revue Internationale de Philosophie* 36 (1956): 144–65.

Baldwin, James Mark. *Social and Ethical Interpretations in Mental Development: A Study in Social Psychology.* New York: Macmillan, 1897.

Bird, G. *William James.* London: Routledge and Kegan Paul, 1986.

Bjork, D. W. *The Compromised Scientist: William James and the Development of American Psychology.* New York: Columbia University Press, 1983.

———. *The Philosophical Psychology of William James.* Ed. M. H. De Armey and S. Skousgaard. Washington, D.C.: Center for Advanced Research in Phenomenology, 1986.

———. *Reflections on the Principles of Psychology: William James after a Century.* Ed. M. G. Johnson and T. B. Henley. Hillsdale, N.J.: L. Erlbaum, 1990.

Bloor, David. *Knowledge and Social Imagery.* 2nd ed. Chicago: University of Chicago Press, 1991.

Boring, E. G. *A History of Experimental Psychology.* 2nd ed. New York: Appleton-Century-Crofts, 1957.

———. *Sensation and Perception in the History of Experimental Psychology.* New York: Appleton, 1942.

Braithwaite, R. B. *Scientific Explanation: A Study of the Function of Theory, Probability and Law in Science.* Cambridge: Cambridge University Press, 1953.

Brentano, Franz. *Psychologie vom empirischen Standpunkt.* Leipzig: Duncker and Humblot, 1874.

Brown, H. *William James on Radical Empiricism and Religion.* Toronto: University of Toronto Press, 2000.

Brozek, J., and H. Gundlach, eds. *G. T. Fechner and Psychology.* Passau: Passavia Universitätsverlag, 1988.

Bryce, Lord James. *The American Commonwealth.* London: Macmillian, 1883.

Buell, Lawrence. *The Environmental Imagination: Thoreau, Nature Writing and the Foundation of American Culture.* Cambridge, Mass.: Belknap Press of Harvard University Press, 1995.

Cameron, Sharon. *Writing Nature.* New York: Oxford University Press, 1985.

Carnap, Rudolph. *Meaning and Necessity.* 2nd ed. Chicago: University of Chicago Press, 1956.

Cavell, Stanley. *Conditions Handsome and Unhandsome: The Constitution of Emersonian Perfectionism.* Chicago: University of Chicago Press, 1990.

———. *In Quest of the Ordinary: Lines of Skepticism and Romanticism.* Chicago: University of Chicago Press, 1988.

———. *Senses of Walden.* New York: Viking, 1972.

———. "Thinking of Emerson." In *The Senses of Walden: An Expanded Edition.* San Francisco: North Point Press, 1981.

Caws, Peter, ed. *Two Centuries of Philosophy in America.* Oxford: Blackwell, 1980.

Clendenning, John. *The Life and Thought of Josiah Royce.* Nashville, Tenn.: Vanderbilt University Press. 1999.

Colapietro, Vincent. "Entangling Alliances and Critical Traditions: Reclaiming the Possibilities of Critique." *Journal of Speculative Philosophy* 12 n.s., no. 2 (1998): 114–33.

———. "Peirce the Contrite Fallibilist, Convinced Pragmaticist, and Critical Commonsensist." *Semiotica* 111-1/2 (1996): 75–101.

———. "Tradition: First Steps Toward a Pragmaticistic Clarification." In *Philosophy in Experience: American Philosophy in Transition,* ed. Richard E. Hart and Douglas R. Anderson, 14–45. New York: Fordham University Press, 1997.

Samuel Taylor Coleridge. "Dejection: An Ode." In *The Portable Coleridge,* ed. I. A. Richards, 170. New York: Penguin, 1978.

Comte, Auguste. *Cours de philosophie positive.* 6 vols. Paris: Bachelier, 1830–42.

———. *The Positive Philosophy of Auguste Comte, freely translated and condensed.* Trans. Harriet Martineau. London: J. Chapman, 1853.

Conklin, Paul K. *Puritans and Pragmatists: Eight Eminent American Thinkers.* Bloomington: Indiana University Press, 1976.

Croce, Paul Jerome. *Science and Religion in the Era of William James: Eclipse of Certainty, 1820–1880.* Chapel Hill: University of North Carolina Press, 1995.

Cropsey, Joseph. *Polity and Economy: An Interpretation of the Principles of Adam Smith.* The Hague: Martinus Nijhoff, 1957.

Cross, Whitney R. *The Burned-Over District: The Social and Intellectual History of Enthusiastic Religion in Western New York, 1800–1850.* Ithaca, N.Y.: Cornell University Press, 1950.

Cunningham, A., and N. Jardine, eds. *Romanticism and the Sciences.* Cambridge: Cambridge University Press, 1990.

Davidson, Donald. "Afterthoughts, 1987." Appended to the reprint of "A Coherence Theory of Truth and Knowledge." In *Reading Rorty,* ed. Alan R. Malachowski. Oxford: Blackwell, 1990.

———. "On the Very Idea of a Conceptual Scheme." *Proceedings and Addresses of the American Philosophical Association* 47 (1973–74): 5–20.

———. "The Structure and Content of Truth." *Journal of Philosophy* 87 (1990): 279–328.

De Koninck, Charles. *The Hollow Universe.* London: Oxford University Press, 1960.

Devitt, Michael. *Realism and Truth.* 2nd ed. Princeton: Princeton University Press, 1991.

Dewey, John. *The Early Works, 1882–1898.* Ed. Jo Ann Boydston. 5 vols. Carbondale: Southern Illinois University Press, 1967–72.

———. *The Middle Works, 1899–1924.* Ed. Jo Ann Boydston. 15 vols. Carbondale: Southern Illinois University Press, 1976–83.

———. *The Later Works, 1925–1953*. Ed. Jo Ann Boydston. 17 vols. Carbondale: Southern Illinois University Press, 1988–91.
———. *Experience and Nature*. Chicago: Open Court, 1925.
———. *Experience and Nature*. 2nd ed. New York: Dover, 1958.
———. "Experience, Knowledge, and Value: A Rejoinder." In *The Philosophy of John Dewey*, ed. Paul Arthur Schilpp, 517–608. New York: Tudor Publishing Co., 1939.
———. *Freedom and Culture*. New York: Putnam, 1939.
———. *Individualism: Old and New*. New York: Minton, Balch, 1930.
———. *Liberalism and Social Action*. New York: Putnam, 1935.
———. *Logic: The Theory of Inquiry*. New York: Henry Holt, 1938.
———. Review of *The World and the Individual: Second Series*, by Josiah Royce. *Philosophical Review* 11 (1902): 392–407.
Dilthey, Wilhelm. *Einleitung in die Geisteswissenschaften*. Leipzig: Duncker and Humblot, 1883.
Donnelly, M. E., ed. *Reinterpreting the Legacy of William James*. Washington: American Psychological Association, 1993.
Dougherty, Jude P. *Recent American Naturalism: An Exposition and Critique*. Washington, D.C.: Catholic University of America Press, 1960.
Drabkin, I. E., and S. Drake. *Galileo Galilei: On Motion and On Mechanics*. Madison: University of Wisconsin Press, 1960.
Drescher, Seymour. *Dilemmas of Democracy: Tocqueville and Modernization*. Pittsburgh: Pittsburgh University Press, 1968.
Drühe, H. *Psychologie aus dem Begriff: Hegels Persönlichkeitstheorie*. New York: De Gruyter, 1976.
Ebbinghaus, Hermann. *Über das Gedächtnis: Untersuchungen zur experimentellen Psychologie*. Leipzig: Hirzel, 1885.
———. "Über erklärende und beschreibende Psychologie." *Zeitschrift für Psychologie und Physiologie der Sinnesorgane* 9 (1896): 161–205. Reprint, in *Materialien zur Philosophie Diltheys*, ed. Fritjof Rodi and H. U. Lessing, 45–87. Frankfurt: Suhrkamp, 1984.
Eggert, G. H. *Wernicke's Works on Aphasia: A Sourcebook and Review; Early Sources in Aphasia and related Disorders*. New York: Mouton, 1977.
Emerson, Ralph Waldo. *The Collected Works of Ralph Waldo Emerson*. Ed. Robert Spiller. Cambridge, Mass.: Harvard University Press, 1971–.
———. *Selected Essays*. Ed. Larzer Ziff. New York: Penguin Books, 1982.
Fechner, Gustav Theodor. *Elemente der Psychophysik*. 3rd ed. 2 vols. Leipzig: Breitkopf and Härtel, 1907.
———. *Über die physikalische und philosophische Atomenlehre*. 2nd ed. Leipzig: Mendelssohn, 1864.
———. *Zend-Avesta: Gedanken über die Dinge des Himmels und des Jenseits vom Standpunkte der Naturbetrachtung*. 3 vols. Leipzig: Voss, 1851.
Feinstein, H. M. *Becoming William James*. Ithaca, N.Y.: Cornell University Press, 1984.
Finnis, John. *Aquinas: Moral, Political, and Legal Theory*. Oxford: Clarendon Press, 1998.
Flower, Elizabeth, and Murray G. Murphey. *A History of Philosophy in America*. 2 vols. New York: Capricorn Books, 1977.
Ford, P. M. *William James's Philosophy: A New Perspective*. Amherst, University of Massachusetts Press, 1982.

Franzese, S. *L'uomo indeterminato: Saggio su William James.* Rome: D'Anselmi, 2000.

Gale, R. M. *The Divided Self of William James.* Cambridge: Cambridge University Press, 1999.

Gavin, W. J. *William James and the Reinstatement of the Vague.* Philadelphia: Temple University Press, 1992.

George, Robert P. "Kelsen and Aquinas on 'the Natural Law Doctrine.'" *Notre Dame Law Review* 75 (2000): 1625–46.

Geschwind, N. "The Work and Influence of Wernicke." In *Selected Papers on Language and the Brain,* 1–97. Boston: Reidel, 1969.

Giedymin, Jerzy. "Antipositivism in Contemporary Philosophy of Social Science and Humanities." *British Journal for the Philosophy of Science* 26 (1975): 275–301.

Giffert, Arthur C., ed. *Young Emerson Speaks.* Boston: McGiffert, 1938.

Giuffrida, Robert. "Chauncey Wright's Theory of Meaning." *Journal of the History of Philosophy* 16 (1978): 313–24.

Greene, M. *Hegel on the Soul.* The Hague: Nijhoff, 1972.

Griswold, Charles L. *Adam Smith and the Virtues of Enlightenment.* Cambridge: Cambridge University Press, 1999.

Habermas, J. "Rortys Pragmatische Wende." *Deutsche Zeitschrift für Philosophie* 5 (1996): 715–42.

———. *Wahrheit und Rechtfertigung.* Frankfurt: Suhrkamp, 1999.

———. "Wahrheitstheorien." In *Vorstudien und Ergänzungen zur Theorie des Kommunikativen Handelns,* 127–86. Frankfurt: Suhrkamp, 1984.

Heidelberger, M. *Die innere Seite der Natur: Gustav Theodor Fechners wissenschaftlich-philosophische Weltauffassung.* Frankfurt: Klostermann, 1993.

Hempel, Carl. "Methods of Concept Formation." In *International Encyclopedia of Unified Science,* 23–38. Chicago: University of Chicago Press, 1953.

Henckmann, "Einleitung." In Herbart, *Lehrbuch zur Einleitung in die Philosophie* [1834], ed. W. Henckmann. Hamburg: Meiner, 1993.

Henderson, Lawrence J. *The Fitness of the Environment: An Inquiry into the Biological Significance of the Properties of Matter.* New York: Macmillan, 1913.

Henrich, Dieter, ed. *Hegels philosophische Psychologie. Hegel-Studien: Beiheft 19.* Bonn: Bouvier, 1979.

Herbart, Johann Friedrich. *Psychologie als Wissenschaft: Neu gegründet auf Erfahrung, Metaphysik und Mathematik.* 2 vols. Königsberg: Unzer, 1824–25.

———. *Sämtliche Werke in chronologischer Reihenfolge.* Ed. K. Kehrbach and O. Flügel. 19 vols. 1887–1915. Reprint, Aalen: Scientia, 1964.

———. *Über die Möglichkeit und Nothwendigkeit, Mathematik auf die Psychologie anzuwenden* [1822]. In *Sämtliche Werke,* vol. 5, 100–103.

Hereth, Michael. *Alexis de Tocqueville: Threats to Freedom in Democracy.* Trans. George Bogardus. Durham, N.C.: Duke University Press, 1986.

Hering, E. *Über das Gedächtniss als eine Funktion der organisirten Materie.* Vienna: Gerold, 1870.

Hertz, Heinrich. *Principles of Mechanics Presented in a New Form.* Trans. D. E. Jones and J. T. Walley. London: Macmillian, 1899.

Hickman, Larry A., ed. *Reading Dewey: Interpretations for a Postmodern Generation.* Bloomington: Indiana University Press, 1998.

Holmes, Oliver Wendell. *The Collected Works of Justice Holmes: Complete Public Writ-*

ings and Selected Judicial Opinions of Oliver Wendell Holmes. Ed. Sheldon M. Novick. 3 vols. Chicago: University of Chicago Press, 1995.

———. *The Essential Holmes: Selections from the Letters, Speeches, Judicial Opinions, and Other Writings of Oliver Wendell Holmes, Jr.* Ed. Richard A. Posner. Chicago: University of Chicago Press, 1992.

Holmes, Oliver Wendell, and Harold J. Laski. *Holmes-Laski Letters: The Correspondence of Mr. Justice Holmes and Harold J. Laski 1916–1935.* 2 vols. Cambridge, Mass.: Harvard University Press, 1953.

Hook, Sidney. *American Philosophers at Work.* New York: Criterion Books, 1956.

Hookway, Christopher. *Truth, Rationality, and Pragmatism.* Oxford: Clarendon Press, 2000.

Hussey, Edward. "Aristotle's Mathematical Physics." In *Aristotle's* Physics: *A Collection of Essays,* ed. L. Judson, 213–42. Oxford: Clarendon Press, 1991.

James, William. *The Meaning of Truth: A Sequel to Pragmatism.* New York: Longmans, Green, 1909.

———. *A Pluralistic Universe: Hibbert Lectures at Manchester College on the Present Situation in Philosophy.* New York: Longmans, Green, 1909. Reprint with introduction by H. S. Levinson, Lincoln: University of Nebraska Press, 1996.

———. *A Pluralistic Universe.* Cambridge, Mass.: Harvard University Press, 1977.

———. *Pragmatism and the Meaning of Truth.* Cambridge, Mass.: Harvard University Press, 1975.

———. *Pragmatism: A New Name for Some Old Ways of Thinking.* New York: Longmans, Green, 1907.

———. *The Principles of Psychology.* 2 vols. New York: Henry Holt, 1890. Reprint, New York: Dover Publications, 1950.

———. *The Principles of Psychology.* Cambridge, Mass.: Harvard University Press, 1981.

———. *The Varieties of Religious Experience.* New York: Longmans, Green, 1902.

———. *The Will to Believe and Other Essays in Popular Philosophy.* New York: Longmans, Green, 1897; reprint, New York: Dover Publications, 1956.

———. "The Will to Believe" (1897). In *Pragmatism and Other Writings,* 191–218. New York: Penguin Books, 2000.

Kim, Jaegwon. *Philosophy of Mind.* Boulder: Westview Press, 1996.

Klee, Robert. *Introduction to the Philosophy of Science: Cutting Nature at Its Seams.* Oxford: Oxford University Press, 1997.

Koch, S., and D. H. Leavy, eds. *A Century of Psychology as Science.* New York: McGraw-Hill, 1985.

Kraushaar, Otto F. "Lotze as a Factor in the Development of James's Radical Empiricism and Pluralism." *Philosophical Review* 48 (1939): 455–71.

———. "Lotze's Influence on the Pragmatism and Practical Philosophy of William James." *Journal of the History of Ideas* 1 (1940): 439–58.

———. "Lotze's Influence on the Psychology of William James." *Psychological Review* 43 (1936): 235–57.

———. "What James's Philosophical Orientation Owed to Lotze." *Philosophical Review* 47 (1938): 517–26.

Kuklick, Bruce. *A History of Philosophy in America, 1720–2000.* Oxford: Oxford University Press, 2002.

———. *The Rise of American Philosophy.* New Haven, Conn.: Yale University Press, 1977.

Kusch, M. *Psychologism: A Case Study in the Sociology of Knowledge.* London: Routledge, 1995.

Lamberth, D. C. *William James and the Metaphysics of Experience.* Cambridge: Cambridge University Press, 1999.

Lamberti, Jean-Claude. *Tocqueville and the Two Democracies.* Trans. Arthur Goldhammer. Cambridge, Mass.: Harvard University Press, 1989.

Lange, Friedrich Albert. *Geschichte des Materialismus und Kritik seiner Bedeutung in der Gegenwart.* 2 vols. Iserlohn: Baedeker, 1873–75.

Laslett, Peter. *Philosophy, Politics, and Society,* series 1. Oxford: Blackwell, 1956.

Latour, Bruno. *Pandora's Hope: Essays on the Reality of Science Studies.* Cambridge, Mass.: Harvard University Press, 1999.

Lawler, Peter Augustine. *The Restless Mind: Alexis de Tocqueville on the Origin and Perpetuation of Human Liberty.* Lanham, Md.: Rowman and Littlefield, 1993.

Le Conte, Joseph. *Evolution: Its Nature, Its Evidence, and Its Relation to Religious Thought.* 2nd rev. ed. New York: Appleton, 1897.

Lepore, Ernest, ed. *Truth and Interpretation: Perspectives on the Philosophy of Donald Davidson.* Oxford: Basil Blackwell, 1986.

Lewis, C. I. "Pragmatism and Current Thought." *Journal of Philosophy* 27, no. 9 (1930): 238–46.

Lewtontin, Richard. *The Triple Helix.* Cambridge, Mass.: Harvard University Press, 2000.

Lindsay, Robert B., and Henry Margenau. *Foundations of Physics.* New York: John Wiley and Sons, 1936.

Lopez, Michael. "*The Conduct of Life:* Emerson's Anatomy of Power." In *The Cambridge Companion to Emerson,* ed. Joel Porte and Saundra Morris, 243–66. Cambridge: Cambridge University Press, 1999.

Lotze, R. H. *Kleine Schriften zur Psychologie: Eingeleitet und mit Materialien zur Rezeptionsgeschichte Versehen.* Ed. R. Pester. New York: Springer, 1989.

———. *Medicinische Psychologie oder Physiologie der Seele.* Leipzig: Weidmann, 1852.

Mach, Ernst. *Beiträge zur Analyse der Empfindungen.* Jena: Fischer, 1886.

———. *Die Mechanik in ihrer Entwicklung: historisch-kritisch dargestellt.* Leipzig: F. A. Brockhaus, 1883; 2nd ed. 1889.

———. *Populär-wissenschaftliche Vorlesungen.* Leipzig: Barth, 1896.

———. *The Science of Mechanics: A Critical and Historical Account of Its Development.* 6th ed. Trans. Thomas J. McCormack. LaSalle, Ill.: Open Court Pub. Co., 1960.

Machiavelli, Niccolò. *The Prince.* Trans. Harvey Mansfield. Chicago: University of Chicago Press, 1998.

Madden, Edward. *Chauncey Wright and the Foundations of Pragmatism.* Seattle: University of Washington Press, 1963.

Malachowski, Alan R., ed. *Reading Rorty.* Oxford: Blackwell, 1990.

Manent, Pierre. *Cours Familier de Philosophie Politique.* Paris: Fayard, 2001.

———. *Tocqueville and the Nature of Democracy.* Trans. John Waggoner. Lanham, Md.: Rowman and Littlefield, 1996.

Mansfield, Harvey C. *Taming the Prince: The Ambivalence of Modern Executive Power.* Baltimore, Md.: Johns Hopkins University Press, 1989.

Mansfield, Harvey C., and Delba Winthrop. "Liberalism and Big Government: Tocqueville's Analysis." In *Tyranny and Liberty,* 1–31. London: Institute of United States Studies, 1999.

Margolis, Joseph. "Reconstruction in Pragmatism." *Journal of Speculative Philosophy* 13 (1999): 221–39.

Marquardt, Odo. *Transzendentaler Idealismus, romantische Naturphilosophie, Psychoanalyse.* Cologne: Dinter, 1987.

Marx, O. "Nineteenth-Century Medical Psychology: Theoretical Problems in the Work of Griesinger, Meynert, and Wernicke." *Isis* 61 (1970): 355–70.

Matthiesen, F. O. *The James Family: Including Selections from the Writings of Henry James, Senior, William, Henry, and Alice James.* New York: Vintage Books, 1980. First published 1947.

Mayr, Ernst. "Teleological and Teleonomic: A New Analysis." *Boston Studies in the Philosophy of Science.* Vol. 14, *Methodological and Historical Essays in the Natural and Social Sciences,* 91–117. Ed. Robert S. Cohen and Marx W. Wartofsky. Boston: D. Reidel, 1974.

McDermott, John. *The Culture of Experience: Philosophical Essays in the American Grain.* New York: New York University Press, 1976.

McDowell, John. *Mind and World.* Cambridge, Mass.: Harvard University Press, 1996.

McTaggart, John McTaggart Ellis. Review of *The World and the Individual: Second Series,* by Josiah Royce. *Mind* 11 n.s. (1902). Reprint, *Critical Responses to Josiah Royce, 1855–1916,* vol. 2, 49–55.

Meynert, T. *Psychiatrie: Klinik der Erkrankungen des Vorderhirns begründet auf dessen Bau, Leistungen und Ernährung.* Vienna: Braumüller, 1884.

Murphy, M. *The Development of Peirce's Philosophy.* Cambridge, Mass.: Harvard University Press, 1961.

Musil, Robert. *On Mach's Theories.* Trans. Kevin Mulligan. Washington, D.C.: Catholic University of America Press, 1982.

Myers, G. E. *William James: His Life and Thought.* New Haven, Conn.: Yale University Press, 1986.

Newton, Isaac. *Mathematical Principles of Natural Philosophy and His System of the World.* Trans. Florian Cajori. 2 vols. Berkeley: University of California Press, 1966.

Niquet, M. *Transzendentale Argumente: Kant, Strawson und die Aporetik der Detranszendentalisierung.* Frankfurt: Suhrkamp, 1991.

Oehler-Klein, S. "Die Schädellehre Franz Joseph Galls in Literatur und Kritik des 19. Jahrhunderts: Zur Rezeptionsgeschichte einer medizinisch-biologisch begründeten Theorie der Physiognomik und Psychologie." *Sömmerring-Forschungen* 8. New York: Verlag, 1990.

Olin, D., ed. *William James: Pragmatism in Focus.* London: Routledge and Kegan Paul, 1992.

Paulsen, Friedrich. "Die Zukunftsaufgaben der Philosophie." In *Die Kultur der Gegenwart.* Vol. I.6, *Systematische Philosophie.* Leipzig: Teubner, 1907.

Peirce, Charles Sanders. *The Collected Papers of Charles Sanders Peirce.* Vol. 1–6 ed. Charles Hartshorne and Paul Weiss; vol. 7–8 ed. Arthur W. Burks. Cambridge, Mass.: Harvard University Press, 1931–58.

———. *The Essential Writings.* Ed. E. C. Moore. Amherst, N.Y.: Prometheus Books, 1998.

———. *The Essential Peirce: Selected Philosophical Writings.* Ed. Nathan Houser and Christian J. W. Kloesel. Bloomington: Indiana University Press, 1992.

———. "A Neglected Argument for the Reality of God." *Hibbert Journal* 7

(1908): 90–112. Also in *Collected Papers of Charles Sanders Peirce,* vol. 6, 452–85.

———. *Peirce on Signs.* Ed. James Hooper. Chapel Hill: University of North Carolina Press, 1991.

Perry, Ralph Barton. *The Thought and Character of William James.* 2 vols. Boston: Little, Brown, 1935.

———. *The Thought and Character of William James.* New paperback ed. with introduction by Charlene H. Seigfried. Nashville: Vanderbilt, 1996.

Pettoello, Renato. *Introduzione a Herbart.* Rome-Bari: Laterza, 1988.

Pieper, Josef. *Scholasticism: Personalities and Problems in Medieval Philosophy.* Trans. Richard and Clara Winston. New York: McGraw-Hill, 1964.

Poggi, Stefano. *Il genio e l'unità della natura: La scienza della Germania romantica (1790–1830).* Bologna: Il Mulino, 2000.

———. *I sistemi dell'esperienza: Psicologia, logica e teoria della scienza da Kant a Wundt.* Bologna: Il Mulino, 1977.

———. "Neurology and Biology in the Romantic Age in Germany: Carus, Burdach, Gall, von Baer." In *Romanticism in Science: Science in Europe (1780–1840),* ed. Stefano Poggi and Maurizio Bossi, 143–60. Boston: Kluwer, 1994.

Pollock, Robert C. "A Reappraisal of Emerson." *Thought* 32 (1957): 86–132.

Potter, Vincent. *Charles S. Peirce on Norms and Ideals.* Amherst, Mass.: University of Massachusetts Press, 1967. Reprint, New York: Fordham University Press, 1997.

Preyer, W. *Die Seele des Kindes: Beobachtungen über die geistige Entwicklung des Menschen in den ersten Lebensjahren.* Leipzig: Grieben, 1882.

Putnam, Hilary. *The Many Faces of Reason.* La Salle: Open Court, 1987.

———. "Pragmatism." *Proceedings of the Aristotelian Society* 95 (1994–95): 291–306.

———. "Pragmatism and Realism." *Cardozo Law Review* 18 (1996): 153–70.

———. *Reason, Truth, and History.* Cambridge: Cambridge University Press, 1981.

———. "Sense, Nonsense, and the Senses: An Inquiry into the Powers of the Human Mind." The Dewey Lectures 1994. *Journal of Philosophy* 91 (1994): 445–65.

———. *The Threefold Cord: Mind, Body, and World.* New York: Columbia University Press, 1999.

Putnam, R. A., ed. *The Cambridge Companion to William James.* Cambridge: Cambridge University Press, 1997.

Quine, W. V. O. "Epistemology Naturalized." In *Ontological Relativity and Other Essays.* New York: Columbia University Press, 1969.

———. "Let Me Accentuate the Positive." Appended to the reprint of "A Coherence Theory of Truth and Knowledge." In *Reading Rorty,* ed Alan R. Malachowski. Oxford: Blackwell, 1990.

———. *Pursuit of Truth.* Rev. ed. Cambridge, Mass.: Harvard University Press, 1992.

———. *Word and Object.* Cambridge, Mass.: MIT Press, 1960.

Randall, John Herman. "The Nature of Naturalism." In *Naturalism and the Human Spirit,* ed. Y. H. Krikorian, 354–82. New York: Columbia University Press, 1944.

Rapp, M. *Der Psychologismusstreit in der deutschen Philosophie.* Freiburg-Munich: Alber, 1994.

Rawls, John. *A Theory of Justice.* Cambridge, Mass.: Harvard University Press, 1971.

Richards, R. J. "The Personal Equation in Science: William James's Psychological and Moral Uses of the Darwinian Theory." In *A William James Renascence: Four Essays by Young Scholars,* ed. M. R. Schwehn. *Harvard Library Bulletin* 30 (1982): 387–425.

Richardson, Robert J., Jr. "Emerson and Nature." In *The Cambridge Companion to Emerson,* ed. Joel Porte and Saundra Morris. Cambridge: Cambridge University Press, 1999.

Robin, Richard S. *Annotated Catalog of the Papers of Charles S. Peirce.* Amherst: University of Massachusetts Press, 1967.

Rorty, R. *Consequences of Pragmatism (Essays: 1972–1980).* Minneapolis: University of Minnesota Press, 1982.

———. "Hilary Putnam and the Relativist Menace." In *Philosophical Papers,* vol. 3. Cambridge: Cambridge University Press, 1998.

———. "Is Truth a Goal of Enquiry? Davidson versus Wright." *Philosophical Quarterly* 45 (1995): 281–300.

———. *Philosophy and the Mirror of Nature.* Princeton: Princeton University Press, 1979.

———. "Pragmatism, Davidson and Truth." In *Truth and Interpretation: Perspectives on the Philosophy of Donald Davidson,* ed. Ernest Lepore. Oxford: Basil Blackwell, 1986. Also in *Objectivism, Relativism, and Truth,* Cambridge: Cambridge University Press, 1991.

———. "Representation, Social Practise, and Truth." In *Objectivism, Relativism, and Truth,* 126–61. Cambridge: Cambridge University Press, 1991.

———. "Transcendental Arguments, Self-References, and Pragmatism." In *Transcendental Arguments and Science,* ed. R-P. Horstmann, 77–103. Boston: Reidel, 1979.

Rosenthal, Sandra B. *Charles Peirce's Pragmatic Pluralism.* Albany: SUNY Press, 1994.

Röttgers, Kurt. "Romantische Psychologie." *Psychologie und Geschichte* 3 (1991): 24–64.

Royce, Josiah. *The Basic Writings of Josiah Royce.* Ed. John J. McDermott. 2 vols. Chicago: Chicago University Press, 1969.

———. "The Decay of Earnestness." *Californian* 3 (1881): 18–25. Reprint, *Fugitive Essays,* 300–321.

———. "The External World and the Social Consciousness." *Philosophical Review* 3 (1894): 513–45.

———. *Fugitive Essays.* Ed. Jacob Loewenberg. Cambridge, Mass.: Harvard University Press, 1920.

———. *Herbert Spencer: An Estimate and Review.* New York: Fox, Duffield, 1904.

———. *The Hope of the Great Community.* New York: Macmillan, 1916.

———. *The Letters of Josiah Royce.* Ed. John Clendenning. Chicago: University of Chicago Press, 1970.

———. "The Mechanical, the Historical, and the Statistical." *Science* 39 n.s. (1914): 551–66. Reprint, *The Basic Writings of Josiah Royce,* vol. 2, 711–33.

———. *The Problem of Christianity.* 2 vols. New York: Macmillan, 1913. Reprint with an introduction by John E. Smith, Chicago: University of Chicago Press, 1968. Reprint with a foreword by Frank M. Oppenheim, S.J., Washington: Catholic University of America Press, 2001.

———. *The Spirit of Modern Philosophy: An Essay in the Form of Lectures.* Boston: Houghton, Mifflin, 1892.

———. *Studies of Good and Evil: A Series of Essays upon the Problems of Philosophy.* New York: Appleton, 1898.

———. *The World and the Individual: First Series; The Four Historical Conceptions of Being.* New York: Macmillan, 1899. Reprint with an introduction by John E. Smith, New York: Dover, 1959.

———. *The World and the Individual: Second Series; Nature, Man, and the Moral Order.* New York: Macmillan, 1901. Reprint, New York: Dover, 1959.

Ryder, John, ed. *American Philosophic Naturalism in the Twentieth Century.* Amherst: Prometheus Books, 1994.

Sachs-Hombach, K. *Philosophische Psychologie im 19. Jahrhundert: Ihre Entstehung und Problemgeschichte.* Freiburg-Munich: Alber, 1993.

Sandel, Michael. *Liberalism and the Limits of Justice.* London: Cambridge University Press, 1982.

Santayana, George. "Dewey's Naturalistic Metaphysics." In *The Philosophy of John Dewey,* ed. Paul Arthur Schilpp, 245–61. New York: Tudor Publishing Co., 1939.

———. *Lotze's System of Philosophy.* Ed. P. G. Kuntz. Bloomington: Indiana University Press, 1971.

Scharff, Robert C. *Comte after Positivism.* Cambridge: Cambridge University Press, 1995.

Scheffler, Israel. "Thoughts on Teleology." *British Journal for the Philosophy of Science* 9 (February 1959): 265–84.

Schilpp, Paul Arthur, ed. *The Philosophy of John Dewey.* 2nd ed. New York: Tudor, 1951.

Seigfried, C. H. *William James's Radical Reconstruction of Philosophy.* Albany: SUNY Press, 1990.

Sellars, Wilfrid. "Pure Pragmatics and Epistemology." *Philosophy of Science* 14, no. 3 (1947): 181–202.

Shapiro, Gary. "'Give Me a Break!' Emerson on Fruit and Flowers." *Journal of Speculative Philosophy* 13, no. 2 (1999): 98–113.

Shook, John R. *Dewey's Empirical Theory of Knowledge and Reality.* Nashville: Vanderbilt University Press, 2000.

Short, T. L. "Peirce's Concept of Final Causation." *Transactions of the Charles S. Peirce Society* 17, no. 4 (Fall 1981): 369–82.

———. "Semeiosis and Intentionality." *Transactions of the Charles S. Peirce Society* 17, no. 3 (Summer 1981): 197–223.

———. "Teleology and Linguistic Change." In *The Peirce Seminar Papers,* ed. Michael Shapiro, vol. 4, 111–58. New York: Berghahn Books, 1999.

———. "Teleology in Nature." *American Philosophical Quarterly* 20, no. 4 (October 1983): 311–20.

Siedentop, Larry. *Tocqueville.* Oxford: Oxford University Press, 1994.

Sigwart, Christoph. *Logik.* 2 vols. Freiburg: Mohr, 1873.

Sleeper, R. W. *The Necessity of Pragmatism: John Dewey's Conception of Philosophy.* New Haven: Yale University Press, 1986.

Smith, John E. *America's Philosophical Vision.* Chicago: University of Chicago Press, 1992.

———. *The Spirit of American Philosophy.* New York: Oxford University Press, 1963.

Sober, Elliott. *The Nature of Selection.* Chicago: University of Chicago Press, 1984.

Spencer, Herbert. *First Principles of a New System of Philosophy.* New York: Appleton, 1881.

Stroud, B. "Transcendental Arguments." *Journal of Philosophy* 65 (1968): 241–56.

Stuhr, John J., ed. *Pragmatism and Classical American Philosophy: Essential Readings and Interpretive Essays.* Oxford: Oxford University Press, 2000.

Stumpf, Carl. *Tonpsychologie.* 2 vols. Leipzig: Hirzel, 1883–90.

———. *Über den psychologischen Ursprung der Raumvorstellung.* Leipzig: Hirzel, 1873.

Swoboda, W. "Physics, Physiology and Psychophysics: The Origins of Ernst Mach's Empiriocriticism." *Rivista di Filosofia* 22–23 (1982): 234–74.

Taylor, E. "W. James on Darwin: An Evolutionary Theory of Consciousness." In *Psychology: Perspectives and Practice,* ed. S. M. Pfafflin et al. *Annals of the New York Academy of Sciences* 1990 (no. 602): 7–33.

Thoreau, Henry David. *Walden.* Princeton: Princeton University Press, 1989.

———. *A Year in Thoreau's Journal: 1851.* New York: Penguin, 1993.

Tocqueville, Alexis de. *Democracy in America.* Trans. by Harvey Mansfield and Delba Winthrop. Chicago: University of Chicago Press, 2000.

———. *Oeuvres Complètes.* 18 vols. Paris: Gallimard, 1951.

Träger, F. *Herbarts realistisches Denken.* Amsterdam: Rodopi, 1982.

Turner, Frederick Jackson. "The Significance of the Frontier in American History." In *The Frontier in American History.* New York: H. Holt, 1920.

Verwey, G. *Psychiatry in an Anthropological and Biomedical Context: Philosophical Presuppositions and Implications of German Psychiatry (1820–1870).* Boston: Reidel, 1985.

Volpicelli, I. *Esperienza e metafisica nella psicologia di J. F. Herbart.* Rome: Armando, 1982.

Wallace, William A. *The Modeling of Nature.* Washington, D.C.: Catholic University of America Press, 1996.

Walzer, Michael. *Spheres of Justice.* New York: Basic Books, 1983.

Weiss, Paul. "Common Sense and Beyond." In *Determinism and Freedom,* ed. Sidney Hook, 231–43. New York: Collier Books, 1958.

Wellmer, A. "Der Streit und die Wahrheit. Pragmatismus ohne regulative Ideen." In *Die Renaissance des Pragmatismus,* ed. M. Sandbothe, 253–69. Weilerswist: Velbrück, 2000.

———. "Wahrheit, Kontingenz, Moderne." In *Endspiele.* Frankfurt: Suhrkamp, 1993.

Wernicke, Carl. *Lehrbuch der Gehirnkrankheiten für Aerzte und Studirende.* Kassel: Fischer, 1881.

Wesson, Robert. *Beyond Natural Selection.* Cambridge, Mass.: MIT Press, 1991.

West, Cornel. *The American Evasion of Philosophy: A Genealogy of Pragmatism.* Madison: University of Wisconsin Press, 1989.

Whitehead, A. N. *Science and the Modern World.* New York: Macmillan, 1925. Reprint, New York: Free Press, 1967.

Wiener, Philip. "Chauncey Wright, Darwin and Scientific Neutrality." *Journal of the History of Ideas* 6 (1945): 19–45.

———. *Evolution and the Founders of Pragmatism.* Cambridge, Mass.: Harvard University Press, 1949.

Wild, J. D. *The Radical Empiricism of William James.* Garden City, N.Y.: Doubleday, 1989.

Wilson, Daniel J. *Science, Community, and the Transformation of American Philosophy, 1860–1930*. Chicago: University of Chicago Press, 1990.

Wilson, Edward O. *Consilience: The Unity of Knowledge*. New York: Knopf, 1998.

Wittgenstein, Ludwig. *Philosophical Investigations*. Trans. G. E. M. Anscombe. Oxford: Blackwell, 1958.

———. *Tractatus Logico-Philosophicus*. Trans. C. K. Ogden. London: Routledge, 1922.

Wolters, Gereon. "Introduction" to reprint of Mach's *Analyse der Empfindungen*, i–xxxii. Darmstadt: Wissenschaftliche Buchgesellschaft, 2000.

Woodward, W. R. "From Association to Gestalt: The Fate of Hermann Lotze's Theory of Spatial Perception, 1846–1920." *Isis* 69 (1978): 572–82.

———. "Introduction" to William James's *Essays in Psychology*, xi–xxxix. *The Works of William James*, ed. F. H. Burkhardt, F. Bowers, and I. K. Skrupskelis. Cambridge, Mass.: Harvard University Press, 1983.

Wright, Chauncey. *Letters of Chauncey Wright with Some Account of His Life*. Ed. James Bradley Thayer. Privately published 1878. Reprint, American Biography Series.

———. *Philosophical Discussions*. New York: Burt Franklin, 1877. Reprint, 1971.

Wundt, Wilhelm. *Grundzüge der physiologischen Psychologie*. Leipzig: Engelmann, 1873–74.

———. *Vorlesungen über die Menschen und Thierseele*. Leipzig: Voss, 1863–64.

Zetterbaum, Marvin. *Tocqueville and the Problem of Democracy*. Stanford, Calif.: Stanford University Press, 1967.

Index Nominum

Index Verborum

Page numbers in italics refer to displays and figures.